Asian Nationalism

The modern world is now made up of nation states, although this was not always the case. Nationalism has re-emerged as a significant and influential political phenomenon.

Asian Nationalism brings together internationally renowned specialists in the field to analyse the dominant experience of Asia in the context of current theories of nationalism. As well as theoretical and empirical material, it features detailed chapter case studies of:

- China, including Taiwan
- Japan
- India
- Pakistan
- Indonesia
- The Philippines

This book contains up-to-date analyses by LSE academics on a theme of great topicality, which is the subject of continuous debate. It will serve as an invaluable resource for senior undergraduates, graduate students and researchers in Politics and Asian Studies.

Michael Leifer is one of the world's authorities on South-East Asia and is Director of the Asia Research Centre at the London School of Economics. He edits Routledge's Politics in Asia series, and is the author of a number of books including the *Dictionary of the Modern Politics of South-East Asia*, also published by Routledge.

Contributors: Anthony D. Smith, Michael Yahuda, Solomon Karmel, Christopher Hughes, Ian Nish, Meghnad Desai, Athar Hussain, Michael Leifer, James Putzel and James Mayall.

Asian Nationalism

Edited by Michael Leifer

London and New York

First published 2000
by Routledge
11 New Fetter Lane, London EC4P 4EE

Simultaneously published in the USA and Canada
by Routledge
29 West 35th Street, New York, NY 10001

Routledge is an imprint of the Taylor & Francis Group

Typeset in Perpetua by Taylor & Francis Books Ltd
Printed and bound in Great Britain by Clays Ltd, St Ives plc

British Library Cataloguing in Publication Data
A catalogue record for this book is available from the British Library

Library of Congress Cataloging in Publication Data
Asian nationalism / edited by Michael Leifer.
Includes bibliographical references and index.
1. Asia–Politics and government–20th century. 2. Nationalism–Asia–
History–20th century. 3. Asia–Ethnic relations. I. Leifer, Michael.
DS35 .A815 2000
320.54'095–dc21   99-086051

ISBN 0–415–23284–8 (hbk)
ISBN 0–415–23285–6 (pbk)

Contents

Contributors

Meghnad Desai is Professor of Economics at the London School of Economics and Political Science (LSE) and President of the British Association of South Asian Studies.

Christopher Hughes is Lecturer in International Relations at the LSE.

Athar Hussain is Deputy Director of the Asia Research Centre at the LSE.

Solomon M. Karmel is Lecturer in Government at the LSE.

Michael Leifer is Emeritus Professor of International Relations and Director of the Asia Research Centre at the LSE.

James Mayall is Director of the Centre of International Studies at the University of Cambridge. He was previously Professor of International Relations at the LSE.

Ian Nish is Emeritus Professor of International History at the LSE.

James Putzel is Acting Director of the Development Studies Institute at the LSE.

Anthony D. Smith is Professor of Ethnicity and Nationalism within the European Institute at the LSE.

Michael Yahuda is Professor of International Relations at the LSE.

Preface

The study of nationalism is an inherent part of the intellectual tradition of the London School of Economics and Political Science (LSE), which has been reflected in the writings of its academic luminaries, past and present. When it was decided to embark on a programme of academic activities under the aegis of a newly established Asia Research Centre, the topic of Asian nationalism came readily to mind as an integrating theme for the first seminar series. Moreover, it was an indication of the critical mass in Asian studies at the LSE that it was possible to find all speakers from within the School. The essays published in this volume constitute revised versions of papers presented during the academic year 1997/1998. The theme of Asian nationalism has not been imposed according to a single orthodoxy of interpretation. Indeed, the contributors to this volume come from a variety of Social Science disciplines, which is reflected in the differences among the respective essays. However, the first chapter by Anthony Smith addresses the subject of alternative models of nation formation and is synoptic in its approach, while James Mayall's concluding chapter reflects on the specific forms of Asian nationalism selected for analysis in this volume with particular reference to international order. The individual states considered are China, Japan, India, Pakistan, Indonesia and the Philippines. In the special case of China, two additional chapters have been included, which deal with ethnic nationalism on the mainland and with Taiwan. This volume marks the first major publication of the Asia Research Centre at the LSE. It is a testament to the quality of collegial collaboration at the School that is also an inherent part of its intellectual tradition. My colleagues and I wish to express our appreciation of the untiring efforts of Joanne Hay, the administrator of the Asia Research Centre, for organising the seminars which led to this book, and for dealing patiently with its contributors.

Michael Leifer,
November 1999

1 Theories of nationalism

Alternative models of nation formation

Anthony D. Smith

In pre-modern eras, human beings lived in all kinds of community and sported a variety of identities – family, gender, clan, caste, class, religion, ethnicity, city-state and empire – and no one kind of community or identity achieved political pre-eminence globally. In the modern world, things are quite different. Though human beings continue to have multiple identities, one kind of community and one type of identity has achieved a political preponderance. Today, the nation, the national state and nationalism have come to occupy the commanding heights of political allegiance and political identity. The world is divided into territorial *states*. These can be defined as sets of autonomous, public institutions with a legitimate monopoly of coercion and extraction in a given territory, and sovereignty in relation to those outside its borders. The contemporary world is similarly divided into *nations*; that is, named populations possessing an historic territory, shared myths and historical memories, a mass, public culture, a single economy and common rights and duties for all members, which are legitimised by the principles of *nationalism*. Nationalism itself can be defined as an ideological movement for the attainment and maintenance of autonomy, unity and identity on behalf of a population deemed by some of its members to constitute an actual or potential 'nation'. These are, of course, only working definitions, but if they are accepted as a starting-point for subsequent analysis, it can be immediately appreciated that states, nations and nationalisms do not often coincide. And in my opinion, this is the immediate cause of so much of the conflict and turbulence that we witness throughout the world today. Here, too, we may find the proximate cause of recurrent 'nationalisms', since it is the aim of all nationalists to create the conditions for a greater congruence between state, nation and nationalism. In this quest, they have been only partly successful; but this serves merely to spur nationalists to greater efforts. Nevertheless, it is testimony to the power of the national ideal, and to the global appeal of nationalism today, that there is hardly a corner of the world that has not been swept by nationalist fervour and ethnic conflict.[1]

Perennialist theories

Why has the 'nation' and its 'nationalism' become so dominant and widespread throughout the world? Put simply, there are four kinds of answer in the literature, and they have given rise to four paradigms or grand narratives of nationalism. The first is usually termed 'primordialism'. This theory holds that the nation is a primordial category, or one founded upon primordial attachments. These may be genetic, as socio-biologists like Pierre Van den Berghe (1995) insist, or they may be cultural, as Edward Shils (1957) and Clifford Geertz (1973) and their followers prefer. In the former case, ethnic ties and nationalisms are derived from the individual reproductive drives which find their expression in 'nepotistic' behaviour in order to maximise their 'inclusive fitness'. The problem here is how far we can extrapolate from small kin groups to the much larger, and more extended, communities of the *ethnie* or nation; and how far these communities' *myths* of presumed ancestry match actual biological ties of descent. In the latter case, the cultural 'givens' of kinship, language, religion, race and territory provide foci for overriding attachments, beyond the calculative nexus, and attest to a deep-seated need for emotional security and life-enhancement. Birth, territory and community are seen as bearers of life, and as such are accorded an awe and loyalty far beyond everyday considerations of interest. The problem here is that by emphasising their primordial character, there is a danger of neglecting the very considerable social and cultural changes to which such attachments are subject, and which so often transform the character of the communities which coalesce around them.[2]

The merit of the primordialist paradigm is that it draws our attention to the long-term significance of popular attachments, kinship and cultural bonds. The primordialist approach asks why it is that so many people are prepared to risk their lives defending 'kith and kin' and 'hearth and home'. And why millions are prepared to lay down their lives for their 'nation'. Of course, this is merely to pose the problem. That it needs to be posed is significant. The reason is that so many would-be explanations of nationalism simply ignore the issue altogether, or else treat it as a secondary matter. However, it is central to the problems posed by the ubiquity and power of nationalism. Besides, many (but not all) nationalists are organic primordialists; and we have also to recognise that many people *feel* that they belong to a primordial *ethnie* or nation, and this 'participant's primordialism' is therefore a central part of the *explanandum* of nations and nationalism. Primordialism cannot furnish an explanation for the widespread appeal of nations and nationalism, but it does highlight the nature and size of the problem.

The second paradigm I shall term 'perennialism'. By this I mean simply that for many scholars, as well as participants, nations are seen as immemorial and/or perennial; and therefore nationalism is simply the ideology and movement for an already existing nation. However, though some perennialists may also be primordialists, many are not; and the former position does not entail the latter. I can argue that nations have been around since the ancient Egyptians and Sumerians, but I do not have to regard them as 'natural', or claim that the nation either itself is, or is based upon, primordial attachments. I can be a perennialist without being a naturalist. I should add that there are two forms of perennialism. The first regards particular nations as *continuous* and *immemorial*, the kind of belief entertained by the nationalists on behalf of their own nation, though not necessarily on behalf of others. The second argues that nations are *recurrent*. They are one of the basic forms of human association and identity throughout recorded history. They emerge and decline, come and go, but they are to be found in every age and continent (see Hastings 1997, chapter 1).

It is a matter of definition of terms, and thereafter of empirical investigation, as to whether there were nations in pre-modern epochs. If one adopts a definition of the nation similar to the one proposed at the beginning to this chapter – one which includes a mass, public culture, a single economy and rights and duties for all members – then one is inclined to think that very few communities in antiquity and the early Middle Ages would qualify as 'nations'. If one were to drop some of these features, then one could certainly find 'nations' in many areas in pre-modern epochs. The difficulty with this position is that the nations of the modern epoch appear to be quite different from those mooted in earlier epochs: they are mass nations, they form legal-political communities with a concept of citizenship, they have compact territorial borders, they legitimate themselves in terms of the ideology of nationalism, and they form part of an international system of national states. All this is relatively novel in historical terms. Though one can cite exceptions – the ancient Jews and Armenians, for example – most pre-modern nations possess none of these features. Thus, while it is important to keep an open mind, I am inclined to think that, as a general paradigm, perennial-ism is flawed.

Modernist theories: socio-economic developmentalism

The other two paradigms are what I call the 'modernist' and the 'ethno-symbolist', and it with these, and with the debates between them, that I shall be mainly concerned in this chapter. Undoubtedly, the current orthodoxy is 'modernist', where it is not 'post-modernist' – I treat the latter as a development of modernism, but intentionally shorn of its explanatory power, and therefore not an explanatory paradigm in itself. Modernism comes in several forms: socio-cultural, economic, political, ideological and constructionist, the labels suggesting the main explanatory thrust or focus of the approach or theory. All modernist approaches hold the following in common:

1   nationalism is an explicitly modern ideology and movement, that is to say, it
     is both novel and relatively recent, i.e. from the eighteenth century onwards;
2   as a social structure and cultural system, the nation is likewise both novel and
     relatively recent, again from the eighteenth century or slightly earlier;
3   as a system, the international order of national states is both novel and
     relatively recent, dating from the nineteenth century, though with intima-
     tions going back to the Treaty of Westphalia in 1648;
4   all three – nationalism, nation and the international order of national states –
     are the product of specifically *modern* conditions; namely, capitalism, bureauc-
     racy, industrialism, urbanisation, secularism and the like. This is what makes
     them qualitatively distinct from any form of community or belief system in
     pre-modern epochs.

The most forthright and original exponent of modernism has been, of course,
Ernest Gellner. His overall purpose has been to demonstrate the sociological
necessity of nations and nationalism in the modern world. Nationalism, he argues,
is logically contingent; it is not given in nature nor is it an intrinsic component of
the human condition. But it is sociologically necessary in a given historical epoch,
that of modernity; today, we *must* live in a modular, nationalist world. The reason
is to be found in the type of society characteristic of modernity: an industrial,
growth-oriented kind of society (Gellner 1964, chapter 7).

Gellner distinguishes between a pre-modern, agro-literate society and one that
is modern and industrial. In the agro-literate society, there was neither room nor
need for nations and nationalism. The vast mass of the population were food
producers, divided into separate, self-sufficient social structures and local
cultures. Above them, and exploiting their labour, the various tiny aristocratic,
clerical, bureaucratic and commercial elites were largely cut off from the mass of
food producers; they possessed a common aristocratic and clerical culture, but
saw no need to spread it downwards or incorporate the peasantry into their way
of life. Even the clergy which might have been tempted to convert the masses to
their revealed truth, had neither the incentive nor the means to do so. By
contrast, in modern, technologically advanced, growth-oriented societies,
populations have to be mobile and literate, fluid and homogeneous. A single
literate culture must come to embrace and unite elites and masses. In these
circumstances, the nation and nationalism act as cement for mobile populations in
industrial societies (Gellner 1983, chapter 2).

How can we explain this great transformation? The answer lies in the peculiar
characteristics of modernisation. Gellner has argued that modernisation, like a
great tidal wave, swept out from its Western heartlands to engulf societies across
the globe; but, crucially, it has done so *unevenly*, sweeping over different areas of
the world at different times, and with varying speed and intensity. Its effects have
been twofold. On the one hand, the great wave of modernisation erodes

traditional structures of family, religion and community. Villagers are driven from the countryside, their livelihoods are destroyed, their religious codes are swept aside, and they become disoriented in the anonymous cities into which they flock in search of homes, jobs and education. This means that whereas in the village local culture had reinforced social structures, in the impersonal life of the city, 'culture replaces structure'. In the city, a new literate, linguistic culture takes the place of the traditional structure of role expectations, forcing the inhabitants to become both numerate and literate. Today 'all men are clerks'; only a literate culture can relate and bind the great mass of immigrants to the city, and turn them into full citizens. And this can only be done through a mass, standardised, public education system under the auspices of the state and its resources. Only by being schooled in a specialist, literate 'high culture', sustained by a public education system, can villagers be turned into effective citizens and become a culturally homogeneous workforce (Gellner 1983, chapter 3).

That is why nations are large. But why, then, are they not as large as empires? The answer lies in a second consequence of the tidal wave of modernisation. For if modernisation erodes tradition, it also creates new kinds of conflict. The newcomers who flocked to the anonymous cities soon compete with the older inhabitants for scarce urban resources – jobs, schools, housing and welfare. If the newcomers resemble the denizens of the city in looks, language, customs and religion, or manage to learn quickly their language, there will only be social antagonism and perhaps class conflict. That was the situation in northern Italy, when southern Italians migrated north to look for jobs and housing. But if the newcomers differ in religion, pigmentation, customs and language, then ethnic antagonism is superimposed on class conflict. This is particularly likely in the later stages of industrialism, when the 'moral chasms' of scriptural religion and pigmentation cannot be bridged. Such an outcome is likely when the intelligentsia on both sides of the cultural divide stir up fear and resentment, and issue a summons to their respective 'proletariats' to secede and set up their own 'nation-states', creating in the process new nations seeking their own states (Gellner 1964, chapter 7; 1983, chapter 6).

Hence, for Gellner, it is not nations that engender nationalism; rather, it is nationalism that invents nations where they do not exist – though it helps to have some pre-existing cultural markers. It is nationalism that demands a culturally homogeneous nation, because the drive for a literate 'high culture' is a necessary component of growth-oriented industrial society. Nationalism's huge contemporary appeal can therefore be attributed, in the final analysis, to the requirements of modern, industrial society. Today, we must all become literate citizens capable of operating the 'industrial machine' and enabling us to 'swim in the sea of industria' (Gellner 1983, chapters 5–6).

In a further development of Gellner's theory, Tom Nairn has argued that we must look to imperialism as the basic mechanism through which the uneven development of capitalism stimulates nationalism. Nairn accepts the existence of ethnic groups and nationalities before 1800, but, like Gellner, he believes that nations and nationalism are phenomena peculiar to the modern world. They are products of the jagged and uneven spread of capitalism resulting from the activities of imperialism in the 'periphery' as it incorporated successive areas of the world, often with great violence, into the capitalist world-system (Nairn 1977, chapter 2).

Nairn explicates his thesis by examining the effects of the bourgeois revolutions and imperialist penetrations in the non-Western world. The result of these massive imperialist intrusions since 1800 was a sense of abject helplessness on the part of the elites in the subjugated peripheries. This was the true meaning of 'underdevelopment'. The peripheral elites possessed neither wealth nor skills nor military might; what could they oppose to the power of imperialism? How could their disgust be turned into effective resistance? The only resource left to the elites in this unequal struggle was numbers, the sheer mass of their native populations. Therefore, they had to appeal to the 'people' for support. They had to invite them into history and write the invitation card in the language and culture of the masses, that is, their vernacular, folk cultures. That is why nationalism is always a profoundly militant, cross-class, populist movement, and why it has found in cultural Romanticism a unifying vehicle for its social and political goals (Nairn 1977, chapter 9).

There are important differences between Gellner's sociological modernism and Nairn's economic developmentalism. Gellner speaks of industrialisation, while for Nairn the uneven development of *capitalism* is what counts. Yet both writers adhere to a materialist determinism: and both derive nationalism and nations from the peculiar character of modern social and economic development. Nothing before the tidal wave of modernisation ultimately matters; pre-existing cultures may help or hinder the process, but in the end nationalism is the child of modernity. Nations do not have navels.[3]

It might be objected that these materialist theories are pitched at a very abstract level of generality. They hardly notice, let alone take into account, the peculiarities of different regions, cultures or periods of history. But this weakness is also a source of strength: in the interests of parsimony, these models aim to capture only the common basic processes in the genesis of nationalism and nations, to answer the fundamental question of 'why nationalism?', leaving it to others to put cultural flesh on the bare bones of socio-economic modernism.

No doubt there is much to be gained from such abstract models. But the cost is high. We are asked to dispense, not only with history, but also with a more nuanced sociology. Take Nairn's dictum that all nationalisms are cross-class and populist, for instance. In theory, nationalist theory, this is true: every modern nationalism appeals to 'the people' as a whole, and identifies the nation with the people. But does that make them in practice inter-class and populist movements?

Nairn himself contrasts the practical, hard-headed nationalism of the Scots with the romantic nationalism of the Welsh. Both, no doubt, appeal to 'the people'. But Scottish nationalism tended to appeal in practice to the middle class, as did early German, Indian and West African nationalisms. Appealing to 'the people' is one thing; bringing them into the movement is quite another. In practice, as opposed to nationalist theory, nationalisms may shy away from populism, because the middle classes fear the consequences of mobilising the lower classes (see Nairn 1977, chapter 5; cf. Brass 1991).

The same problems apply to Gellner's thesis that nationalism is the product of 'exo-socialisation' – of mass, standardised, specialist public education systems. Very few would dispute the fact that mass education is vital to sustain national consciousness and socialise new generations of loyal citizens. But the education in question is not only mass, literacy-based and public; it is also *national*, indeed often national*ist*. It is a necessary instrument of the nationalists, and is instituted when they seize control of the state, as occurred in France of the Third Republic or in Meiji Japan, or when they set up a new state of their own, in the case of Israel or Nigeria, for example. In other words, nationalism precedes and institutes Gellner's mass education systems, rather than the other way round.

More serious perhaps than these specific objections is the observation that nationalisms, and nations, emerge in all kinds of economic milieux – among rich populations and poor ones, in stagnant and mobile societies, and in backward and advanced regions. They may do so for different reasons, but the range of socio-economic circumstances in which nationalisms emerge quite clearly rules out any explanation in terms of relative deprivation. That is the burden of Walker Connor's well-known critique of economic theories of nationalism. Nationalism first emerged, not in the underdeveloped periphery, but in the advanced core, in England, France, the United States and Germany. Moreover, it appeared in backward Serbia and Greece in the early nineteenth century and in advanced Catalonia and Croatia in the twentieth century, in an economically mobile society like Japan and among relatively economically stagnant communities like the Shan and the Somali (Connor 1994, chapter 6; see also Smith 1981, chapter 2).

Such considerations caution us against trying to link nationalism too closely to the processes of socio-economic modernisation. For *nationalism* to emerge, rather than just social discontent, we require additional ingredients, not only the means of mass political organisation, but also the presence and salience of ethnic and cultural ties on which to base a claim to nationhood. In the absence of shared culture and ethnic community, no amount of socio-economic modernisation and social discontent will produce a *nationalist movement*. Hence, it is ethnicity and culture that shape and direct the processes of modernisation, and it is pre-existing ethnic community that determines the answer to the question: '*Who* is the nation?'

Modernist theories: cultural constructionism

Gellner had, of course, reserved a key role for 'high culture', but for him it was the necessary product of a society geared to industrial growth. Hobsbawm and Anderson also trace the emergence of such 'garden' or 'invented' literary cultures, albeit indirectly, to the rise of capitalism. But for Hobsbawm, there is an important intervening political variable: the need for elites to control the newly enfranchised masses in an era of popular mobilisation and democratisation, particularly in Europe and America after 1870. In this scenario, the nation became the most important agent of social control in the time of capitalism: by engineering 'invented traditions' of a largely fabricated national history, symbolism and mythology, the upper classes were able to channel the energies of the masses into new forms of status system and new kinds of community. For Hobsbawm, this kind of cultural invention was particularly prevalent in the fissiparous 'ethno-linguistic' nationalisms of Central and Eastern Europe after 1870, though it was also present in the more inclusive, mass-democratic and civic nationalisms of the early nineteenth century. Nevertheless, though the collapse of communism has produced a spate of divisive ethno-linguistic nationalisms, especially in Eastern Europe and the former Soviet Union, the nation and its nationalism has become increasingly obsolete in an era of vast transnational markets and huge population movements (Hobsbawm and Ranger 1983, 'Introduction' and chapter 7; Hobsbawm 1990, chapters 4, 6).[4]

These expectations are not shared by Benedict Anderson. On the contrary, he argues that nations and nationalism (which are more akin to kinship or religion than to ideology) are destined to be with us for a long time to come. This is because nations are ultimately grounded in the twin fatalities of human existence: death and language. The fear of oblivion drives us to seek some kind of immortality, if no longer in another world, then through our posterity and our community; while the diversity of languages ensures the division of the world into categories which provide the basis for distinctive communities. For Anderson, nations and nationalism are modern phenomena; hence they stand in need of other, more historical, explanatory motors. For nations to emerge, other kinds of community had to recede; the decline of the powerful sacred monarchies and the great religious language communities that had dominated human thought and existence for so long provided the social space in which nations could emerge. The nation, which he defines as 'an imagined political community, and imagined as both finite and sovereign', appeared to vouchsafe to mortals that solace of continuity beyond death which the great religions and dynasties had ensured. But this was really only possible when the old medieval cosmological frameworks had given way to linear conceptions of time in which communities appeared to move through an 'empty, homogeneous time' measured by clock and calendar to an unknown destiny (Anderson 1991, chapters 1–2).

If these were the necessary conditions for the emergence of nations and nationalism, it was the invention of printing and the arrival of the mass produced vernacular book that made it possible to imagine the communities we call 'nations'. Anderson calls this process 'print-capitalism'. When the Latin market was saturated, print-capitalists sought out new vernacular markets, aided by the new Protestant emphasis on the need for each believer to read the scriptures. This encouraged the standardisation of official vernacular languages below Latin but above the level of popular dialects, which in turn gave rise to a vernacular reading public, or 'print-community'. After books came newspapers – 'one-day best-sellers' – which through their social subject-matter, tropes of identification and standardised chronology united readers who would never meet or know one another into the new imagined sociological community of the nation. It was the conjunction of a new technical invention, print, with a new system of production, capitalism, and the fatality of linguistic diversity, that ensured the success of the nation and the diffusion of nationalism across the globe (Anderson 1991, chapter 3).[5]

The nation and the historians

The nation for Anderson is a modern creation, but is it also a product of human imagination? Are we to say that nations exist only in the narratives of their purveyors? That is certainly one reading of Anderson's approach, and it is one that has commended itself to post-modernists like Homi Bhabha. Even Bhabha, however, distinguishes the performative narratives of the nation of everyday life from the pedagogical narratives of nationalist tradition (Bhabha 1990, chapter 16). Anderson, too, would surely accept the created reality of the nation and agree with Adrian Hastings' observation that the multiplication of books may enable people to imagine themselves members of a nation, but it could never be 'a matter of groundless imagining – rather a growth in realisation of, and preoccupation with, certain important shared characteristics' (Hastings 1997, 22).

But, if that is the case, if nations exist outside the discourse and artefacts that re-present them to an audience, then what are their distinctive, shared characteristics and where are we to look for their social and cultural foundations? This returns us to our earlier question, '*who* is the nation?', but equally to another question debated by some historians, '*when* is the nation?'

For most historians, nationalism has been a decidedly European, and a largely modern phenomenon. Elie Kedourie, for example, dated its appearance pretty precisely to Fichte's *Addresses to the German Nation* of 1807, in which the German Romantic philosopher sought to inculcate a national Will and a love of linguistic purity among German-speakers following Napoleon's crushing defeat of the Prussians at Jena the year before. For Kedourie, this German Romantic nationalism was a product of Kantian ethics and Herderian linguistic populism, and it possessed a special appeal for the excluded intelligentsia of the German principalities, and after them for the restless, alienated youth of Eastern Europe, the Balkans and subsequently the Middle East and South Asia. But the ultimate cause of that Fichtean striving for unattainable perfection on earth, of which nationalism's doctrine of the collective Will was so striking and successful an exemplar, was the quest for epistemological and moral certainty that had characterised the European philosophical tradition from Descartes to the Enlightenment, and whose ultimate origins were to be traced to the heterodox, antinomian Christian millennialism of the Middle Ages with its quest for salvation on earth in God's kingdom of saints. Only in the modern, secular world, the nation had replaced the elect, and historical progress the saving arm of God. Even outside Europe, the excluded intellectuals, or 'marginal men', exposed to European philosophy and historical scholarship in the wake of imperial regimentation, sought to assuage the discontents of their colonial status by adopting, and adapting, the millennial doctrines of European nationalism, leaving in their wake a trail of terror, massacre and mass destruction (Kedourie 1960 and 1971, 'Introduction').[6]

If nationalism is a wholly modern, secular doctrine, what of the nation? Must we accept the modernist contention that nations are the product of nationalisms and therefore entirely modern, that is, both recent and novel, phenomena? Kedourie's answer here is not entirely unambiguous, for he concedes the prior existence, at least in Africa and Asia, of ethnic ties and sentiments, not to mention collective religious traditions. Other historians would argue the same for Europe. Hugh Seton-Watson, for example, distinguishes between the 'old, continuous nations' of France, England, Spain, Sweden, Hungary, Poland and perhaps Russia, from those created by the nationalists, 'nations by design', as Charles Tilly maintains, formed in the wake of long periods of interstate warfare concluded by treaties, or through the colonial division of conquered overseas territories (Tilly 1975, 'Conclusion'; Seton-Watson 1977, chapters 1–2).

The latter nations, of course, all post-date the French Revolution. But the 'old, continuous nations' can be traced back in some cases to the fourteenth and fifteenth centuries, long before print-capitalism had created a literate middle class. Liah Greenfeld, it is true, regards England in the early sixteenth century as the first example of a nationalism that equates the nation with 'the people' as a whole, and sees in the Reformation and its biblical literature and martyrology the forgers of English nationhood, the first of the great roads to modernity opened up by different modes of nation formation (Greenfeld 1992). For Adrian Hastings, however, the first nations – England, Ireland, Scotland, France and Spain – emerged in the Middle Ages with the creation of vernacular languages from more fluid oral ethnicities. Hastings regards the nation as a peculiarly Christian, or more accurately, a Judaeo-Christian creation. The spur to the formation of nations in Europe was provided, not only by the sanction that Christianity gave to vernaculars, but by the powerful biblical prototype of the ancient Jewish nation which Christianity carried and purveyed to a wide popular audience by means of the Bible and prayer book, in its weekly services and annual festivals (Hastings 1997, chapters 1, 9).

Against these increasingly 'perennialist' views which decouple nation formation from modernisation, Susan Reynolds and John Breuilly present powerful cautionary tales. Reynolds takes Seton-Watson to task for the teleological framework which sees medieval communities as foreshadowing or even containing the lineaments of modern nations, with an inexorable movement carrying them forward into modernity. Instead, she views the kinds of political community prevalent in medieval Western Europe as *regnal*, being based on the attachment to dynastic houses of communities of common custom and descent. One is nevertheless tempted to ask how far such regnal ties and communities provided the matrix for subsequent national identities in the same areas, and whether there are any lines of continuity, or bases of recurrence, between them. It is partly a matter of definitions, but equally of the theoretical framework employed to analyse empirical cases, problems that can equally be raised in relation to other parts of the world like Japan and Sri Lanka (Reynolds 1984, chapter 8).[7]

At the other end of the historical spectrum, John Breuilly claims that we would do well to confine nationalism to the political sphere, and regard it as a strictly political movement for the seizure of state power. By divorcing it from questions of culture and identity, we can analyse national appeals in fairly instrumental and rational terms, as arguments for legitimating, co-ordinating and mobilising a variety of sub-elites in their quest for state power. Breuilly concedes, however, that to succeed and overcome the alienation caused by the split between the modern state and civil society, nationalists must appeal to historicist visions of the kind proposed by Herder; for they seem to offer a solution, albeit a specious one, to the discontents characteristic of modern politics and society. For Breuilly, nationalism only appears in the context of modern citizenship and the modern centralised state; he sees little use for perennialist approaches which suggest an historical continuity between *ethnies* and nations that lacks firm institutional bases, whether dynastic or religious, and which overlooks the totally new historical context of the modern state and citizenship in favour of a misplaced 'retrospective nationalism' (Breuilly 1993, chapters 1–3).

This kind of state-centred modernism offers a powerful corrective, but its vision seems unduly restrictive. Can we realistically sever identity concerns such as historicism seeks to address from political movements, and seal nationalism hermetically in the domain of politics? Such an approach inevitably misses the fundamental emotional level of mass appeal that gives nationalism its wide resonance. Further, while 'political' versions of modernism rightly highlight the impact of the modern, centralised state on society as a general precondition, they cannot explain the formation and distinctive character of particular nations and nationalisms in purely political terms.[8]

Ethno-symbolism

At this point in the discussion, we seem to have reached a theoretical impasse. The question is both historical and sociological. Can we avoid the dangers of reading modern nations and nationalism back into past epochs, while giving a more convincing account of which nations have emerged, and why? If modernist theories fail to address this question, and if perennialist approaches simply assume either the necessary recurrence of nations in general or the immemorial continuity of particular nations, can we furnish a more differentiated and nuanced socio-historical account of the formation and character of those nations that did in the end succeed in maintaining themselves – as well as those that did not?

This is where the approach favoured by John Armstrong and myself may offer some insights. I shall call this approach, for want of a better term, 'historical ethno-symbolism'. It suggests a twofold starting-point for the analysis of nation-formation: first, the importance of historical clusters, or heritages, of myths, memories, values and symbols for cultural community formation; and second, the vital role of ethnic ties and ethnic communities, or *ethnies*, in providing a basis for the emergence and persistence of nations. An *ethnie* may be defined as a named human population with a common myth of descent, shared historical memories, one or more elements of common culture, a link with an historic territory, and a measure of solidarity, at least among the elites. This definition suggests a connection between the two starting-points: the centrality of what Armstrong calls 'myth-symbol complexes' to the identification and persistence of *ethnies*. I would add the important role of historical memories and traditions, or 'ethno-history', the subjective history of the members of a community, and especially memories of heroes and 'golden ages'. Among myths, those of origins and ethnic election occupy a pivotal role in the self-definition and persistence of *ethnies*; while symbols, or what Armstrong, following Fredrik Barth, calls 'symbolic border-guards', play a crucial part in arousing collective emotions and ensuring cultural differentiation over the *longue durée* (Armstrong 1982, chapters 1, 9; Smith 1986, chapters 1–2).[9]

Armstrong argues that two principles of social organisation, one based on kinship, the other on territory, help to explain the divergence between Islamic and Christian European patterns of ethnic identification. Armstrong traces a series of influences on ethnic identity, from broad nomadic or sedentary lifestyles and their typical nostalgias, to world religious civilisations, imperial *mythomoteurs*, urban patterns of settlement, types of central administration and religious organisation, through to the most particularistic level of language differences. At each of these levels beyond the first, loosely bounded kinds of ethnic identification emerge, often combining with or sliding into class and religious identities. Armstrong offers no theory of the formation of ethnic communities, which, in perennialist mode, he equates with pre-modern nations, or of the emergence of nationalism and of modern nations based on its ideology; instead he suggests only a complex matrix of levels and factors that combine to form different kinds of ethnic identity, sensitising us to the range of historical influences at work (Armstrong 1982, chapter 9).[10]

My own approach owes more to the historians and sociologists than the anthropologists. Using the definitions of nation and nationalism which I proposed at the beginning to this chapter, it contends that many modern nations are formed around pre-existing, and often pre-modern, ethnic cores or dominant *ethnies* which over a period of time succeeded in incorporating outlying or 'peripheral' *ethnies* or 'ethnic categories'. Unlike the modernists, but like Armstrong and John Hutchinson, I tend to see the formation of modern nations taking place from this base over the *longue durée*; unlike Armstrong, I do not regard nations as 'perennial' either in the sense of continuity (though *particular* nations may be able to point to considerable continuities from the Middle Ages) or in the sense of necessary recurrence (though some pre-modern *ethnies* have resembled modern nations in certain key respects). In other words, most nations are, like the ideology and movement of nationalism, modern in the sense of being recent, though not wholly novel; but most nations are at the same time formed over long time-spans and are based on pre-existing ethnic ties and sentiments in the same area. Of course, there have been attempts to create modern nations fairly swiftly and with few pre-existing ethnic or cultural resources, as in many recent African states; but their success is by no means assured, and they are often threatened by internal ethnic conflicts and secessionist ethno-nationalisms (Smith 1998, chapter 8; Hutchinson 1994, chapter 1; cf. Horowitz 1985).

As this suggests, the differences between *ethnies* and nations are not absolute; indeed, the formation of nations on the basis of one or more *ethnies* is a relatively long, drawn out set of processes, such as increasing territorialisation, centralisation of collective myths and memories, growth of a territory-wide mass, public culture, increasing economic unification and legal standardisation. Such processes are uneven, and may be reversed; one can think of *ethnies* like the ancient Jews who, in the Second Temple period, came close to our definition of 'nation', but who thereafter, as a Diaspora community, lost some of those features (historic territory, economic unity, mass, public culture) that they had increasingly possessed prior to the destruction of Jerusalem in AD 70. This suggests that the nation is not a fixed, once-for-all state of being, but a moving target; and that is why nationalism does not cease after the attainment of independence, but is continually renewed as men and women seek to achieve their visions of nationhood (Grosby 1991; Smith 1994).

This leaves open the possibility that some nations may exist prior to the modern epoch, and that nations and nationalism should not be too closely linked to the condition of modernity or the processes of 'modernisation'. Indeed, Adrian Hastings has put forward a powerful argument to the effect that the first nations, notably England, Ireland and Scotland, emerged at least by the fourteenth century, if not earlier, even if the Reformation gave a huge boost to mass involvement through church liturgies and Bible readings. This supports a limited form of perennialism: some modern nations may indeed be able to trace their origins back to medieval epochs, or in a few cases like the Armenians, Greeks and Jews, to ancient *ethnies*. This may also hold for some nations in the Far East and South-East Asia; the Japanese and Vietnamese, for example, are able to trace their cultural heritages back to dynastic periods, and to pre-modern ethnic communities (Lehmann 1982; Hastings 1997).

None of this should be taken as supporting the nationalist contention that nations have always existed, 'primordial' entities in nature, slumbering until their appointed hour of regeneration by nationalist 'awakeners'. The truth of modernism is that most nations are recent; the error of modernism is to think that they are therefore wholly novel. Once we recognise the links between many modern nations and pre-modern *ethnies*, we can begin to build up an account of the ways in which they were formed from pre-existing ethnic ties and symbolic networks, and thereby shed light on their distinctive character.[11]

There are two main ways in which *ethnies* have formed the basis for modern nations, and two main routes to the formation of modern nations (I leave aside the third *pioneering* route found in immigrant societies). The first type of ethnic base is 'lateral'. These are mainly upper-class ethnic communities whose boundaries are ragged and extensive, but who, as Gellner portrays them, have no cultural need for or interest in the lower classes they exploit. The second type is the 'vertical' *ethnie*. This is a much more compact demotic community with high barriers to entry, in which all classes share, more or less, in a common (often religious) culture. Examples of the 'lateral' type include the ancient Hittites, the Aryans of India, the Normans and the French; and of the 'vertical' type, the Jews, Irish and Sikhs (Smith 1986, chapter 4).

The first Western nations tended to be based on 'lateral' *ethnies*, though closer inspection reveals a more mixed type in which the aristocratic (Norman or Frankish) *ethnie* conquered territories inhabited by various pre-existing demotic *ethnies* (Anglo-Saxons or Gauls). There have, of course, been many aristocratic ethnic states from ancient Egypt to Han China and Japan; what was peculiar about the Western European 'lateral' or aristocratic *ethnies* was their ability to create strong states that could incorporate both outlying regions and the middle classes of subordinate *ethnies*, and thereby create a new cultural amalgam in compact territorial states. Thus the Norman aristocracy in England managed to create a centralised state and incorporate the Saxon elites, adopting much of their standard law, ecclesiastical organisation and linguistic culture. By the late thirteenth century, wars with neighbours – Wales, Scotland and France – began to create cross-class national loyalties, on which the later Tudor monarchy's centralising state and Reformed Church could build in its wars with Spain. In France, from the twelfth century the Frankish Capetian kings were gradually able to extend their possessions around the Ile de France to include most of northern and central France, and from the later part of the thirteenth century much of Languedoc and Provence. In this process, the role of the Church, notably the archbishop of Rheims, in legitimating the monarchy in an era of feudal wars was pivotal; the Church helped to secure the small but expanding French kingdom, a fact that Joan of Arc later intuitively grasped, before it became subordinate to the French state. Even more than in England, a Parisian French linguistic culture was filtered down to the middle classes and to outlying regions by an increasingly centralised bureaucratic state, though it met with strong resistance from many regions like Brittany and Provence even after the Revolution (see E. Weber 1979; Armstrong 1982; Hastings 1997, chapters 2–4).

Such processes of *bureaucratic incorporation* could be found elsewhere – in Spain, Sweden, Hungary, Poland and, later, in Russia and Japan, under the aegis of 'official' nationalism – but in most of these cases, with the exception of a largely mono-ethnic Japan, they met with little success. It was, therefore, in, and from, an increasingly powerful West that the successful Anglo-French model of the 'nation' became canonical for so many penetrated and colonised areas of the world. At the same time, this very success spurred the diffusion of an alternative route to nationhood, one of *vernacular mobilisation* of 'the people'. This route proved especially popular with smaller, subject ethnic communities – in Eastern Europe, and parts of Asia and Africa. Here, 'vertical' *ethnies*, subject to imperial or colonial rule, as well as a variety of ethnic categories which were stirred into communal forms of social existence by ethnic neighbours and by processes of modernisation (urbanisation, commerce, secular education and bureaucratic penetration), became an object of attention for both colonial or imperial rulers and indigenous intellectuals and professionals. Members of these subject *ethnies* and ethnic categories, educated in the intellectual mores and cultures of their rulers but unable to assimilate into their society and political life, returned to their native communities and cultures which they then sought to modernise and politicise. Here they joined forces with other indigenous intellectuals who sought in the histories and cultures of their own *ethnies* a means of reconciling the authority and values of science and technology purveyed by the modern state with those of traditional religion. Together with many neo-traditionalists who rejected Western ways, they began to rediscover, authenticate and appropriate the 'ethno-histories' and linguistic cultures of their communities, thereby helping to restore their pride and dignity (See Smith 1995, chapter 3).

However, on their own, the native intelligentsias were powerless. As Nairn has demonstrated, they needed a broader social base, and this meant activating the small traders, clerks, artisans and peasants through a process of *vernacular mobilisation* – educating and politicising them in their vernacular languages and cultures. In many cases, this necessitated using native religions and redirecting popular religious sentiments into political channels. But in the process, the secular, and often civic, nationalism of the intelligentsia was frequently subtly transmuted into an ethnic nationalism with a strong religious aura that was more attuned to the needs and outlook of the mobilised 'people'. We can trace such processes of vernacular mobilisation and ethno-historical appropriation by intellectuals and professionals among many peoples from Poles, Germans, Czechs and Serbs to Arabs, Armenians, Sikhs, Burmese and Sinhalese – processes that have transformed these demotic *ethnies* by degrees from objects of history into self-determining political nations (see Smith 1991, chapters 2–3).

Ethnic and civic nations

These two routes to nationhood have formed the great majority of the world's nations. Apart from the 'plural' nations forged by pioneering settlement on the basis of immigrant fragment-*ethnies*, most people today reside in nations created on civic-territorial or on ethnic-genealogical foundations. Ideal typically, in the 'civic' nation, members are related through territorial birth and residence; they possess citizenship in a territorial political community, and are integrated by a unified legal system and a mass, public culture (usually in an official language). In the 'ethnic' nation, members are related through myths of common descent, and are distinguished from outsiders by vernacular languages and customs, traditional religions and a strong sense of native history. In the civic nation, barriers to entry are low: it is only necessary, at least in theory, to have resided in the national territory for a prescribed period and to speak the language and adopt the culture of the nation, to become a co-national through the application of *ius soli*. Whereas in the ethnic nation, again in theory, the barriers to entry are correspondingly high: only those born of the same ethnic 'stock' and able to trace their genealogies back to the prescribed generations, can be admitted to the circle of the ethno-nation. Like the metics of ancient Athens, those unable to meet the requirements of *ius sanguinis* are relegated to the status of (more or less welcome) guests – *Gastarbeiter* – or outsiders (see Brubaker 1992).[12]

That these distinctions do have consequences, especially for the reception of immigrants, is demonstrated by the contrast of contemporary French and German national policies. But, even here, we need to be careful. If German citizenship laws and ethnic policies can be gradually eroded, French civic attitudes and policies can be equally, if quite differently, exclusive. From the time of the Jacobins, French civic nationalism has insisted on stripping ethnic and religious minorities within its territories of their ethno-religious heritages and assimilating them entirely into French culture as the price for admission to French citizenship. Perhaps we are dealing here with a variant of the civic and the ethnic ideal of nationhood: what we may term a 'cultural' type of nationhood makes membership of the nation dependent on possession of, and assimilation into, the language, culture and history of the dominant ethnic nation to the exclusion of all else, thereby constituting a mixed type (mixed, because it mingles civic membership and territorial residence with dominant vernacular culture and ethno-history) (see Citron 1988).

Closer inspection suggests that many nations fall into this mixed category and that therefore we are dealing not so much with exclusive types of nationhood but with a complex continuum which mingles several variables and along which particular instances can be ranged only for analytical purposes. This is important, because given instances of nations may change 'type' over time, moving back and forth, from the 'civic' end of the spectrum on one variable to the 'ethnic' on another, combining elements in various permutations according to context. In this way, we see that all nations are permeated, in varying degrees, by both civic and ethnic features and criteria, and sometimes appear as 'cultural' variants of both (see Breton 1988).

Perhaps this unending duality, civic and ethnic, can be found even at the level of wider continental identities and communities like that of ASEAN and the EU. Certainly, the current debates centred around European citizenship, and who constitutes a 'European', suggest that these issues are about to be played out again, this time on a much broader canvas and with even higher economic and political stakes. Once again, cultural issues, though largely underplayed, form the unstated background to European policy debates and legal directives (see Smith 1995, chapter 5).

Conclusion

Mention of the idea of a European 'cultural identity' which, however tacitly, derives so much of its meaning from an analogy with national identities, suggests that we are unlikely to witness the imminent supersession of nationalism, let alone nations, despite the massive globalising economic and political pressures of the late twentieth century. The current proliferation of ethnic nationalisms, which have helped to spawn at least twenty new states since 1989, may in time abate and dissipate its momentum. But we are likely to witness other 'waves' of nationalism in other areas of the world, even if they do not succeed in breaking through the crust of the inter-state system in quite the same way. In any case, the basic *national* structuring of the 'inter-national' system is unlikely to wither away, as sovereign states continue to legitimate their existence through appeals to the 'nation' or the 'people'; the ideal of national self-determination may not give much comfort to particular ethnic secession movements, but it has been incorporated into the very structure of cultural and political pluralism that provides the basic framework of the world's inter-state system (see Mayall 1990).

The underlying reason for this state of affairs must be sought both in the increasing recognition of the moral equality of nations and in the deep influence exerted by the frequently pre-modern but basically *uneven* distribution of ethnic ties and cultural resources to this day; a contradiction that, in conjunction with gross inequalities of political and economic power, generates so many of the rivalries and conflicts which beset our world. A world of competing nation-states, fuelled by uneven ethno-cultural resources and political power, is unlikely to wither away. Rather, the pressures of economic and political globalisation are more likely to feed reactive cultural and political nationalisms through the 'demonstration effect' of successful movements and the dense communicative networks of ethno-cultural communities that feel liberated or threatened by new opportunities. In such an interdependent world of unsatisfied, but hopeful, ethnic nationalisms, the chances of transcending a world of nations must remain a dream of liberal cosmopolitans.

Notes

1 There is no agreement among scholars over the definition of basic terms and concepts in the field; see, for example, Connor 1994 (chapter 4). My own definitions are discussed more fully in A. D. Smith 1983 (chapter 7) and 1991 (chapters 1, 4).

2 For a defence of 'primordial' approaches, see Grosby (1994); for a discussion and critique, see A. D. Smith (1998, chapter 7).

3 Nairn has, as he says, taken the notion of 'uneven development' from Gellner's early analysis, but transferred it to capitalism. For the analogy of Adam's navel, see Gellner (1997, chapter 15).

4 Hobsbawm (1990) contrasts the two types of nationalism, which are also stages: the first, the mass civic-political type, flourished in Europe from 1830 to 1870, the second, the small-scale ethno-linguistic type, from 1870 to 1914, reappearing again in the 1960s.

5 Anderson goes on to apply these basic ideas in various parts of the world. But he warns that nationalism is 'modular': it varies with period and place, and hence no single theory can adequately explain the variety of nationalisms, nor encompass the many historical factors that are involved in different culture areas and periods.

6 As the example of Mau Mau shows, the marginal men in Africa and Asia adapted European doctrines to pre-existing ethnic customs and practices. For Kedourie, Tilak's use of ancient Hindu motifs is a particularly powerful example of the ways in which nationalists used, and subverted, history for their political purposes.

7 For Asia generally, see Tonnesson and Antlov (1996). For Sri Lanka, see Roberts (1993) and for Japan, see Lehmann (1982).

8 For similar state-centred versions of modernism, which focus on nationalism as a product, and expression, of the modern, reflexive state, or more generally of political and military factors, see Giddens (1985, chapters 4, 8) and Mann (1995). The origins

of this political thesis can be traced to the writings of Max Weber, especially on ethnic groups (see Weber 1968, I, ch. v).

9 For Barth's transactional account of ethnicity, see Barth (1969, 'Introduction'). For the definition of *ethnie*, see A. D. Smith (1995, p. 57).

10 While firmly opposing primordialist assumptions, Hutchinson (1994, chapter 1) finds the presence of recurrent ethnicity in the historical record, and, unlike Hobsbawm and Breuilly, admits the possibility of some continuities between pre-modern ethnic ties and modern nations.

11 This is disputed by Breuilly (1996) on the ground that, in the absence of institutional carriers, any links between pre-modern *ethnies* and modern nations must be fragmentary and tenuous. For my response, see A. D. Smith (1998, chapter 8).

12 There is a large literature on this subject, much of it normative and philosophical. See especially Miller (1995) and the symposium edited by O'Leary (1996). Billig (1995), however, demonstrates how the same basic nationalist motifs and attitudes pervade even the most civic and democratic nation-states.

References

Anderson, Benedict (1991) *Imagined Communities: Reflections on the Origins and Spread of Nationalism*, London: Verso.

Armstrong, John (1982) *Nations Before Nationalism*, Chapel Hill: University of North Carolina Press.

Barth, Fredrik (ed.) (1969) *Ethnic Groups and Boundaries*, Boston: Little, Brown and Co.

Bhabha, Homi (ed.) (1990) *Nation and Narration*, London: Routledge.

Billig, Michael (1995) *Banal Nationalism*, London: Sage.

Brass, Paul (1991) *Ethnicity and Nationalism*, London: Sage.

Breton, Raymond (1988) 'From ethnic to civic nationalism: English Canada and Quebec', *Ethnic and Racial Studies* 11(1): 85–102.

Breuilly, John (1993) *Nationalism and the State*, 2nd edn, Manchester: Manchester University Press.

—— (1996) 'Approaches to nationalism', in Gopal Balakrishnan (ed.) *Mapping the Nation*, London and New York: Verso: 146–74.

Brubaker, Rogers (1992) *Nationalism Reframed: Nationhood and the National Question in the New Europe*, Cambridge: Cambridge University Press.

Connor, Walker (1994) *Ethno-Nationalism: The Quest for Understanding*, Princeton: Princeton University Press.

Gellner, Ernest (1964) *Thought and Change*, London: Weidenfeld and Nicolson.

—— (1983) *Nations and Nationalism*, Oxford: Blackwell.

—— (1997) *Nationalism*, London: Weidenfeld and Nicolson.

Geertz, Clifford (1973) 'The integrative revolution', in Geertz, Clifford, *The Interpretation of Cultures*, London: Fontana.

Giddens, Anthony (1985) *The Nation-State and Violence*, Cambridge: Polity Press.

Greenfeld, Liah (1992) *Nationalism: Five Roads to Modernity*, Cambridge, Mass.: Harvard University Press.

Grosby, Steven (1991) 'Religion and nationality in antiquity', *European Journal of Sociology* XXXII: 229–65.

—— (1994) 'The verdict of history: the inexpungeable tie of primordiality – a response to Eller and Coughlan', *Ethnic and Racial Studies* 17(1): 164–71.

Hastings, Adrian (1997) *The Construction of Nationhood: Ethnicity, Religion and Nationalism*, Cambridge: Cambridge University Press.

Hobsbawm, Eric (1990) *Nations and Nationalism Since 1780*, Cambridge: Cambridge University Press.

Hobsbawm, Eric and Ranger, Terence (eds) (1983) *The Invention of Tradition*, Cambridge: Cambridge University Press.

Horowitz, Donald (1985) *Ethnic Groups in Conflict*, Berkeley and Los Angeles: University of California Press.

Hutchinson, John (1994) *Modern Nationalism*, London: Fontana.

Kedourie, Elie (1960) *Nationalism*, London: Hutchinson.

—— (ed.) (1971) *Nationalism in Asia and Africa*, London: Weidenfeld and Nicolson.

Lehmann, Jean-Pierre (1982) *The Roots of Modern Japan*, London and Basingstoke: Macmillan.

Mann, Michael (1995) 'A political theory of nationalism and its excesses', in Sukumar Periwal (ed.) *Notions of Nationalism*, Budapest: Central European University Press: 44–64.

Mayall, James (1990) *Nationalism and International Society*, Cambridge: Cambridge University Press.

Miller, David (1995): *On Nationality*, Oxford: Oxford University Press.

Nairn, Tom (1977) *The Break-up of Britain: Crisis and Neo-nationalism*, London: New Left Books.

O'Leary, Brendan (1996) 'Symposium on David Miller's *On Nationality*', *Nations and Nationalism* 2(3): 409–51.

Reynolds, Susan (1984) *Kingdoms and Communities in Western Europe, 900–1300*, Oxford: Clarendon Press.

Roberts, Michael (1993) 'Nationalism, the past and the present: the case of Sri Lanka', *Ethnic and Racial Studies* 16(1): 133–66.

Seton-Watson, Hugh (1977) *Nations and States*, London: Methuen.

Shils, Edward (1957) 'Primordial, personal, sacred and civil ties', *British Journal of Sociology* 7: 113–45.

Smith, Anthony D. (1981) *The Ethnic Revival in the Modern World*, Cambridge: Cambridge University Press.

—— (1983) *Theories of Nationalism*, 2nd edn, London: Duckworth and New York: Holmes and Meier.

—— (1986) *The Ethnic Origins of Nations*, Oxford: Blackwell.

—— (1991) *National Identity*, Harmondsworth: Penguin.

—— (1994) 'The problem of national identity: ancient, medieval and modern?', *Ethnic and Racial Studies* 17(3): 375–99.

—— (1995) *Nations and Nationalism in a Global Era*, Cambridge: Polity Press.

—— (1998) *Nationalism and Modernism*, London: Routledge.

Tilly, Charles (ed.) (1975) *The Formation of National States in. Western Europe*, Princeton: Princeton University Press.

Tønnesson, Stein and Antlov, Hans (eds) (1996) *Asian Forms of the Nation*, Richmond: Curzon Press.

Van den Berghe, Pierre (1995) 'Does race matter?', *Nations and Nationalism* 1(3): 357–68.

Weber, Eugene (1979) *Peasants into Frenchmen: The Modernisation of Rural France, 1870–1914*, London: Chatto and Windus.

Weber, Max (1968) *Economy and Society*, New York: Bedminster Press.

2 The changing faces of Chinese nationalism

The dimensions of statehood

Michael Yahuda

The question of 'face' may be understood in various ways. It has long been asserted that one of the differences between the cultures of East Asia and those of the West is that the former is concerned with 'face' or social standing and prestige whereas the latter is more 'guilt' orientated. Typically, today's Chinese spokesmen on foreign affairs refer to the period of foreign invasion and modern penetration of their country as the century of 'shame and humiliation'. Another way in which the concept of 'face' has been applied to the Chinese is as a mask, behind which the person's true identity is concealed. Bette Bao Lord, the wife of the American ambassador in Beijing in the late 1980s, used her appearance as an ethnic Chinese and her excellent command of the language to interview many Chinese people about their experiences. She concluded that the Chinese had become so accustomed to hiding behind successive masks that they were no longer sure of their true identity.[1] In this chapter I shall argue that perhaps the same is true of the manifestations of Chinese nationalism.

A substantial literature has appeared in recent years which seeks to chart new developments in Chinese nationalism and the Chinese people's sense of their identity. This reflects both new uncertainties on the Chinese mainland and new relationships that have emerged within and between the different Chinese communities resident outside the People's Republic of China (PRC), as well as between these communities and the mainland.[2] Rather than assess these writings and the new thinking that has emerged on the subject, I shall focus primarily on the issue of statehood. In other words, I shall not dwell much on the questions of ethnicity, culture and community, but shall examine one aspect of how the Chinese have sought to grasp what Gellner has called 'the national principle' of seeking to make 'the cultural and the political unit congruent'.[3]

Specifically, this chapter will address the following questions about Chinese statehood: on what basis are the claims for its formation or existence made? What should be its territorial bounds? Who is included among its members or citizens and why? What purposes should the Chinese state serve? And what should be the character of its relations with the wider world?

The imperial legacy

The questions just posed are of a modern character as they are predicated on the acceptance of the sovereign state as was developed first in Europe and then made universal over the nineteenth and twentieth centuries.[4] Of course, China has a long history of statehood and perhaps an even longer claim to a sense of political community. The West's thinking of China in cultural terms as a civilisation sometimes obscures this point. Lucian Pye's observation that 'China is a civilization pretending to be a state' points up some of the problems in the adaptation to modern statehood, but it plays down the significance of China's long history of pre-modern statehood.[5] In the 1960s, Joseph Levenson famously argued that the key transition to modernity in China was the move from culturalism to nationalism as the legitimate basis for organised political life.[6] However, he too underplayed the elements of statehood and nationhood that were evident in China's pre-modern era.

We should not forget that one of the ways in which China is distinctive is that it has the world's longest tradition of continuous statehood. Stretching back to ancient times, China has been a state that was centrally administered in accordance with an enduring civic ethos, laws, administrative hierarchy and so forth.[7] Although it was not a state in the modern sense of having the attributes of sovereignty, territorial integrity with clearly defined borders and conducting diplomacy with other equally sovereign states, nevertheless, the pre-modern Chinese state had a long-standing territorial domain that was usually referred to as the eighteen provinces. Even though for about half of the period of recorded Chinese history this domain was divided between two or more states, the idea, or perhaps one should say the ideal or myth, of a single, unified, cultural, imperial China prevailed as the only desirable, and indeed legitimate, China. That took the form of a single, centrally administered state.

The effectiveness of the Chinese tradition of administration and the Confucian trained scholars who served the state can be seen in the fact that throughout history, all conquerors of China have had to turn to the Chinese state in order to administer the country. In time, of course, as the conquerors settled down they became sinified – or at least that is the myth. Like all myths, this contains much that is true, but it nevertheless obscures some important truths. As we shall see, much of the basis for the claims put forward by the rulers of the PRC for the legitimacy of the current territorial domain of the Chinese state rests on this myth. Spokesmen for the PRC claim that all previous dynasties were in effect Chinese and that all the people who inhabit these vast territories are and always have been members of the Chinese family regardless of their ethnicity or what they believe. Yet the historical record suggests a more complex reality.

One example that can be cited is the case of the Mongol dynasty, known in China as the Yuan dynasty, which ruled from 1279 to 1368. Although the Yuan dynasty followed within China many of the traditional Chinese administrative practices, it employed many non-ethnic Chinese and superimposed upon the administration a Mongolian hierarchy. The armed forces were organised along Mongol lines. Mongol armies reached into Korea and were only stopped from reaching Japan by the Kamikaze wind that sank their ships. It also sent armies into South-East Asia. Curiously, contemporary Chinese spokesmen who like to argue that traditionally the Chinese were not militarily aggressive, disavow this example as 'Mongol' rather than Chinese in character. However, in other contexts these same people affirm the Yuan dynasty as inescapably Chinese. Also of interest is that during this period, many within the Confucian Chinese officialdom refused to serve the Mongol 'Son of Heaven' and others deliberately eschewed public careers. It was argued at the time that the Mongols were uncivilised and that their autocratic style of rule owed too much to their nomadic tradition rather than being based on proper Confucian virtue. The defeat of the Mongol dynasty and the founding of the Ming dynasty (1369–1644) was widely seen at the time, and subsequently, as a restoration of proper Chinese rule.[8] Indeed, when the Ming in turn were defeated by the Manchus – another nomadic people, but from what is now called the north-east – to establish the Qing (1644–1911), long-standing secret societies kept alive an anti-Manchu orientation.

It was not until the advent of the Qing dynasty – which was in part the successor to the Mongol dynasty as well as to the Ming dynasty, which it overthrew – that the emperor in Beijing could claim to rule over the vast tracts of land of Inner Asia that were the domains of the Mongols, the Tibetans and the Turkic-speaking peoples who lived on the western side of the Pamirs and the Mountains of Heaven (Tian Shan). As Evelyn Rawski and others have shown, the Manchu claimants to the throne in Beijing had their own separate order of kingship and nobility and it was in that capacity that they were able to establish ritual authority over the Mongol nobles and over Tibet. Although much was still contested, general authority of a feudal kind was established prior to the enthronement of the founder of the Qing in China proper. Among the titles of the Qing emperor was the Mongolian, Khan of Khans.[9] It followed from this perspective that when the dynasty came to an end then so ended the titular claims of its successor in Beijing to Mongolia. Seen from this point of view, the Mongolian nobles had every right to proclaim independence upon the fall of the Qing.

The Sinitic perspective could hardly be more different. Once on the imperial throne, the Qing assumed the attributes of a Chinese dynasty despite their different ethnic background. Other precedents could be cited for this. Hence the emperor ruled as a Chinese emperor and it was that which gave him authority. The emperor's position in China was at the top of a hierarchical pyramid in which personal-feudal and bureaucratic power were combined with the claim to ethical authority, and in which the social and cosmic orders were seen as fused. His supremacy had to be recognised not only by all Chinese, but by the so-called less civilised or barbarians on the outside. They too had to accept a kind of lord–vassal relationship. From earliest times it was understood within the Chinese scheme of things that a form of concentric hierarchy radiated out from the emperor (or the 'Son of Heaven' as he was known), and even though it became more tenuous with geographic distance, the principle of subordination as expressed in the form of tribute remained. It demonstrated Chinese superiority, but also imperial impartiality and benevolence or paternalistic generosity. Typically, Chinese records would show such generosity at times of peace and Chinese power. For example, the founder of the Ming dynasty issued instructions that the mountains and rivers of Korea, Annam (Vietnam) and Champa (eastern Tibet, now incorporated in Sichuan Province) be included on Chinese maps and that they be marked with stone inscriptions. He also undertook to offer sacrificial rites on their behalf. In accordance with Chinese views of the proper order, foreign rulers were described in Chinese records as having been conferred with titles and the attributes of office, demonstrating that they too had a place in the Chinese scheme of things. It should be recognised that this was not always the triumph of form over substance, as contenders for disputed thrones in maritime South-East Asia sometimes found it useful to strengthen their legitimate claims by gaining the ritualistic endorsement from the Chinese emperor.[10]

Nevertheless, the tributary rites could disguise the true character of relations in which the form of Chinese superiority masked what was in reality a system of exchange that favoured the barbarian. Typically, the Chinese would claim in their own literature that this merely yielded to the materialism indicative of less cultured people. Meanwhile, it was possible that outsiders could topple a dynasty by military means, but in so far as they sought to establish themselves as rulers, they would soon find that the only way to do so was in the time-honoured Chinese way. Indeed, that was precisely what happened to the Manchu Qing dynasty who in the end became thoroughly sinicised.[11] Nevertheless, the point to stress here is that Chinese official records regarding territorial claims and the character of relations with foreign rulers cannot be taken at face value. It is clearly anachronistic to use them as a basis for territorial claims in the way that contemporary rulers of the PRC are wont to do.

A wide range of methods were deployed by the emperors in dealing with non-Chinese rulers of other places. When strong enough, the Chinese could subdue the nomadic barbarians by force.[12] 'When less strong,' in Fairbank's words, 'they could refuse contact or buy peace by payments of grain, silk or even princes given in marriage. When weak, the more numerous Chinese could still assimilate the rather smaller number of barbarian invaders.'[13] These practices were not dissimilar from those of other traditional empires, as was the way in which divisions among nomadic tribes and peoples were cultivated for imperial ends in what the Chinese called 'using barbarians to control barbarians'. When the

Chinese imperium itself was split, its different constituents could engage in the state-craft of diplomacy, warfare and balance of power politics as recognised within the European experience.[14] Perhaps it was precisely because of the experience of the breakdown of unity and order, and the extent to which this challenged deeply-held Chinese beliefs to do with orthodoxy and harmony which fused the cosmic and the social, that the ideal of unity has continued to exercise a powerful grip on the Chinese political imagination to this day.

Chineseness was understood in cultural terms that encompassed the 'little tradition' of daily life – the settled cultivation of agricultural land and a sophisticated pre-industrial urban living – approximating to what anthropologists define as culture, as well as the 'major tradition' associated with cultivated Confucian hierarchy. In principle, non-Chinese could become Chinese through a process of assimilation which mainly involved adopting the practices of the 'little tradition'. Indeed, many people in China today who are regarded as ethnic Han Chinese include ethnic peoples who were assimilated in this way in past generations. Yet the external contrast with the Other, the barbarian, was also an important element in the traditional Chinese sense of identity. The attitude to the outsider was fraught with ambiguities. On the one hand, the barbarian could be sinicised; on the other hand, 'when the sense of cultural superiority was threatened the elite appealed to categorical differences in [racial] nature to expel the barbarian and seal the country off from the perverting influences of the outside world'.[15] This outlook, together with an appreciation of the highly sophisticated achievements of their own civilisation – as the only civilisation – contributed to the profound sense of the superiority and endurance of the Chinese way.

Nevertheless, traditional China was more than a civilisation whose distinctiveness should be defined in largely cultural terms. Chinese civilisation may be said to centre upon statehood. Levenson was only partially right in describing the transition into the modern era as that from culturalism to nationalism. Moreover, there is much that is variable and contested in the Chinese tradition of statehood affecting both its internal and external dimensions. Not surprisingly, modern Chinese nationalists have differed among themselves and over time as they have sought to understand the legacy of the past and adapt to the dynamic challenges of modernity as mediated by the West.

The modern transformation

The emergence of Chinese nationalism and the development of the Chinese modern state is intrinsically linked with meeting the challenge of the West, or rather that of modernity. There has been a tendency to confuse the two – a confusion that of course is not unique to China, but which has been a particular obstacle to Chinese attempts to establish their political identity. The imperialist and colonial assault by Western countries that in China is primarily remembered for the hundred years of 'shame and humiliation', was accompanied by the spread of industrialism and its associated political ideals and forms of organisation (of which the military assaults were themselves a part). However, these manifestations of modernity were also seen as examples of Westernisation. In China the revolutionary transformations of the twentieth century took a strongly national turn with the preservation of the nation (which was equated with the preservation of the state) as being the primary aim. Hence Chinese attempts to come to terms with the modern world have been described as 'anti-Western Westernization' – a concept which neatly captures the contradictory impulses invoked by the process of modernisation.[16]

In the 150 years or so since the West broke down the doors of entry into China, Chinese leaders have provided successive political doctrines around which it was hoped that the people could coalesce with a coherent view of their national identity at home and of their rightful place in the wider world: none has endured and all have been found wanting. Interestingly, once the Qing officials and the Confucian literati appreciated from about 1860 that the Western maritime challenge was unlike anything that had been previously experienced in Chinese history, two approaches were articulated that have echoed down the years without resolution to the present day. On the one side were reformers who argued that it was necessary to adapt to Western ways if China were to strengthen itself and once again acquire the power and wealth to repel aggressors and re-establish its significance as a major centre of power and culture in the world. On the other side were those who argued, on moral grounds, that this was tantamount to 'Westernisation' which would inevitably undermine the key values that the reformers claimed to uphold.[17] This polarity highlights a fundamental paradox in Chinese approaches to modernisation/Westernisation. Namely, that as long as they maintained that the values of their political system were fundamentally different from those of the modern/Western world, China would be isolated and would fall behind technologically, making it vulnerable as a power. On the other hand, carrying out programmes of modernisation/Westernisation meant that they risked subverting the very values that these were designed to protect. This paradox is as true today for the adherents of 'socialism with Chinese characteristics' as it was for the upholders of the Confucian way in the latter part of the nineteenth century.

It is generally agreed that modern Chinese nationalism was sparked off by the defeat of China by Japan in 1895. This was the point at which the fear of the loss or the death of China (conceived as both a state and a nation) took hold. Theories of Social Darwinism filled many Chinese with foreboding.[18] The universalistic principles on which ultimately the political culture of the Qing state rested were becoming an obstacle to China's integration into international society. After the defeat of the xenophobic Boxer uprising in 1900, even the Qing belatedly turned to constitutionalism as a new basis for establishing legitimate government. However, it was a case of too little too late. Sun Yat-sen (who had been energised by the still earlier defeat by France in 1885), the father of the Chinese Republic, and who alone has the distinction of being still honoured as a founding father by both the Nationalist Party and the Communist Party, famously first blamed China's misfortunes on the Manchus as alien rulers who supposedly sacrificed Chinese territory and rights to foreigners in order to preserve dynastic rule. It was China's defeat by Japan and the consequent secession of the island of Taiwan that proved to be useful to Sun in gaining adherents to his first political association, the China Revival Society (*Xing Zhong Hui*). He later changed his position and ceased to attack the Manchus because of the separatist implications that followed from excluding ethnic groups on the territorial periphery from mainstream China. Subsequently, he claimed that China was made up of five main nationalities (*minzu*): the Han Chinese, the Manchus, the Mongols, the Tibetans and the Hui (Muslim peoples). Apart from anything else, this was aimed at ensuring the retention of Chinese claims to the territories ruled by the Qing. Interestingly, the term *minzu* (meaning 'nation', but literally meaning 'race') was only introduced into the Chinese lexicon in 1899, and the concept of *minzu zhuyi* (nationalism) was first used in 1901 and by Sun in 1904.[19] In itself this demonstrates the modernity of the concept for the Chinese. Sun, however, always claimed the superiority of the Han Chinese and in effect adopted an assimilationist approach. Indeed, he has been described as having espoused the doctrine of racial nationalism.[20]

Sun also took a maximalist position in staking out the territorial claims of the modern Chinese state. In his *Three Principles of the People*, published in 1924, he listed a range of territories that had been 'lost' to China which included Korea, Vietnam, Taiwan, Mongolia, Burma, the Ili Basin, unspecified territories to the north of the Heilongjiang (or Amur River), the Ryukyu Islands, Bhutan and Nepal. Tributary relations were seen as the equivalent of colonies. In all cases they were said to have been lost as a result of foreign encroachments aided and abetted by Chinese or local traitors. Clearly, the claims to these territories were based not only on the rights to succession to the Qing as the rulers of a sovereign state called China, but also on the claim that the international agreements underpinning their loss were 'unequal' and therefore invalid. There was no question of self-determination as a principle. Moreover, the claims were ultimately based on a particular reading of history asserted to be authoritative and unchallengeable. Yet even leaders as different as Chiang Kai-shek and Mao Zedong, who basically followed Sun's position on China's territorial claims, showed themselves in practice to be selective and inconsistent in the ways in which they upheld or gave up these claims.

In his talks with Edgar Snow in 1936, Mao Zedong argued that after the defeat of Japan:

the Outer Mongolian Republic will automatically become part of the China Confederation, at their own will. The Mohammedan and Tibetan peoples, likewise will form autonomy republics attached to the Chinese federation ... Burma, Indo-China, Korea and Mongolia are illegally annexed parts of China which must be restored to it.[21]

Leaving aside Mao's temporary flirtation with the ideas of federation or confederation, it is clear that he shared with Sun a basic vision of the territorial bounds of the Chinese state as the successor to the Qing. Like him, and indeed Chiang Kai-shek, Mao's goal was not to dismantle the remnants of the Qing empire, but to transform them into a modern Chinese state. In fact, by placing the emphasis on how China had been victimised as a result of territories unjustly lost, and on its entitlement to restitution of past wrongs, as well as on its right to overcome past injustices and resume its greatness, these leaders also hoped to build a sense of national unity which was felt to be missing. On the fall of the Qing, Sun Yat-sen famously described China as a 'loose sheet of sand'. This did not imply that the Han Chinese people had no sense of self to distinguish themselves from foreigners. On the contrary, the recent Boxer uprising had demonstrated only too clearly the depth of a nativistic xenophobia. What was at issue for Sun was the prevalence of localist and familial loyalties and solidarities and the absence of a sense of national cohesion and organisation. The attempt to cohere around the symbol of statehood and the sense of grievance about lost territories may be seen as part of the effort to establish the elusive sense of national solidarity.

The establishment of a national solidarity involved above all claiming succession to the territorial bounds of Qing rule. Yet the question of succession to the Qing was fraught with problems in the sense that much of the legacy of the past had to be repudiated if modernity and a new powerful statehood could be embraced. The attempt to set up a republic in 1912 was widely perceived to have failed as China fragmented into warlord satraps. However, as in the case of nationalist movements elsewhere, many 'modern' intellectuals attempted to establish a vernacular literature with which to reach the broader masses beyond the classically educated elite. They also attempted to establish a 'new' and modern learning system openly derived from the West. The May Fourth Movement is regarded as the high-water mark in the establishment of the new modern ideals in China. The movement began in 1919, interestingly enough, by students and other urbanites demonstrating against a warlord government that stood accused of selling out China's birthright to the Japanese and thereby preventing it from regaining the German concessions at the Versailles peace conference. The movement called for the enthronement of 'Messrs Science and Democracy' and it repudiated past Chinese culture in self-consciously iconoclastic ways. Although the May Fourth Movement has served ever since as a symbol for open, political, intellectual debate and as the beacon pointing China towards the modern world of science and democracy (especially in the many darker nights of political oppression that were to prevail for much of the rest of the century), it could not ultimately serve as a basis for promoting national identity because of its wholesale denigration of the Chinese past.[22]

The weaknesses of the Kuomintang (National Party) under Chiang Kai-shek coupled with the continued division of China and the Japanese invasions seemingly destroyed whatever chance Sun Yat-sen's doctrine of *The Three Principles of the People* may have had to provide the appropriate political blueprint for establishing a modern Chinese state. Curiously, it was the universalistic doctrine of Marxism, or rather its Bolshevik variety, that was eventually to prevail as the political doctrine. But much of its appeal in China stemmed from highly nationalist considerations. Since most intellectuals and nationalists were convinced that China had to carry out a social revolution to meet the challenge of modernity posed by the West, the Bolshevik-Marxist approach promised a way of not only catching up with the advanced technology of the West, but of also superseding it by moving towards the socialist stage while the West still belonged to the previous historical era of capitalism.[23] In the event, it was the doctrine as purportedly sinicised by Mao Zedong that was to prevail. The day of triumph of Mao's revolution was hailed on 1 October 1949 in highly nationalist terms. Mao declared, 'The Chinese people have stood up. Never again will they be humiliated!' Indeed, whatever his claims to be a revolutionary, Mao took pride in his achievement as the unifier of the country and frequently compared himself to that other great unifier in Chinese history – the equally tyrannical first emperor of Qin of 221 BC.

Ambiguities of the territorial basis of statehood

Statements made by the PRC's leaders concerning territorial claims and rights to specific borders often invoke history and appear to be well founded and unchallengeable. However, not only are these historical claims frequently of doubtful validity, but they have not always been pursued with consistency, and indeed they have sometimes been quietly abandoned altogether. At earlier stages in the struggle for power, the Chinese Communist Party (CCP) had assumed positions that it later abandoned as it came closer to seizing state control. For example, Mao stated to the Second Congress of the Chinese Soviet Republic (in Jiangxi) in January 1934 that the presence of comrades from Taiwan, Korea and Annam proved the Party's commitment to allowing minorities to form their own states.[24] After arriving on the outskirts of Inner Mongolia at the end of the Long March, Mao issued an appeal in December 1935 to the peoples of Inner Mongolia, who were then under Japanese occupation, in which he promised 'to preserve the glory of the epoch of Ghengis Khan, prevent the extermination of their nation and embark on the path of national revival and obtain their independence as enjoyed by such people as those of Turkey, Poland, the Ukraine and the Caucasus'.[25] Even in Yan'an, the CCP chose to recognise that the anti-Japanese resistance on Taiwan constituted a separate national liberation movement by a distinct Taiwanese nation (*minzu*).[26] The CCP position on Inner Mongolia shifted as its troops gained local ascendancy and established the Inner Mongolian Autonomous Region in 1947 under the leadership of Ulanhu. It was in that capacity that the region was incorporated into the unitary state of the PRC. The CCP's change of position with regard to Taiwan was a result of the 1943 Cairo Conference in which Roosevelt and Churchill agreed that Taiwan, among other territories taken by Japan, should be returned to China. Chiang Kai-shek himself had not claimed Taiwan to be a part of the Chinese Republic in the draft constitutions of 1925, 1934 and 1936. It was only once Roosevelt and Churchill suggested that Japan should restore the territories it had captured in the course of the Second World War that Chiang insisted upon and secured their agreement to the restoration of territories captured in 1945.

Chinese inconsistency with regard to official policy and Taiwan is evident even after the establishment of the PRC. Christopher Hughes has noted how the character of the official claims to Taiwan have waxed and waned in accordance with the varying prominence given to the nationalist or revolutionary elements in CCP belief and governance. The significance of the Chinese claims to Taiwan faded when the revolutionary ideological tide was at its peak and then rose as that tide ebbed to be replaced by a stronger emphasis on nationalism. Thus the 1954 and 1975 Constitutions do not mention Taiwan specifically, whereas the 'liberation' of Taiwan is mentioned for the first time in the preamble to the March 1978 Constitution (during the brief ascendancy of Mao's hapless successor, Hua Guofeng), and again as 'reunification' in the preamble to the 1983 Constitution (under Deng Xiaoping). Hughes has observed that:

> In emphasising the call for national unification at the time of his succession, Deng thus located himself in an unbroken tradition of leaders and would-be leaders of the Chinese nation, stretching back to Sun Yat-sen and forward to Jiang Zemin, who link the issue of the integrity of the Chinese nation with the legitimacy of party dictatorship.[27]

The way China's communist leaders have handled their claim to Outer Mongolia or the Mongolian (People's) Republic is even more striking in its inconsistency. Chinese nationalists had long disputed the legitimacy of its independence in 1911 and again in 1921 on the grounds that this was obtained by a conspiracy between foreigners and unrepresentative or traitorous Mongol noblemen. What is more, they regarded its independence as spurious since they saw Mongolia as a satellite or protectorate of the Soviet Union. However, during the Yan'an period when Mao led the relatively weak Chinese Communist Party and was seeking to cultivate Stalin, Mao ignored China's claim to Mongolia and avowed that relations between the two countries were one of 'complete equality'.[28] After the establishment of the People's Rebuplic, Mao found that in making a much needed treaty with the Soviet Union in 1950 that like Chiang Kai-shek in 1945, he too was forced to recognise the independence of the Mongolian People's Republic. Four years later in 1954 (after Stalin's death) when Mao felt to be in a stronger position, he privately raised the question of China's territorial claims to Mongolia with Khruschev who was visiting Beijing, only to be told that he should address himself to the Mongolians.[29] Ten years later in 1964, Mao publicly listed Mongolia as among the territories that had been unjustly seized by the Russians from China and for which the Chinese had not yet settled the account. From 1966 until 1988, the Soviet Union maintained up to six armoured divisions and advanced strike aircraft in Mongolia, thereby transforming the country from simply a terrritory claimed by China into one that constituted a direct security threat to the Chinese heartland.

It might be thought that China's leaders would be keen to change the status of Mongolia at the first oppotunity. Yet after the disintegration of the Soviet Union in 1991, the PRC leaders showed no inclination to raise the question of Mongolian independence. Notwithstanding their sudden strategic superiority, nor the evident rise of nationalistic passions in China, no moves were made to put pressure on Mongolia to accept Chinese claims. On the contrary, in August 1991 (the same month in which the Soviet Union expired) the Chinese President, Yang Shangkun, visited the Mongolian Republic and signed a number of agreements, and the following year a border agreement was signed.

A similar pattern emerged in China's dealing with the territorial and border disputes with the Soviet Union, and after the fall of communism, with Russia. As already mentioned, when sketching out China's territorial claims in his *Three People's Principles* in 1924 Sun Yat-sen referred in vague terms to the territories north of the Heilongjiang (Amur River), implying not only that he questioned the borders established by the 'unequal' treaties of 1858 and 1860, but that he claimed the areas going back to the Treaty of Nerchinsk of 1689. The purpose of that treaty was not to set a border in the modern sense, but rather to stop Russian penetration into the Amur River valley area. Forty years after Sun, Mao raised the issue in 1964 at the height of the Sino–Soviet polemics by way of showing his support for Japanese territorial claims against the Soviet Union. Mao told a visiting Japanese delegation: 'About a hundred years ago, the area east of [Lake] Baikal became Russian territory, and since then Vladivostok, Khabarovsk, Kamchatka and other areas have been Soviet territory. We have not yet presented our account for this list.'[30] Again, as with the case of Mongolia, even though the Chinese side came to enjoy tremendous strategic latitude after the fall of the Soviet Union, China's leaders happily signed border agreements with Russia and the three new Central Asian states based on the borders set by the 'unequal treaties' that were supposedly invalid. Good relations were established while Deng was still politically active, but even after he became incapacitated by advanced age his successors, who might have been thought to be anxious to bolster their legitimacy by banging the nationalist drum, signed new border agreements in 1996 (resolving some of the remaining minor disputes), that were also based on the same old unequal treaties.

Such flexibility, however, is not in evidence regarding the PRC's maritime claims. These have basically been inherited from the Republican era, including the dotted line that stretches deep into the South China Sea in the shape of a tongue. Although this may be seen as an unexceptional assertion of historic or traditional rights that are not necessarily exclusive, it is striking that PRC spokesmen have not chosen to clarify the position in public. A recent study of PRC maritime claims which concludes that many of them are better established than those of rival state claimants, nevertheless observed that: 'Lack of clarity about the nature of PRC claims in the South China Sea has remained a feature of PRC statements or commentary upon the subject.' The author cited by way of example an official Chinese protest at a Malaysian occupation of one of the disputed islands, that was quoted as saying: 'China has indisputable sovereignty over the Nansha [Spratly] islands and the nearby waters and the natural resources in these areas belong to China.'[31] Many other such statements could be cited, and the point about them is that their nationalistic tone is deeply reinforced within China by the absence of open discussion of the strengths and weaknesses of China's claims in comparison to those made by other countries. Archaeological finds are also invoked as to suggest a long history of development and operation in the largely uninhabitable reefs and islets that make the bulk of the Spratly chain that spread over several hundred miles. For example, a discovery of a wide range of Chinese ceramics going back as far as the Tang dynasty was reported in the official New China News Agency on 28 November 1997 as follows:

> The archaeological survey once again proved: The Chinese people discovered the Xisha [Paracel] Islands first, and beginning no later than the Tang dynasty, have been continually developing and operating in various islands in the South China Sea including the Xisha Islands. *These cultural relics and materials have irrefutably proven that the Xisha Islands have been China's sacred territory since ancient times.* [Emphasis added]

The emotive, nationalist language that is used in this quotation may in fact reflect the PRC's relative maritime weakness and lack of familiarity with maritime practices, as opposed to the greater flexibility shown in advancing territorial claims in Inner Asia where China's deep-seated continentalist orientation made possible a more lenient and self-confident approach. Typically, that language also overlooks key points in International Law and totally disregards any claims that other countries may have to the area.

What is even more striking is the way in which the claims to Mongolia have been quietly set aside while those for Taiwan have been intensified. Perhaps the key difference in the divergent treatment of Mongolia and Taiwan, however, is the link between nationalist claims and the national interest as defined by the CCP leadership in the relevant period. Once the Soviet Union had disengaged from Mongolia and China's leaders no longer feared security threats from the north, there was no longer an urgent need to press the issue of unification. Moreover, to have done so would have jeopardised the goal of assuaging the concerns of neighbours about the depth of the commitment of China's leaders to cultivating a peaceful, international environment as a necessary corollary of their commitment to economic development through reform and openness. This approach was all the more necessary in the wake of the Tiananmen Square tragedy that had occurred only two years before. The Taiwan issue, by contrast, bore directly upon matters involving the legitimacy of CCP rule and on China's emergence to full great power status. Not only was there the question of completing the victory of the civil war, but it was also a question of sustaining the claim to the unity of the Chinese state. The fact that the process of democratisation in Taiwan had weakened the latter's commitment to the principle of 'one China' was in itself no reason for the CCP to do so. Self-determination that could lead to separatism had no place in Beijing's lexicon. As the then Foreign Minister Qian Qichen put it in 1996, ' the future of Taiwan is not a matter to be decided by the 21 million people of Taiwan, but it is to be decided by the 1,200 million people of China'.[32] Finally, the Taiwan issue involves the United States and the cluster of questions that concern China's emergence as a great power of international significance. As seen from Beijing, without American support Taiwan would have joined the mainland many years ago and, ultimately, it is that support that continues to enable Taiwan to stand apart. CCP leaders tend to see the American support for Taiwan as an instrument for containing China and for limiting its rise to its rightful standing in world affairs. Thus the question of Chinese *irredenta* may be seen as turning ultimately upon the political calculation of interest rather than necessarily upon the high matters of principle in which Chinese claims are usually advanced.

Patriotism and nationalism

According to the PRC political lexicon, *minzu zhuyi* (nationalism) within China refers to the ethnic nationalities of which officially China has fifty-six. Nationalism is therefore a divisive and pejorative concept – a view that is reinforced by the traditional Marxist disdain for it. *Aiguo zhuyi* (patriotism, or literally, 'love-state-ism' and, therefore, better understood as 'state nationalism') by contrast is much encouraged. As interpreted by the leaders of the PRC it calls for uncritical devotion not only to the state and its institutions, but also to the leadership of the CCP. For example, on receiving the child Panchen Lama whom the Chinese had chosen as against the candidate favoured by the Dalai Lama, Jiang Zemin was officially reported to have instructed him that he must be 'patriotic' and that involved loving China's leaders.[33]

This kind of 'patriotism' is particularly useful to the leadership not only because they can use it to demand loyalty to the person, but also because the leaders themselves determine its whole character. It is they who 'control' history and they are able to ensure that history serves their purpose. Not surprisingly, Chinese official histories have been so suffused with the need to serve whatever happened to suit the needs of current leaders that it has given rise to peculiar anachronisms. For example, contemporary historians apparently feel it incumbent upon them to show that the current territories encompassed by the borders of the PRC have always belonged to China and that the inhabitants have always been members of something known as the 'Chinese family'. Consequently most of the wars between the Chinese and the various peoples of the steppe are described as a form of civil war caused by reactionary or traitorous elements among the ruling classes. Strange distinctions are drawn between people of apparently the same ethnic group, some of whom reside on the Chinese side of the border and are described as members of the Chinese family and those on the other side of the border who presumably belong to a different family.[34]

This approach leaves no room for the exercise of self-determination or for different ethnic groups to develop their own accounts of their history. Tibetan, Mongolian or Uighur accounts of their history are dismissed out of hand or regarded as inherently subversive and designed to destroy the unity of the Chinese people. The perpetrators are stigmatised as 'splittists'. Consciously or not, it has the effect of elevating the Han view of history and the Han sense of cultural superiority with its assimilationist tendencies. Paradoxically, the manifestations of both the extreme leftism in the Maoist era in the Great Leap Forward of 1959–1961 and the Cultural Revolution of 1966–1976 and of the rampant commercialism since 1978 have tended to accentuate Han assimilation-ist tendencies. The leftist tendency was impatient with what were regarded as the feudalist exceptions applied to the non-Han and it carried out the socialist policies based on class analysis without exception. The commercial revolution that has swept China since 1978 also left little room for exceptional treatment of minority nationality sensibilities. A familiar complaint in Xinjiang and Tibet is that the new commercialism has favoured the Han at the expense of the locals. The new commercialism has also encouraged further Han migration into peripheral areas formerly dominated by the non-Han. In some cases the policy was begun in the late Qing, when the lands of Manchuria and Inner Mongolia were opened up to Han migrants. That policy has been continued in the PRC so that Han people outnumber the Mongols in Inner Mongolia by 7 or 8 to 1. In 1949 the Han accounted for about 7 per cent of the population of Xinjiang, by 1996 the proportion had risen to over 40 per cent, making the Han the largest nationality. This fact may help to account for the rise of ethnic nationalism in these areas at a time when the direct dictatorial or totalitarian controls of the Maoist era have been progressively loosened.

The emphasis on the Han has also evoked a kind of racial or ethnic patriotism that has transcended state boundaries. Despite their opposition to dual nationality, China's leaders have used important state occasions such as National Day to call upon the patriotism of the Chinese overseas (most of whom are citizens of other countries) as ' fellow descendants of the Yellow Emperor' to contribute to the Chinese economy. At the time of the Cultural Revolution, especially between 1966–1967, these same ethnic Chinese were expected to carry out revolution too.

The Deng era has witnessed a profound shift from ideological politics to those of commerce and patriotism. The emphasis on reform and openness has enabled China to focus on modernisation, and it stresses one dimension of the agenda as set by the May Fourth Movement. But it has not addressed the other key issue of political reform, or the 'Mr Democracy' as the co-respondent of 'Mr Science'. The Chinese patriotism from above may have accommodated considerable change and displayed unexpected flexibility in settling the territorial problems in the north and the west and it may yet prove able to address the maritime problems in the east and the south. But the innate conservatism built into the idea of preserving CCP rule is unlikely to meet the demands of a fast changing society into the twenty-first century. Indeed, as long as modern globalisation is equated with Westernisation China's integration into the international community will be less than complete and modern Chinese will continue to find it difficult to articulate what significance should be attached to the rise of their country other than its elevation in status.

Moreover the emphasis on the ill-defined concept of 'socialism with Chinese characteristics' does little or nothing to indicate to what ends China's growing weight in international affairs will be applied. The legacy of the past would place China at the 'centre', but that is no longer possible. So far China's spokesmen have done little more than call for the self-serving ends of demanding that their government be allowed a free hand at home and be granted the entitlements which it claims abroad. The Chinese have yet to articulate a view about the universal values and purposes that would be served by China's assumption of the international greatness that its leaders and intellectuals crave. Thus to return to the imagery with which I began this chapter, China's leaders have presented various masks or faces to delineate the identity of the Chinese state, but it is as yet unclear to the Chinese people or to others as to what is exactly the true identity.

Notes

1 B. B. Lord, *Legacies: A Chinese Mosaic* (New York: Fawcett Columbine, 1990) p. 120.
2 To cite but a few: Tu Wei-ming (ed.), *The Living Tree: The Changing Meaning of Being Chinese Today* (Stanford: Stanford University Press, 1994); L. Dittmer and S. Kim (eds), *China's Quest for National Identity* (Ithaca, NY: Cornell University Press, 1993); J. Unger (ed.), *Chinese Nationalism* (Armonk: M. E. Sharpe, 1996); and G. A. Hoston, *The State, Identity and the National Question in China and Japan* (Princeton: Princeton University Press, 1994).
3 E. Gellner, *Nations and Nationalism* (Oxford: Basil and Blackwell, 1990) p. 1.
4 For accounts of this development and the character of international relations to which it gave rise, see H. Bull and A. Watson (eds), *The Expansion of International Society* (Oxford: Oxford University Press, 1984).
5 L. W. Pye, 'Erratic state, frustrated society', *Foreign Affairs*, vol. 69, no. 4 (Fall 1990), p. 58.
6 This is the principal theme of his trilogy, *Confucian China and its Modern Fate* (Berkeley: University of California Press, 1958, 1964 and 1965).
7 The general book on imperial China that best attests to this is E. Balazs, *Chinese Civilization and Bureaucracy* (New Haven: Yale University Press, 1964).
8 For an extensive treatment of the Yuan period see the relevant sections in J. K. Fairbank and D. Twitchett (eds), *The Cambridge History of China, Volume VI* (Cambridge: Cambridge University Press, 1987).
9 E. Rawski, 'Reenvisioning the Qing: the significance of the Qing period in Chinese history', *Journal of Asian Studies*, vol. 55, no. 4 (November 1996), pp. 820–50. See also P. Crossley, 'The rulerships of China', *American Historical Review*, vol. 97, no. 5 (December 1992), pp. 1468–83. For a spirited rejoinder, see Ping-ti Ho, 'In defense of sinicization: a rebuttal of Evelyn Rawski's "Reenvisioning the Qing" ', *Journal of Asian Studies*, vol. 57, no. 1 (February 1998), pp. 123–55. For an earlier account that looks at the subject more broadly, see O. Lattimore, *Inner Asian Frontiers of China* (New York: American Geographical Society, 2nd edn, 1951). For a balanced account, see Joseph Fletcher, 'Ch'ing Inner Asia c. 1800', in J. K. Fairbank and D. Twitchett (eds), *The Cambridge History of China, Volume 10, Late Ch'ing 1800–1911, Part I* (Cambridge: Cambridge University Press, 1986), pp. 35–106.
10 For further discussion of this see, Wang Gungwu, 'Early Ming relations with southeast Asia: a background essay', in J. K. Fairbank (ed.), *The Chinese World Order: Traditional China's Foreign Relations* (Cambridge, Mass: Harvard University Press, 1968), pp. 34–62.
11 The account in this paragraph has followed the standard account to be found in John K. Fairbank's 'Introduction: the old order', in Fairbank and Twitchett (eds), *The Cambridge History of China, Volume 10, Part I*, especially pp. 29–32.
12 This is the theme of Iain Johnston's study of the Ming. See his *Cultural Realism: Strategic Culture and Great Strategy in Chinese History* (Princeton: Princeton University Press, 1995).
13 Fairbank and Twitchett, *The Cambridge History of China, Volume 10, Part I*, p. 19.
14 M. Rossabi (ed.), *China Among Equals: The Middle Kingdom and its Neighbors, 10th–14th Centuries* (Berkeley: University of California Press, 1983).
15 F. Dikotter, *The Discourse of Race in Modern China* (Hong Kong: Hong Kong University Press, 1992), p. 29.
16 The theme is argued at some length in I. C. Ojha, *Chinese Foreign Policy in an Age of Transition: The Diplomacy of Cultural Despair* (Boston: Beacon Press, 1969).

17 For accounts of the first attempts at reform in the face of the Western challenge, see M. C. Wright, *The Last Stand of Chinese Conservatism: The Tung-Chih Restoration, 1862–1874* (Stanford: Stanford University Press, 1957); Yen-p'ing Hao and Erh-min Wang, 'Changing Chinese views of Western relations, 1840–95', in Fairbank and Twitchett (eds), *The Cambridge History of China, Volume 11, Late Ch'ing 1800–1911, Part II* (Cambridge: Cambridge University Press., 1980), pp. 142–201.

18 These included leading intellectuals of the significance of Liang Qichao and Yen Fu. See Hao Chang, 'Intellectual change and the reform movement, 1890–8', in Twitchett and Fairbank (eds), *The Cambridge History of China, Volume 11, Part II*, p. 296 and 298.

19 See Dikotter, *The Discourse of Race*, pp. 108–9. See also C. Hughes, *Taiwan and Chinese Nationalism: National Identity and Status in International Society* (London: Routledge, 1997), p. 3.

20 Dikotter, *The Discourse of Race*, pp. 123–5.

21 E. Snow, *Red Star Over China* (London: Victor Gollancz Ltd., 1937), p.102. This statement was watered down in later versions of this famous work.

22 For a general account, see Chow Tse-tsung, *The May Fourth Movement: Intellectual Revolution in Modern China* (Cambridge, Mass: Harvard University Press, 1960). For particular analyses of its significance in the light of subsequent developments, see Vera Schwarz, *The Chinese Enlightenment: Intellectuals and the Legacy of the May Fourth Movement of 1919* (Berkeley: University of California Press, 1986); and Lin Yu-sheng, *The Crisis of Chinese Consciousness: Radical Anti-traditionalism in the May Fourth Era* (Madison: University of Wisconsin Press, 1979).

23 J. R. Levenson, 'Marxism and the middle kingdom', in J, R. Levenson (ed.), *Modern China: An Interpretive Anthology* (London: Collier-Macmillan Ltd., 1971), pp. 229–36.

24 Hughes, *Taiwan and Chinese Nationalism*, pp. 13–14.

25 CCP Central Archive Library, *Zhonggong Zhongyang Wenjian (CCP Central Documents), Volume X (1934–35)* (Beijing: Party Press, 1988), p. 880. This was translated and shown to me by Mr Temtsel Hao, to whom I express my gratitude.

26 F. Hsiao and L. Sullivan, 'The Chinese Communist Party and the status of Taiwan, 1928–1943', *Pacific Affairs*, vol. 52, no. 3, pp. 446–67.

27 Hughes, *Taiwan and Chinese Nationalism*, pp. 14–15.

28 Snow, *Red Star*, p. 102.

29 D. J. Doolin, *Territorial Claims in the Sino-Soviet Conflict, Documents and Analysis* (Stanford: Stanford University Press, 1965), pp. 43–5. See also T. Strobe (trans. and ed.), *Khrushchev Remembers, Volume 2* (London: Penguin Books, 1977), pp. 335–6.

30 Doolin, *Territorial Claims*, pp. 43–4.

31 G. Austin, *China's Ocean Frontier* (NSW: Allen and Unwin Australia Pty Ltd., 1998), p. 208.

32 BBC Summary of World Broadcasts, Part 3, *The Far East*, January 6, 1996.

33 New China News Agency: Beijing, January 13, 1996.

34 W. Gungwu, 'Pre-modern history: some trends in writing the history of the song', in M. B. Yahuda, *New Directions in the Social Sciences and Humanities in China* (Basingstoke: Macmillan Press, 1987), pp. 1–27; especially pp. 7–14.

3 Ethnic nationalism in mainland China[*]

Solomon M. Karmel

> This frontier post brings me sorrow,
> Once before I came through here.
> Ice and snow slash muscles and skin,
> The wind howls without end;
> For a hundred *li* there are no people,
> Grass and trees lie untended ...
> The world is filled with happy places,
> Why linger here, on and on?
>
> (Wang Can, AD 177–217, *Seven Poems of Lament*)[1]

The Chinese names for the western provinces in China imply their position in the Chinese empire: Tibet is not called 'the land of snows', as it is in Tibetan, but rather 'Xizang', which means 'western storehouse' or 'western treasure-house'. China's communist leaders have attempted to profit with only limited success from this vast western territory – a treasure-house of minerals and resources, but one that is largely uninhabited and impoverished – in their forty years of rule over the region. Xinjiang, the huge region populated by Uighur (pronounced 'vigour'), Hui (pronounced 'h-weigh'), and other Muslim peoples in the north-west of what is now China, means in Chinese, 'new border' or 'new frontier'. Yet many of the Muslims who live in this 'new frontier' have fought to make large parts of it into independent regions.

The frontier regions to the west, Inner Mongolia and Ningxia to the north, and to a lesser extent Manchuria to the north-east and Yunnan to the south-west, have their own identities and cultures that are significantly different from those of the Han areas of China. None the less, the Chinese name for China means literally 'central nation', and the Chinese are therefore the 'people of the central nation'. These frontier regions are territories, far to the west or north, which add to the power of the 'centre' and the belief is that they should always be ruled by the central authorities.

---

[*] Some information in this chapter on Tibet updates the author's previously published article, 'Ethnic tension and the struggle for order: China's policies in Tibet', *Pacific Affairs*, 68: 4 (Winter 1995–1996), pp. 485–508.

This chapter focuses on the Tibetan plateau and Xinjiang Province, and looks at the sources for ethnic nationalist tensions in Mainland China. First, I provide a brief historical overview of 'imperial legacies', including destructive policies under Mao Zedong, which give the native peoples of these regions many reasons to resent the authorities in Beijing. I then hone in on the primary reasons why ethnic tensions during the reform period appear to be increasing rather than decreasing. In conclusion, I discuss the potential implications of currently rising tensions in Tibet and Xinjiang.

An historical overview

At moments of strength in China's imperial history, Tibet was a protectorate of China, with some Chinese administrators claiming 'suzerainty' over this 'protectorate' in exchange for concessions to the sovereign authority of Tibetan lamas on questions of rites, ceremony and religion. The status of Tibet during these periods of imperial expansion has parallels to Western feudalism but few similarities to contemporary relations between nations or states in any world region. Ironically, China's power over Tibet was also strongest when China itself was not ruled by 'Han' Chinese but rather by 'foreign' emperors of the Mongolian (Yuan) and Manchurian (Qing) dynasties. Yet Tibet's submission to the Mongols (in 1207, nullified by 1358) and to the Manchurians (especially during the late seventeenth and early eighteenth centuries) are important markers in China's official historiography on its claims over Tibet.

Through the nineteenth and early twentieth centuries, as the Qing dynasty unravelled and revolutions tore China apart, Tibet governed itself in the few large towns where it could be considered governed. On the other hand, its introspective, dispersed, monastic leadership maintained no significant relations with any established state. Hence, on the eve of Mao Zedong's 1951 military invasion, Tibet was a more or less united, feudalistic territory under the decentralised control of the Dalai Lama; but while it enjoyed *de facto* independence, it did not enjoy *de jure* 'statehood' in the United Nations. After Tibet's 1951 'peaceful liberation' (by China's People's Liberation Army, in a quick, violent battle against local troops), it was eventually broken into separately governed sections by the Chinese authorities. Today, these include the 'autonomous region' of Tibet, which has never been remotely autonomous since the 1951 occupation and especially since a 1959 military crackdown; the Qinghai Tibetan autonomous region; and a prefecture added to Sichuan that dramatically increased the size of Sichuan Province. 'Autonomous' prefectures of Gansu and Yunnan Provinces are also on the Tibetan plateau and have large Tibetan populations.

The Chinese promoted a brave new world in Tibet soon after the military occupation. Communes were carved out of fragile hills and forests, and nomadic herdsman were told to abandon their lifestyle and grow grain. During the Great

Leap Forward (1959–1961) and the Cultural Revolution (1966–1976), autocratic economic management caused hundreds of thousands of people to starve to death in Tibet's first recorded famines.[2] During a military crackdown in 1959, long before the excesses of the Cultural Revolution, the Dalai Lama already had had enough. Fearing for his own life and his land, Tibet's political and spiritual leader fled to exile in India. Soon after, during the disastrous Great Leap Forward, millions starved to death throughout China, but there is evidence to suggest that the famine was particularly destructive in Tibet. Official statistics suggest that Tibetans were the only nationality in China whose population growth was not only checked but reversed (that is, the population of Tibetans decreased) during the famine.

During the Cultural Revolution, Chinese policies towards Tibet were even more destructive than those towards the rest of China. In the name of a higher religion, Maoist leaders persecuted Tibetan monks and others who were labelled members of the 'exploiting' classes in Tibetan society. By the mid-1970s, authorities had killed or starved hundreds of thousands of people on communes, in prisons, and in labour reform camps. From 1966 to 1976, hundreds of monasteries that had survived earlier military campaigns were blown up or burned to the ground.[3] Some partisan estimates claim that one in every ten Tibetans had been imprisoned at one time or another between 1959 and the first few years of the reform period,[4] but no accurate records can be garnered on related issues from the Maoist period.

Deng Xiaoping promoted less destructive policies towards Tibet, on the advice of Hu Yaobang, a reformist who would later be purged. Totalitarian policies towards religion, education and collectivisation were largely reversed. In interviews in Beijing and Lhasa in the late 1980s and 1990s, several university-educated Tibetans informed me that the economic and political situation in their homes and villages improved dramatically under Deng and in the post-Deng period. Yet even today, Tibetans have reasons to feel that they have no political control over their 'autonomous region', and many are socially alienated from the Han Chinese who speak a different language, tend to be atheist, occupy superior economic and political positions in Tibet's cities, and are in general from a different culture than the Tibetans. Anti-Chinese sentiment among Tibetans is still strong.

Chinese empires have occupied Xinjiang on and off since the Han dynasty, and the Qing dynasty secured Xinjiang in the second half of the nineteenth century.[5] Yet there were four major rebellions against Qing rule. One culminated in an independent state of East Turkestan from 1867–1877.[6] During the Republican era, Chinese warlords who ruled Xinjiang, 'brought economic rapacity to perfection', and forbid Muslims to perform the pilgrimage to Mecca, probably in an attempt to stop money from leaving the country.[7] Warlords also annexed semi-autonomous fiefdoms. All of this led to violent revolts against Chinese rule. In

1931, in retaliation for one revolt, the Chinese burned to the ground the ancient city of Hami (then called Kumul). Other bloody revolts led to retaliatory crackdowns in Urumqi and elsewhere.

Some revolts were at least temporarily successful. In 1933–1934, independence leaders overthrew Chinese warlords in Kashgar. During the Second World War, the Ili revolt in Kashgar, led by a Kazakh, resulted in the creation of a second 'Turkish-Islamic Republic of East Turkestan'.[8] In order to regain control, the Guomindang signed an impressively democratic peace treaty with the independence leaders of East Turkestan. But the Guomindang never carried out most of the concessions in the treaty after it re-annexed Kashgar.[9]

Reports of demonstrations in Muslim areas have reached the outside world almost continuously since communist 'peaceful liberation'. Opposition also persisted among activist exiles outside the country. Before the collapse of the Soviet Union, the Secretary General of the national government in East Turkestan in the 1940s, Isa Yusuf Alptekin, worked in exile in Istanbul to drum up resistance to communist forces. He met regularly with the leaders of all of Turkey's major political parties. After the dismantling of the Soviet state, revolutionaries established a Uighur 'liberation organisation',[10] and Erkin Alptekin has continued his family's leadership in the 'liberation' struggle using the Kazakh capital, far closer to China's north-western border, as his base.

Sources for continued tension in Tibet and Xinjiang

Sources for continued tension in ethnic minority regions like Tibet and Xinjiang include, since around 1988, (1) the largest outpourings of ethnic nationalist protest and dissent, in Tibet since 1959, and in Xinjiang since the Cultural Revolution; (2) a problematic international situation, which poses new challenges to Chinese authority in Tibet and Xinjiang; (3) a national development plan that permits great disparity in 'open door' policies in coastal and inland regions, with more centralised control of the weak and vulnerable economies of national minority regions; (4) the continued ethnocentric, or 'ethno-nationalist' attitudes of the Chinese leadership towards the value of Tibetan and Islamic Central Asian culture; and finally, (5) residual, 'leftist' ideas on religion and class struggle, apparently revived by conservatives to attack independent cultural traditions and figures of authority among ethnic minorities. Details on these sources for newly imposed restrictions and their results are provided below.

Crisis, ethnic conflict, and the threat of revolt

Between the autumn of 1987 and March of 1989, by the government's own count, opponents of Chinese authority led twenty-one riots of varying sizes in the Tibet Autonomous Region. The demonstrations of 1987 and 1988 were the largest since 1959, and at least some officials (both Chinese and Tibetan) may have feared for their own lives during the protests. The Panchen Lama said that at one protest in April 1988, police beat monks 'during their attempts to rescue local leaders whose lives were threatened by rioting separatists'.[11] While most Chinese officials would simply leave Tibet in the event of a successful transition to independence, a large number of Tibetans currently serving the government – especially those who must enforce order at the grassroots – may view the prospect of such a transition with some apprehension.

It should be emphasised, however, that most protests during this period were non-violent, and the majority of those arrested in recent years for demonstrations, protests and 'counter-revolutionary' or 'splittist' activities have been non-violent activists. Still, a 'bunker' mentality emerges from the propaganda. In the words of Yan Mingfu, then chief of the Communist Party's United Front department: 'The consciousness of minorities, their sense of pride, nationalism and self-respect is getting stronger and stronger. This means the work among nationalities will become more onerous.'[12]

Since the lifting of Martial Law in Tibet in April 1990, there has been a diminished troop presence on the streets of Tibet's largest cities and towns. Nevertheless, all major roads leading to and from strategic sites contain large army bases, and the political atmosphere in Tibet is generally somewhat more 'militarised' and tense than elsewhere. For example, independent analysts abroad listed 1993 as the worst year for political arrests and trials in China since 1990, and in 1993 almost 80 per cent of the documented arrests and sentences for political crimes in the People's Republic of China (PRC) occurred in Tibet. In 1994, the number of officially acknowledged arrests for pro-separatist or counter-revolutionary activities rose by over 90 per cent in the Tibet Autonomous Region; more recently, reports by Amnesty International document cases of over 600 people in Tibet regarded by the organisation as political prisoners.[13] In addition, the largest non-governmental educational institution in Lhasa was closed down in April of 1994, with all of its students expelled and the Tibetan director arrested on 'counter-revolutionary' charges.

The second half of the 1990s have been somewhat more quiescent, and the political and social atmosphere in Lhasa is more relaxed. There are fewer signs of large troop movements; there is a more developed restaurant and night life (dominated by Chinese-run businesses); and more emphasis on commercial construction. But even in this period of tenacious development and comparative political stability in Tibet (and in all of China), small, unorganised protests against China's political and economic presence continue all over Tibet.

As a result, according to Gyaincain Norbu, the current governor of the Tibet Autonomous Region (TAR), there is a need for 'increased vigilance' to counter the separatism that has sprung up in the mid- to late 1990s. This is due in large part to (1) new efforts by exiled separatists to dispatch 'special spies', build 'underground reactionary organizations, and intensify the infiltration of political thoughts and religion' in Tibet; and (2) the 'spread [of] secessionist activities to the agricultural and grazing areas' of Tibet.[14]

Scattered reports and speeches by Tibet's alarmed leadership strongly suggest that rebellions in pastoral and border areas may indeed be increasing. In 1991, dozens of Tibetan farmers from the Dri region of Qinghai (Amdo) protested outside provincial offices in Xining, with a long banner which proclaimed in Tibetan: 'Return our snowlands – Give us back our grasslands – Leave us be – We are dying of hunger.' In 1993, judicial authorities issued prison sentences ranging from thirteen to fifteen years to other farmers who displayed a Tibetan flag and disrupted a political education meeting with independence slogans. In March 1994, a group of protesters from Baxoi County hung anti-Chinese banners and slogans in public locations of Chamdo Prefecture, and were sentenced to twelve years of prison for the county's first publicised case of 'counter-revolutionary sabotage'. In June 1994, paramilitary police placed a cordon around Shar Bumpa, a rural nunnery in the mountains near Lhasa, in response to a demonstration by five nuns. In the first quarter of 1995, Amnesty International documented over 123 arrests for a series of peaceful, pro-independence protests in monasteries and nunneries of Tibet, most of which were located outside of Tibet's two largest cities.

Foreigners were banned from Xinjiang briefly in the spring of 1990, just as I planned to tour the region, because of unrest and rioting near Kashgar. Official reports claimed that only twenty-two people were killed and thirteen wounded during the uprising; yet reports from outside travellers suggested that the true death toll may have reached sixty,[15] and over 6,000 people were reportedly arrested.[16]

Again, after the collapse of the Soviet Union, the struggle against Chinese rule in Xinjiang became somewhat more organised, with a reinvigorated 'liberation' movement ('the United National Revolutionary Front'), now based in Kazakhstan. 1996 saw the beginning of a campaign to assassinate government officials and religious leaders seen as loyal to Beijing.[17] For example, in November, a Uighur carried out a machine gun attack on Chinese police which left sixteen officers dead.[18] In February 1997, during the Chinese New Year celebrations, perhaps 10,000 people rioted in Yining City; nine people were killed, 198 injured, and after widespread looting the town fell under martial law. The riots began as protests against Chinese rule, and China blamed them on 'Uighur militants'. Just before the local police force carried out a capital punishment sentence on three convicted leaders of the riots, in April 1997, they fired on a crowd which gathered outside the jail in a struggle to free the death row convicts.[19] Since February 1997, Uighur sources claim that dozens of protests have occurred elsewhere. Uighurs were executed for planting home-made bombs on public buses in Urumqi during the funeral rites in Beijing for

Deng Xiaoping.[20] In late September, non-violent occupations of government offices by Uighur nationalists have taken place in Shanshan, Hoxud, Hutubi and elsewhere.[21] In December 1997, between seven and thirteen Uighur people were executed for 'crimes against the state', apparently related to the February uprising in Yining. There are no truly independent sources which list the specific crimes of the accused, yet they are said to have included both non-violent and violent anti-Chinese activities, ranging from shouting slogans calling for an independent East Turkestan to murder. China's version is that they included a 'gang of seven [not thirteen] who killed 13 people and committed more than 10 robberies to "fan ethnic hatred and create an atmosphere of terror" '.[22]

Xinjiang's current Party Secretary, Wang Lequan, suggested as recently as December 1997, that public security in Xinjiang is not improving. He cites, as an important new threat to law and order, the collusion between political separatists and unsanctioned yet increasingly respected religious organisations and authorities.

> [P]ublic security has not fundamentally improved ... In Xinjiang, in addition to ordinary public order problems that also exist in other parts of China, there are national separatist forces and illegal religious forces. These two forces and criminal elements are using one another. Regarding criminal elements as their allies, the national separatist forces have created an atmosphere of terror by carrying out terrorist activities.

The Xinjiang Party Secretary has also suggested that attacks against public security forces and other government organisations have become frequent and serious: 'Today, whoever comes out to struggle against the national separatists and against criminal elements will often suffer revengeful attacks by criminal elements.'[23] In general, Wang Lequan suggests that 'the struggle between separatists and anti-separatists will be a protracted, fierce and arduous one. ... We must be prepared to fight separatists for a long time to come.'[24]

While violent and non-violent protests in Xinjiang receive international support from Kazakhstan and elsewhere, they are fuelled primarily by the resentment of locals who have no contacts abroad. Further, protests appear to be spontaneous and bereft of prominent leadership. Domestically manufactured weapons of violent protest include home-made bombs and stolen or black-market guns and grenades.[25] The tools of non-violent protest include illegal signs, graffiti and banned books.

The new international situation

Tibet's Party Secretary, Chen Kaiyuan, refers to international changes in the post-Cold War era to explain changes in China's policies towards Tibet: 'Especially under the influence of the international macro-environment, separatist activities have intensified in Tibet and the situation of the anti-separatist struggle has sharpened. These factors are causing political instability.' In a classified speech attributed to Chen Kaiyuan, he specifically refers to the break up of the Soviet Union and 'peaceful evolution' in Eastern Europe as an alarming precedent for China and for the TAR Party leaders he addressed.[26]

Similarly, Gyaincain Norbu, the current Governor of Tibet, stated in 1992 that changes in Eastern Europe and the former Soviet Union had given rise to speculation that Tibetan independence might be only five to ten years away. 'But the speculation will not come true.' Meanwhile, China's official press claims that the Dalai Lama's supporters harbour 'a hidden motive': 'They want to take advantage of [turmoil] to split China. To be frank, they want to bring about another "Bosnia-Herzegovina" in China! But China is not Yugoslavia.'[27]

International problems for China's mini-empire include the break-up of the Soviet Union (caused in large part by ethnic nationalism), ethnic conflicts in Eastern Europe (for example, Yugoslavia), the rise of Muslim states on China's north-western border, and democratisation in dozens of countries. As a result of all of these changes, powerful nations, international bodies and national minority groups themselves hold higher expectations for the rights of Chinese-ruled minority nationalities and citizens. The Dalai Lama and his supporters are tremendously heartened by these international changes. In a 1993 interview, the Dalai Lama listed three reasons for his renewed hopes for Tibet. These are: (1) 'representatives of totalitarianism have become a minority' in the world; (2) almost all communist authoritarian regimes have collapsed; and (3) the government-in-exile has received more international support in the past few years, especially from the West.[28] Vaclav Havel, an imprisoned dissident in the era of Soviet strength, became the first of many heads of state to receive the Dalai Lama. Since the late 1980s, the Dalai Lama has visited Mongolia and several nations of Eastern Europe (including the newly independent Baltic states). He has met with two American Presidents and heads of state in the UK, Australia, Canada, Africa and Latin America.

Other international changes bear directly on the Tibet question. Top leaders of Taiwan, for example, note that reunification strained Germany's economic and social fabric, and that the East European path away from socialism is far more arduous than most had realised. For this and other reasons, authorities in Taiwan are increasingly distancing themselves from the Mainland, and increasingly sympathetic to leaders elsewhere in 'greater China' who wish to do the same. Taiwan's new geopolitical view has led to a diplomatic breakthrough in Taiwan's relations with the Dalai Lama's government in exile.[29]

Ethnic separatists in Xinjiang have clearly received a boost from the birth of five Muslim republics between Russia and China in the early 1990s. Again, separatists have moved the base of their activities from Turkey to Kazakhstan, where they are publishing a separatist newspaper and lobbying for an independent nation carved out of Muslim regions of China.[30] Their efforts are winning supporters among local politicians. As recently as January 1998, several Kazakh opposition parties called upon the government to break off diplomatic ties with China if Beijing continues its 'political repression' of Uighurs. Their new call for action was in response to the execution of several Uighurs in Urumchi who were political dissidents opposed to Chinese rule.[31]

Most reports from China on efforts to bolster 'stability' on Xinjiang's borders focus on meetings between defence and government ministers of China and Kazakhstan, but the situation in smaller Tajikistan may be a more immediate cause for worry. The post-Soviet leaders there are facing a civil war led by forces that operate from bases on the Afghani border, and China's defence authorities may be working to bolster the defences of Tajikistan's government to prevent a 'spill-over' of Afghan's radical movements elsewhere into Central Asia.[32]

Not surprisingly, then, Chinese government leaders blame current problems of order in Xinjiang in large part on foreign aid received by 'ultra-nationalists' from unspecified foreign powers.[33] Immediately following the February 1997 riots in Yining, Jiang Zemin met with the top leaders of Kazakhstan in Beijing, and the role of Kazakhstan's anti-Chinese movements and political parties must surely have been a subject of discussion.[34] In the words of Xinjiang's regional Party Secretary:

> Xinjiang is in the front line of the struggle against the attempt of the international reactionary forces to 'Westernize' or 'divide' our country ... After the drastic change in Eastern Europe and the disintegration of the Soviet Union, the international hostile forces have regarded Xinjiang as a major region against which they pursue their strategy of 'Westernizing' or 'dividing' China. Their aim is to separate Xinjiang from our great motherland. All separatist and illegal religious activities and reactionary and separatist sabotage activities that have taken place in recent years are closely related to and echo with the international hostile forces.[35]

In this quotation and others, it is often suggested that the US (the primary, unspecified 'Western power') is China's most hostile enemy, even in Xinjiang. It is true that an office called the East Turkistan National Freedom Center was established in Washington in July 1995, with the goal of attracting as much attention in Congress and in the US at large as the Tibet issue has attracted. Yet regional authorities should have greater reason to fear anti-Chinese movements launched from Muslim Central Asia, especially in Kazakhstan, Tajikistan or Afghanistan.

Restrictions on 'non-coastal' China

Throughout China's reform era, the 'open door' has been more open for coastal provinces and cities than for central and western regions, and this has prevented dramatic change in minority regions. Generally, Deng Xiaoping's reforms called for a separation of Party from government administration and greater autonomy for the provinces. Yet Tibet and (to a somewhat lesser extent) Xinjiang, with their less-trusted local cadres and constant disturbances, remain rigidly centralised.

In terms of the economy, central government planning has a greater influence on Tibet than regional plans and budgets. Central government subsidies in the TAR are over six times higher than regional tax revenues. The TAR also brings in over 90 per cent of its commodities from other provinces, so regional pricing policies can influence events only slightly. Furthermore, since many of the expensive development projects in Tibet have a military component, they are generally conceived and planned by military authorities appointed in Beijing.[36]

Chen Kaiyuan relies upon his superiors in the central government and his allies in the military, armed police, security and judicial organs – themselves following higher orders – as his primary bases of authority. Meanwhile, propaganda organs in Tibet continue to emphasise 'upholding the Party's democratic centralism'. Throughout China, people have protested that democratic centralism 'creates additional procedures', 'adds more bosses', 'causes unnecessary wrangling', and 'creates obstacles'; yet in Tibet, even in the management of enterprises, democratic centralism and 'subordinating partial interests to general interests' is hailed as a key to economic and political success. 'We must strictly forbid the practice of cliquism and the development of measures designed to counter the policy of the higher authorities.'[37]

Tibet is landlocked, and large portions of it are uninhabitable due to extreme altitudes and limited water supplies. It is therefore not surprising that Tibet would be one of the poorest regions of China. Yet the result of the extreme centralisation, the limited development of border trade, the restrictions on tourism, and the comparative emphasis on military objectives is that development proceeds much more slowly than elsewhere and improves the lives of new Chinese immigrants more than it does the lives of Tibetans. Tibet is not just 'one of the poorest regions of China': it is by far the poorest. Centralisation and the emphasis on traditional state-owned industrial units as primary recipients of government subsidies also mean that resource extraction and primary industries receive special emphasis, and the resulting 'development' is frequently unsustainable.

Eyewitness accounts of once wild, fertile regions of the countryside reveal deforestation of thousands of acres of ancient woodlands (tens of billions of US dollars worth of trees have been cut since 1959); desertification of grasslands (especially during communisation, but continuing under reform); and extinction or near extinction of once abundant wildlife. When I visited closed regions of the Tibetan plateau in western Sichuan, the logging industry ploughed onward, with deep cuts into many old growth forests that I passed and rivers often clogged with felled evergreens.[38] Chinese redwood and bamboo forests on the Tibetan plateau in western Sichuan and Qinghai are disappearing rapidly, and largely as a result the giant panda, a native to the far-eastern regions of the plateau, faces extinction.[39] Today the punishment for killing endangered animals is occasionally severe and China at least is working (under adverse Chinese population pressures and deforestation policies) to save the panda.[40] However, there still is limited enforcement of new endangered species regulations.

Why do the Chinese authorities wish to maintain control over Xinjiang, which is not quite as destitute as Tibet, but is none the less almost as poor? One of the most important reasons is that they hope to keep extracting oil from the region with the help of large, state-owned corporations which answer directly to bureaucracies in Beijing. Xinjiang's proven oil reserves are said to exceed two billion tons, with natural gas reserves totalling 360 billion cubic metres. Through discoveries and new technology, authorities are hoping to nearly double these figures by 2000, and already, 30 per cent of China's total oil reserves are said to be located in Xinjiang. Much of these reserves have yet to be tapped, but by 2000 China expects Xinjiang's total oil output to rise from 9 per cent to about 16 per cent.[41] In the last three years of the twentieth century, moreover, China has invested more than 90 billion yuan (US$10.8 billion) in the petrochemical, oil and mining sectors in Xinjiang. The China National Petroleum Corporation – a state industrial organisation run directly by the central government – provided 20 billion yuan of the 90 billion.[42] One Chinese economist has bluntly described Xinjiang as China's future 'filling station', and Xinhua, the official propaganda organ of the Chinese Communist Party (CCP), has hailed it in exactly these terms.[43] Other 'strategic resources' of Xinjiang include uranium and gold.

The Chinese government has instituted policies to push Xinjiang's Muslim peoples to become more integrated into China's national economic development programme and industrialisation process. The government is struggling to bring electricity to villages, and to provide them with asphalt roads and safe drinking water. It is clear that as the GDP of the regional economy increases at the same rate or more quickly than that of the rest of China, there is a great deal of wealth which trickles down to the rest of the population. Some development policies are also specifically designed to apply to Muslim peoples. For example, former herdsmen who begin work in agriculture, mining, construction, transportation and processing are exempt from agricultural, industrial and commercial taxes for three to five years.

Yet Xinjiang's slow start under reform, its relatively conservative administration, and its focus on short-term resource extraction all contribute to a growing disparity of wealth between the average Muslim in the province (especially in rural areas) and the average Han Chinese, in Xinjiang and elsewhere in China. Among the poverty-stricken counties where the per capita income of farmers falls below 300 yuan (US$36), 81 per cent are autonomous minority areas, and Xinjiang's poverty is only exceeded on the Tibetan plateau.[44] Thirty of Xinjiang's counties were still below China's low poverty line in 1996 (personal income 530 yuan per year, or around US$65), with about one-sixth of Xinjiang's rural population unable to afford sufficient food and clothing.[45] While development has led to gross environmental problems elsewhere in China, in regions where 'development' plans centre around central government national security goals and resource extraction, the environmental degradation can be that much more pronounced.

In Xinjiang, desertification and overgrazing in steppe regions is a serious problem. This has not been helped by the effort that has been made to turn Xinjiang into a cotton basin, and increase Xinjiang's cotton production by 200,000 tons, particularly in the last half-decade of the 1990s.[46] Other problems stem from the legacy of China's nuclear competition with the US and the Soviet Union. The desert region around Lop Nor is now poisoned by the twenty-three above-ground nuclear tests which took place between 1964 and 1981, before the Chinese began testing underground.[47]

Despite the boom experienced throughout China in the 1980s and 1990s, Xinjiang is said to be suffering from an unusual number of economic problems, ranging from rising unemployment due to bankrupt state firms (and those that are most strapped for funds are located in China's far west), to disputes over handling of water and pasture land. The regional government has admitted to 'clumsy' handling of these and other economic issues.[48] Xinjiang borders on eight countries, including Russia, Afghanistan, Pakistan, Mongolia, India, and three new Muslim republics; yet its international trade in 1995 was worth a paltry US$1.4 billion. Again, comparative poverty in China's driest, landlocked, desert regions is to be expected. Yet the government admits that many of the economic problems of Xinjiang are related to politics, including internecine management of 'sensitive' borders by Chinese authorities:

> [M]anagement of the border ports has been chaotic and weak, with a forest of overlapping units and organs, and the practice of arbitrary imposition of fines, production quotas and fees has had disastrous consequences. Business people have 'fled' the border ports one after another. The authorities have therefore had to close down a number of border ports for rectification, including even ... long-standing ones ... [T]he formalities required have been too detailed and complicated, with more than twenty official chits being needed for obtaining approval for the transit of only one batch of goods.[49]

In short, if Tibet and Xinjiang are to develop economically and politically at anywhere near the pace of regions further east, differences in 'open door' policies across different regions of China will have to be significantly narrowed. The problem is that Beijing still looks upon the open door, for Tibet and Xinjiang, in communistic terms. Beijing works with a heavy hand to 'protect' these regions from the outside world and from enemies within; but the resulting 'stability' is unlikely to be long-lasting.

Han Chinese ethnocentrism and political domination

Socially and politically enforced ignorance is a problem for the Chinese empire. The Han Chinese, for the most part, are crowded together in central China or along the eastern and southern coasts. In some provinces and many cities in these regions, the Han comprise close to 100 per cent of the population. Thus, many Han Chinese have no contact with other nationalities, and are not even remotely aware of what 'popular opinion' towards central government rule might be in far-away Tibet or Xinjiang. Some large cities – Beijing, for example – do have small Uighur and Tibetan populations. Yet the contact between these groups and the Han still tends to be minimal, and the relationship between individuals rarely approaches the level of classmate, office-mate or friend.

With no other sources of information, the Han whom I interviewed from large population centres tend to trust central authority propaganda. The propaganda claims unequivocally that development projects and reforms have helped 'civilise' and modernise the distant, 'backward' border areas. The Han gifts of modernisation and 'peaceful liberation' from the feudal past have led to universal or near-universal satisfaction with central control. Surprisingly, even college students, for example, who are generally very sceptical towards or disgusted by the government's proclamations on other issues, tend to believe the propaganda on the nationalities question. In the long run, ignorance breeds foolish policies from the centre and anger among the minority groups.

The cultural biases of China's leaders in Tibet parallel those of China's leadership during the Maoist era, when propaganda on Tibetan culture focused exclusively on the cruelty and barbarism of Tibet's old society, the strong love of Tibetans for the 'motherland' (China), and the need for a universally positive transformation in Tibet under Beijing's version of communism.

A 1992 'White Paper' on Tibet set down the renewed official propaganda line on Tibetan culture: Tibet 'is now experiencing earth-shaking changes in a gradual shift from medieval, extreme backwardness to modernization'. Torture and forced confessions are still common in Chinese prisons in Tibet and elsewhere; yet the extensive focus on this particular issue in 'feudal' Tibet suggests that the idea of a 'cultural revolution' – a liberation from feudal ethics and norms –

remains as important in China's accounts of 'peaceful liberation' as any other achievement in Tibet. The White Paper discusses torture in 'feudal' Tibet.[50]

The official view of Tibet's traditional barbarity expressed by top officials occasionally severely damages relations with even the most Sinofied elements of the Tibetan population. Two hundred Tibetans from the National Minorities Institute in Beijing are said to have boycotted classes in January 1992, because Jiang Ping, a National People's Congress (NPC) representative and Vice-Chairman of the United Front Work Department, referred to the idea of rich cultural traditions in Tibet as 'useless nonsense'.

Meanwhile, statements issued by the Xinhua News Agency against the Dalai Lama are often degrading, militant and overtly threatening to Tibetans still living in Tibet. These statements claim that before liberation, the Dalai Lama celebrated his birthday by eating 'fresh human intestines, heads, skins, and blood'; that he has 'slid further and further down the evil path of betraying the motherland'; that he was followed out of the country by 'a cohort of assassins'; and that if he does not halt his secessionist struggle, 'the outcome will be like what the Buddhists often say: "The sea of bitterness has no bounds".'[51]

The focus on Tibet's cultural 'liberation' leads to an official historicism that contradicts the official line for other parts of China. The sweeping leftism of the Great Leap Forward period, for example, is denounced as a tragic moment in Chinese history except with respect to Tibet, where the policies of the period were most severe: 'The Democratic Reform that started in Tibet in 1959 buried the darkest and most corrupt feudal serfdom.' Deng Xiaoping described Mao Zedong's rule as only '70 per cent good and 30 per cent bad', but Tibetans are said to still regard Mao as a Bodhisattva.[52]

The most permanent act of destruction in Tibet during the Cultural Revolution involved the demolition of hundreds of monasteries and religious sites. In recent years, the official attitude towards Tibetan culture continues to extend to architecture. Maps of the Lhasa Valley Development Project (1980–2000) show an imminent, nearly complete disappearance of the old city of Lhasa.

Gyaincain Norbu (the current regional government leader, himself a Tibetan) has even suggested that central government support has 'helped ethnic cadres grow to maturity'. Han Chinese regions, by contrast, have little to learn from Tibet. A rare article on 'the outstanding contribution of the Tibetan people to China' discusses Tibet's religious, medical and military contribution to 'feudal' China, but then stops abruptly at 1951, as if a post-'liberation' contribution to 'modern' China is unworthy of discussion.

Because Tibet is perceived as a feudal, backward, frigid frontier, the settling of Tibet by Han Chinese is presented as a great sacrifice. The Dalai Lama has accused China of attempting a 'cultural genocide' of Tibet through immigration and policies outlined above. Yet when asked by foreign officials if Han Chinese were settling in the region in an attempt to overwhelm the native population, one top official (Raidi) allegedly said that 'the question sounded like a joke': 'Since the region is located on a frigid plateau and lacking in oxygen, how could it be possible that many people from outside the region would come and settle here?'[53]

Throughout the period of reform, Tibetans have occupied the highest level positions in the regional, prefectural, and village *governments* of Tibet, but usually not the highest level positions in the Communist Party or its Propaganda Department, the military, the armed police and the public security forces. Official policy attracts 'qualified' candidates from elsewhere to work in Tibet, with Tibetans themselves regarded as technically or politically unqualified for a host of positions in the Party, the government, the military and public industry. It is now officially considered 'reactionary' to complain of the 'large-scale immigration' of Han cadres into Tibet.[54]

Tokenism – placing a handful of minority people in visible positions to suggest racial fairness and equality – is evident in Chinese propaganda, with Tibetans often serving as spokesmen for their superiors or as examples highlighted by superiors. In the military stationed in the TAR, for example, the highest-ranking *Tibetan* is Major General Jiama Zedong, 'son of a serf' and a Deputy Commander of the Tibet Military District. Names of other officers with the same rank are rarely mentioned. Jiama serves underneath a Han Commander of the TAR and a Han regional People's Liberation Army (PLA) Political Commissar. In the court system, Basang Pingduo, *Deputy* Chief of the Tibetan high court, often serves as a spokesman for judicial organs and policies, although the highest authority in the courts is a Han Chinese.[55] The CCP's strongest warnings against dissent are usually promulgated by Raidi, a *Deputy* Party Secretary who more often than Hu Jintao and Chen Kaiyuan has laid down the Party's hard line through the 1990s. Yet, despite repeated public attempts to demonstrate 'unswerving loyalty', central authorities passed over Raidi, a Tibetan, in favour of Chen Kaiyuan (then a lower-ranking, Han Chinese outsider) when they chose Hu Jintao's successor.

The government has suggested publicly, moreover, that some of the Tibetan cadres who have managed to attain positions of authority are not yet politically reliable. '[A] small number of cadres have failed to firmly establish a Marxist viewpoint towards nationalities and religion, their understanding has been blurred, and they have assumed an ambiguous attitude in the struggle against separatism.' Regional government plans to attract more 'reliable' personnel from other provinces may reduce the percentages of Tibetans in positions of authority even further. According to Chen Kaiyuan, the loyalty of rural cadres is especially questionable.[56]

In Xinjiang as in Tibet, the regional government leader, Abdulahat Abdurixit, is a member of a national minority group (the Uighurs); yet he is only the *Deputy* Secretary of the regional Party committee, and more extensive power is held by the regional Party Secretary, Wang Lequan, a Han Chinese. Further, while the majority of people in government are from Muslim minorities, the majority of the 'leading members of the autonomous region' who are listed in government propaganda have Chinese, not Uighur or Muslim names.[57]

Like Tibet, Xinjiang is looked upon as a 'hardship post' for Chinese cadres, and those who 'volunteer' to serve there, regardless of incentive structures that induce them to do so, are looked upon as heroes. Thousands of graduates from military academies in the armed forces and armed police units, for example, have been called upon to volunteer for Xinjiang and Tibet; anyone volunteering for such 'hardship' posts is not billed as interested in Xinjiang or Tibet *per se*, but rather is regarded to be properly inculcated with 'the spirit of hard struggle' and service to the motherland.[58]

The problem of tokenism in the government, the Party and military leadership is almost as widespread as in Tibet. Propaganda organs claim that '470 junior ethnic officers have been trained at the PLA's Army University in Xinjiang. The command now sends five to ten regiment and division commanders from ethnic minorities to study in the PLA's higher military institutes each year.'[59] Yet the commander of the Xinjiang military (and the commander of the Lanzhou Military region under which he serves) are both Han Chinese, as are the vast majority of ranking officers in the region.

Residual communist ideas on religion and class struggle

In other provinces, 'experts' (technocrats) are supposed to have triumphed over 'reds' (Maoists, staunch communists). But in Tibet, in the words of Raidi, as of 1994, an ideological 'campaign' was being waged against those who were not red:

> The attitude of leading cadres to the anti-splittist struggle is the fundamental political criterion for judging whether they are qualified or not ... Tibet is under the rule of the Communist Party and will stay that way forever ... All localities and units should strengthen ideological and political work under their jurisdiction, improve inner management and plug all loopholes. In the light of ideological problems existing among workers and staff members, proper efforts should be made to conduct, in a timely and thoroughgoing fashion, an ideological and political campaign among them.

Other documents echo Raidi's stated view that the importance of 'correct ideology' should be a primary (or *the* primary) criterion upon which cadres in Tibet will be judged.[60]

Policies towards Tibetan Buddhism in China were most brutal during the Cultural Revolution, yet currently authorities are employing restrictive policies never previously implemented. In 1992, for example, the government began its efforts to dictate the selection process for replacements of high-level lamas, or living Buddhas. In September of that year, the seventeenth Living Gyalwa

Karmapa, leader of the Karma Kagyu school of Tibetan Buddhism, became 'the first reincarnated living Buddha approved by the related department of the central government', the Bureau of Religious Affairs of the State Council. Efforts to dictate the selection process of the Gyalwa Karmapa and recently, the Panchen Lama, appear to have backfired.[61] Other recent restrictions include a new ban on monks from entering tea houses, restaurants, dance halls and cinemas. Elsewhere in China residency restrictions have been relaxed, but in Tibet, authorities have instituted a new requirement that monks ask for leave before travelling on a pilgrimage or for other reasons. Any monk absent fifteen days would be dismissed. (To circumvent this restriction, monks often travel in lay clothes.) An additional ban on unsanctioned teachings states that lamas must obtain permission from Chinese authorities for any sermon to over 100 people. 'Democratic Management Committees' have been established in all of Tibet's major monasteries. They appoint monks within the monastery to work with the authorities, and they force monks to serve as informers or face punishment. In May 1994, Communist Party members were told to remove any signs of religion from their homes, including altars, rosaries, shrines and pictures of the Dalai Lama. Finally, a recent government work report in the Tibet Autonomous Region suggested placing new restrictions on the building of temples and the recruitment of members: 'The practice of indiscriminately building temples and recruiting monks and nuns must be resolutely checked.' There apparently will be a more rigorous 'examination and approval' process by a 'Nationality Religion Committee' before new projects and new members are approved.

The government leaders fear not only the independent religious activities of lamas, monks, nuns and laymen, but also the secret religious beliefs and sympathies of cadres. '[D]o not believe the Dalai Lama or cherish any illusions of the Dalai Lama,' said Chen Kaiyuan to his regional Communist Party subordinates in 1993. 'Party members must be able to distinguish between believing in the Party and believing in Buddhism. They must be atheists and do not worship any religion.'[62]

At the beginning of the reform era, the promotion of 'class struggle' virtually disappeared as a tenet of Chinese communist ideology. Post-Tiananmen praetorians have revived the dormant language of class struggle to divide Tibetan leaders and weed out those who are deemed less dedicated to the Chinese nationalist cause. In the words of Chen Kaiyuan,

> At this time, there [are] a very small number of places or work units where long ago overthrown members of the exploiting classes, reactionaries or children of supporters of reactionary views are resurfacing. They are turning up ... to reject the cadres from working class famil[ies]. Restoration of reactionary rule will not be permitted ... In Party construction, we must continue to attract a large number of enlightened elements in the working

class, as well as other laboring people and intellectuals, to preserve the purity and vitality of the Party ranks.

Chen Kaiyuan's return to class-based rhetoric appears as one more method of testing the unity and unswerving loyalty of subordinates in an era of hostile Party-people relations. 'In organizational building, we must not abandon the Party's class viewpoint. The more we carry out reforms and open to the outside world, the more we should emphasize the need to be strict with Party members.'[63]

In Xinjiang, China's government regards religious organisations as profoundly threatening, for many good reasons: Islam and communism have never been compatible, and almost all of the Islamic revivalist movements to emerge worldwide since the late 1970s have been fiercely anti-communist. Further, Islam is the primary force which unites the non-Han Chinese people of Xinjiang Province. Finally, Islamic temples and study centres are virtually the only elements of 'civil society' in Xinjiang; that is, they are the only formal organisational structures with anything approaching autonomy from state control. Not surprisingly, then, they are a focus of government ire:

> In an attempt to realize their reactionary goal of promoting separatism, a handful of national separatists and leading elements of religious extremist forces have used the legal status of religion to openly oppose China's regulations and policies on religion; peddle Pan-Islam; instigate religious fanaticism; [fan] reactionary public opinion; ... hoodwink some people who have little common sense, no knowledge of the truth and only a naive love for religion, and coerce them into committing criminal activities. They are taking advantage of religious activities to disseminate reactionary religious ideas, preach 'jihad', and imbue religious people with ideas that undermine national unity and disrupt the motherland's unification; they discriminate against, attack and exclude non-religious people; they run underground scripture study centers and martial arts centers; they interfere with administrative, judicial, educational and planned parenthood activities in the name of religion; they openly organize and carry out religious activities and expound scriptures outside the sites for religious activities; they lure and coerce juveniles into religion and religious activities; they even go so far as to use religious activities as a cover to organize reactionary gangs and constantly engineer violent, terrorist and disruptive activities detrimental to the country's safety. All the disturbance, chaos, and violent terrorism cases that have occurred in our region in the past few years are almost without exception connected to illegal religious activities.[64]

In spite of a claimed support for freedom of religion in Xinjiang and elsewhere, the government authority quoted above would hope to 'gradually diminish the influence of religion' in Xinjiang Province.[65]

Even with the government efforts to crack down on religious activities, religious institutions are said to be burgeoning in Xinjiang Province. According to religious figures, there are supposedly 10,000 mosques in Xinjiang, compared to around 6,000 to 7,000 before the Cultural Revolution.[66]

Meanwhile, Xinjiang's Communist Party leadership has emphasised that 'this region is in the primary stage of socialism';[67] in Xinjiang this has translated to more restrictions on 'non-state' enterprises than exist elsewhere in China. Regional government leaders admit that among leaders in Xinjiang 'some people still have not got rid of the ultra-left ideology in their minds and have not fundamentally solved the problem of confusion in regard to "capitalism" and "socialism".'[68]

Conclusion

Nationality questions have destroyed the old Soviet Union, and it is understandable that they would tear apart the Russian empire sooner than they would the Chinese one. While Russians comprised less than half the population of the Soviet Union, China is over 90 per cent Han Chinese. Nevertheless, despite cases of assimilation by non-Han nationalities in China, the Chinese still have a nationalities problem that one day could separate parts of the west into independent states.

Although it is possible that the Han will eventually overwhelm the native populations, comparatively few Han Chinese live in nationality regions. According to the minority peoples themselves, in Xinjiang, a Chinese population of 200,000 in 1949 grew by 1990 to 6 or 7 million of the 16 million residents; if one considers all of what is now Inner Mongolia, the Han population outnumbers the Mongolian population by 8.5 million to 2.5 million; finally, in all of what the Dalai Lama considers to be Tibet (Tibet, Qinghai, parts of western Sichuan), there already may have been about 7.5 million Han to 6 million Tibetans at the beginning of the 1990s.[69] The imbalance now must be greater. However, most of the Han Chinese are concentrated in or near large capital cities or on the borders of other Chinese provinces. Hundreds of thousands of them are contract workers or soldiers who plan to leave and to return to provinces they consider to be their real homes. In vast areas within these regions, especially outside provincial capitals and especially among permanent residents, China's 'minority' groups actually comprise a culturally independent and sometimes alienated majority.

Such 'autonomous' regions, including Xinjiang, Tibet, Qinghai, Inner Mongolia and Ningxia together comprise almost exactly half (49 per cent) of China's current territory.[70] Including every national minority region and 'autonomous' prefecture, the national minority regions comprise almost two-thirds (64 per cent) of Chinese territory.[71] Many of the nationality peoples who populate these giant, sparsely populated areas of the country (especially in Xinjiang, Tibet and Qinghai) have different languages, different religions, independent histories and different cultures from those of the Han Chinese. Some of the people, especially in Tibet and Xinjiang, refuse to learn the Chinese language. Moreover, they do not have much contact with the Han Chinese or need for their 'aid' outside the capital or the borders of each province.

Of all of the nationality groups currently under the domination of the Chinese government, the Tibetan community seems to attract the most international publicity and has the most organised government-in-exile, led by Tenzin Gyatso, the fourteenth Dalai Lama of Tibet. In 1991, he advocated several non-violent proposals to create peace in Tibet and autonomy from Chinese troops, if not outright independence:

- The entire Tibetan plateau would be demilitarised.
- The manufacture, testing and stockpiling of nuclear weapons and other armaments on the Tibetan plateau would be prohibited.
- The Tibetan plateau would be transformed into the world's largest natural park or biosphere. Strict laws would be enforced to protect wildlife and plant life ...
- The manufacture and use of nuclear power and other technologies which produce hazardous waste would be prohibited.[72]

Few people in Tibet have access to news or proposals from the Dalai Lama, but people do know that he is alive in exile in India. From what I can tell through interviews of both religious and secular Tibetans, he is popular and supported, except among a small handful of elite, atheist, Sinofied Tibetans (many of whom do not speak Tibetan) with positions of authority in Lhasa and outside the Tibet Autonomous Region. Thus, if some regions of China do manage to break away from central government control as independent entities, Tibet, or some part of it, will probably be first in line at the United Nations.[73]

While the separatist movement in Xinjiang is aided by a revived nationalist separatist movement abroad, it may have a harder time gaining international recognition than Tibet has had. Its exile movement has become very vocal only in recent years; Western powers might fear its association with Islamic revivalism; and, most important, the native peoples of Xinjiang are more difficult to define as members of one 'ethnos'. The Uighurs are the dominant Muslim group, but in some towns and villages, they are not in a majority even among the 'national minorities'.

Still — despite the far-superior numbers and power of Han China and other problems of resources and internal rivalries within the minority communities — due to increased outside influence, decentralisation, corruption, and even democracy, distant, isolated nationality groups are likely to become increasingly vocal. It remains to be seen whether the end result of increased ethnic identity and nationalism will be generally positive (as seems to be the case in the now more democratically run Baltic states, for example) or negative (for example, the civil war in the former Yugoslavia during much of the 1990s, or the current situation of Chechnya).

Regardless of one's views on independence for Tibet and Xinjiang, one would hope that the increasing prominence of ethnic nationalist movements in these two locations will not provoke a crackdown that further impoverishes them. One would also hope that any increased autonomy would not lead to introspective, 'anti-Chinese', reactionary politics in these geographically isolated locales. An 'increased Chinese presence' in Tibet and Xinjiang is an inevitable result of industrialisation and increased trade across adjacent lands, but a more liberal, autonomous and enlightened management of this presence, and of everything from environmental policy and schooling to immigration and tourism, is certainly to be encouraged.

Notes

1 Translated by Ronald C. Miao, in Wu-Chi Liu and Irving Lo (eds), *Sunflower Splendor* (Bloomington: Indiana University Press, 1975), pp. 42–3.
2 One estimate claims that over 300,000 Tibetans starved in famines which followed Chinese rule. See Robbie Barnett, 'Taking the lid off the roof of the world', *China Now*, no. 133 (Spring 1990), p. 23.
3 Chinese policies towards Tibet between 1951 and 1976 are reviewed in Melvyn C. Goldstein, *The Snow Lion and the Dragon: China, Tibet, and the Dalai Lama* (Berkeley: University of California Press, 1997); John F. Avedon, *In Exile from the Land of Snows* (New York: Vintage Books, 1986); and George N. Patterson, *Requiem for Tibet* (London: Aurum, 1990).
4 James D. Seymour, 'China', in Jack Donnelly and Rhode E. Howard (eds), *International Human Rights Handbook* (New York: Westport, Connecticut, 1987), p. 82.
5 For a well-written, officially approved view of Xinjiang's history and its people see *Xinjiang: The Land and the People* (Beijing: New World Press, 1989) (no author cited).
6 Andrew D. W. Forbes, *Warlords and Muslims in Chinese Central Asia: A Political History of Sinkiang, 1911–1949* (Cambridge: Cambridge University Press, 1986); see especially pp. 1–47. See also *Xinjiang: The Land and the People*, ibid.
7 Forbes, *Warlords and Muslims*.
8 Ibid., pp. 48–148.
9 The Ili delegates demanded elections for all government posts; total religious freedom; the languages of the Muslims used for all official and social affairs; total artistic and cultural freedom; free trade with other countries; and a national minority army, among other things. The Muslims of Kashgar had as little experience with many democratic institutions as the Chinese, but their leaders at that time were educated nationalists with some surprisingly liberal goals. Chinese negotiators caved in to these demands, but on paper only. Linda Benson, *The Ili Rebellion: The Moslem Challenge to Chinese Authority in Xinjiang, 1944–1949* (New York: M. E. Sharpe, Inc., 1990), pp. 22, 58, 185–7.

10 Robert Kaplan, 'Central Asia: shatter zone', *The Atlantic*, 269(4) (April 1992), p. 30.

11 For information on Tibet's twenty-one 'riots' from 1987–1989, see, for example, 'Tibet-based officer on Lhasa riots and martial law', *China News* (*Zhongguo Xinwen She*), 23 March 1989, in BBC Summary of World Broadcasts (hereafter BBC), 30 March 1989.

12 'Nationalism among minorities growing in China', Reuters, 3 February 1989.

13 Human Rights Watch, *Detained in China and Tibet* (New York: Human Rights Watch, February 1994), p. xi; Amnesty International, *Persistent Human Rights Violations in Tibet*, (Amnesty International, 1995); 'Arrests of Tibetan separatists rose in 1994', Agence France Presse, 22 June 1995; 'Tibet procuratorate work report', *Xizang Ribao*, 13 June 1995.

14 'Speech by Gyaincain Norbu', *Xizang Ribao*, 6 June 1993.

15 *Human Rights Watch World Report 1990* (New York: Human Rights Watch, January 1991), p. 287.

16 The fighting began when several hundred Muslim Kirghiz on a pilgrimage were barred access to a mosque by police. *Amnesty International Report, 1991* (London: AI Publications, 1991), pp. 65–6.

17 Benjamin Kang Lim, 'China says smashes plot to sabotage Muslim region', Reuters, 28 August 1997.

18 'Country alert', The Economist Intelligence Unit, 25 August 1997.

19 Lim, 'China says smashes plot'.

20 Ibid.

21 'Trouble in Xinjiang', The Economist Intelligence Unit, 17 November 1997.

22 'China steps up war on separatism in Muslim region', Reuters, 4 January 1998; Gareth Jones, 'Kazakhstan: Muslim exiles say fight against China rule goes on', Reuters, 12 January 1998.

23 'Xinjiang Party Secretary tells commendation meeting security has not improved', *Xinjiang Daily* (*xinjiang ribao*), 27 December 1997, in BBC, 14 January 1998.

24 'Party chief tells army to be prepared for "protracted" anti-separatist struggle', *Xinjiang Daily* (*xinjiang ribao*), 26 November 1997, p. 1, in BBC, 6 December 1997.

25 'Country alert', The Economist Intelligence Unit, 25 August 1997.

26 'State councillors in Tibet hear anti-separatist struggle has sharpened', Tibet Television, 9 September 1993, in BBC, 22 September 1993; Chen Kaiyuan, 'Ernest implementation of the basic Party line to succeed in Party construction for the new era', speech delivered in the first weeks of 1993 at a Communist Party meeting in the Tibet Autonomous Region; document obtained and released to the international press by the International Campaign for Tibet, 12 February 1993. The speech has not been independently confirmed as genuine, but elements of this speech were subsequently publicly aired by officials, and the evidence suggests that it was genuine.

27 'Tibetan Chairman [Gyaincain Norbu] rules out independence', Kyodo, 14 September 1992, in Foreign Broadcast Information Service, *Daily Report: China* (hereafter, FBIS), 14 September 1992, p. 38; Bao Xin, 'Tibet can never become "China's Bosnia-Herzegovina"', *Liaowang* (Overseas), 21 (24 May 1993), p. 2, in FBIS, 27 May 1993, p. 18.

28 'Barbara Schwepcke, 'Dalai Lama discusses relations with the Chinese', Sueddeutsche Zeitung, 12–13 June 1993, in FBIS, 15 June 1993, pp. 20–1.

29 For details, see Lilian Wu, 'Dalai Lama hopes to establish liason office', Taipei CNA (English), 26 January 1994, in FBIS, 27 January 1994, p. 83; Chu Ke, 'What is the Dalai Lama's intention behind his Taiwan visit?', *Zhongguo Tongxun She*, 6 April 1993,

in FBIS, 8 April 1993, pp. 34–5; 'Taiwan to "fully respect" Dalai Lama's proposal', Taipei CNA, 11 March 1993, in FBIS, 11 March 1993, pp. 62–3.

30 Gareth Jones, 'Kazakhstan: Muslim exiles say fight against China rule goes on', Reuters, 12 January 1998.

31 'Kazakhstan: opposition parties protest at "political repression" against Uighurs', in BBC, 16 January 1998.

32 Robert Karniol Bangkok, 'China and Tajikistan in bilateral pact on military cooperation', Jane's Information Group, 9 October 1996.

33 'Xinjiang Party Secretary tells commendation meeting security has not improved', Xinjiang Daily (xinjiang ribao), 27 December 1997, BBC, 14 January 1998.

34 Tom Korski, 'Jiang to discuss ethnic riots with Kazakhstan leaders', Reuters, 20 February 1997.

35 Wang Lequan (regional Party Secretary), 'Conscientiously implement the guidelines … of the Party's 14th Central Committee …', Xinjiang Daily (xinjiang ribao), 31 October 1996, in BBC, 30 November 1996.

36 The dilemmas of economic reform in Tibet under a vastly limited version of 'market socialism' are detailed in Sun Yong (ed.), Tibet: Development and Reform under the Non-Typical Dual Structure [Xizang: Feidianxing Erjiegouxia de Fazhan Gaige] (Beijing: China Tibet Publishing House, 1991).

37 Deng Zhujia, 'Roundup', Xizang Ribao, 4 July 1994, p. 3, in FBIS, 19 July 1994, pp. 49–53 (51).

38 Vaclav Schmil, in his book The Bad Earth, says that 30 per cent of western Sichuan's forest cover and 68 per cent of Aba Region's forest have been felled in the last 40 years. Cited in Robbie Barnett, ibid., pp. 22–3.

39 For more information on the giant panda, see George B. Schaller, The Last Panda (Chicago: University of Chicago Press, 1993). For more information on China's environmental crisis generally, see Vaclav Smil, China's Environmental Crisis: An Inquiry into the Limits of National Development (New York: M. E. Sharpe/East Gate Books, 1993).

40 Galen Rowell, 'The agony of Tibet', Greenpeace (March/April 1990), pp. 6–11. The Chinese are primarily responsible for the environmental problems of Tibet, and these problems are the central theme of Rowell's excellent article. However, to the Chinese government's credit, there is now relatively extensive propaganda admonishing people on the frontier against killing animals for sport. In fact, the government occasionally administers the death penalty against those who kill giant pandas, rare felines and other endangered species.

41 'Xinjiang to be China's "filling station" ', Xinhua, 31 December 1996.

42 'China to invest $10.8 billion in Xinjiang oil sector', Reuters, 8 January 1998.

43 'Xinjiang to be China's "filling station" '.

44 Zhang Xia, 'Nation to boost minority economies', China Daily, 3 December 1996.

45 'Xinjiang pledges to eliminate poverty by the end of the century', China News Agency (zhongguo xinwen she), 31 October 1996, in BBC, 4 November 1996.

46 Zhang Xia, 'Nation to boost minority economies'.

47 'China reportedly to turn Lop Nor nuclear test desert into oasis', Xinhua, 29 November 1997, in BBC, 3 December 1997.

48 'China steps up war on separatism in Muslim region', Reuters, 4 January 1998.

49 'Xinjiang's border protests described', People's Daily (renmin ribao), 5 October 1996, p. 2, in BBC, 20 November 1996.

50 On the 1991 exhibition in Beijing: 'Tibet's social, historical articles on display', Xinhua, 18 May 1991. Admittedly, the White Paper on Tibet also focuses on expanded health care, education and other issues. For a complete text: 'China on its ownership and human rights in Tibet', Xinhua, 22 September 1992.

51 Information on the Beijing boycott: 'Tibetans stage boycott', *Tibet Press Watch*, 4(1) (February 1992), p. 2; for Xinhua quotations: Ren Haiping, 'It is not too late to return after going astray', *People's Daily* (overseas), 28 September 1992, p. 3, in FBIS, 29 September 1993, p. 30.

52 On 1959 'reforms': Dorje Tsedain, 'Tibet: human rights and China's sovereignty', *Beijing Review*, 9 (28 March 1992), pp. 22–5; Mao as Bodhisattva: Qin Guanglong, *Lhasa: Riots and the Imposition of Martial Law [Lasa: Saoluan yu Jieyan]* (Beijing: PLA Cultural Publishing House, 1990), p. 44.

53 On architecture: at least fifteen historic sites in the old section of Lhasa have been demolished in the past ten years. Most have been replaced by Chinese commercial and public buildings. 'Demolition derby', *Tibet Press Watch*, 4(4) (September 1993), pp. 5–6; 'Urban crisis on the Tibetan plateau', *Tibet Press Watch*, 4(2) (May 1994), pp. 14–15. On 'still-backward' Tibet: 'Tibetans always "grateful" to "inland"', Xinhua, 4 October 1992; 'Report on government work delivered by Gyaincain Norbu', *Xizang Ribao*, 8 June 1995, pp. 1, 3, and 6 June 1994, pp. 1–3; Zhou Xiyin, 'The outstanding contribution of Tibetan people to China' [*Lun Zangzu Renmin dui Zuguo de Zhuyao Gongxian*], *Tibetan Studies [Xizang Yanjiu]*, no. 35 (May 1990); Raidi on 'frigid' plateau: 'U.S. senators complete visit to Tibet', Xinhua, 24 August 1993, in FBIS, 25 August 1993, p. 3.

54 Ni Banggui, 'Fostering correct views on nationalities', *Xizang Ribao*, 4 July 1994, p. 3, in FBIS, 18 July 1994, pp. 77–9.

55 The two Tibetan names cited above are taken from Chinese language sources, and the author has been unable to identify the transliterated Tibetan spelling of the names.

56 On weak Marxist viewpoints: Deng Zhujia, 'The first Tibetan symposium on the theory of leading bodies' ideological and work style building', *Xizang Ribao*, 4 July 1994, p. 3, in FBIS, 19 July 1994, pp. 49–53 (50). Chen's negative views on rural cadres and grassroots organisations are contained in Chen Kaiyuan, 'The basic Party line'.

57 See, for example, 'Xinjiang leader mentions "grim situation" in social stability', *Xinjiang Daily (xinjiang ribao)*, 19 October 1997, in BBC, 18 November 1997.

58 'Army advances "hard struggle," 10,000 volunteer for "difficult" postings', Xinhua, 4 January 1998, in BBC, 7 January 1998.

59 'China says more ethnic officers promoted in Xinjiang region', Zhongguo Xinwin News Agency, 10 October 1996, in BBC Summary of World Broadcasts, 10 October 1996.

60 'Text of speech by Raidi', *Xizang Ribao*, 24 May 1994, pp. 1, 3.

61 The seventeenth Karmapa was said to have been privately approved by the Dalai Lama beforehand. Monks at the Tashilhunpo Lamasery, which is responsible for the selection of the Panchen Lama, have traditionally *not* accepted the Dalai Lama's authority, but their insistence on his participation in the selection process is a strong sign of their dissatisfaction with Beijing's interference. The Dalai Lama participated in the selection process and it was he who first announced the reincarnation of the Panchen Lama on 14 May 1995. This led to the arrest of the chair of the selection committee, and subsequent riots and arrests in Shigatse. The eleventh Panchen Lama and his

family were first 'exiled' by officials from Tibet to Beijing, and then all news about them was suppressed. At the time of writing (2000), their whereabouts are unknown.

62 On new religious restrictions: 'Report on government work', *Xizang Ribao*, 8 June 1995, pp. 1, 3; Testimony of Louisa Coan before Congress; 'Tibet to restrict the number of Buddhist monks, nuns', HK AFP, 2 December 1993, in FBIS, 2 December 1993, p. 53; Daniela Deane, 'Chinese army, police overshadow Tibetan monks', *Washington Post*, 3 July 1991; 'New restrictions on religion reported', *Tibet Press Watch*, 4(3) (July 1992), p. 19. For Chen Kaiyuan's admonitions: Chen Kaiyuan, 'The basic Party line'.

63 Chen quotations ('At this time … '; 'In organizational building … ') in Chen Kaiyuan, 'The basic Party line', pp. 7–8, and 'Chen Kaiyuan speaks', Tibet Television, 12 June 1992, in FBIS, 16 June 1992, pp. 59–60.

64 Quotations are originally by Hasimu Mamuti, Deputy Chief procurator of the Xinjiang Regional People's Procurate, quoted in 'Official calls for reduction of religious influence, "clear-cut stand" separatists', *Xinjiang Daily (xinjiang ribao)*, 27 October 1997, in BBC, 21 November 1997.

65 Ibid.

66 Jane Macartney, 'Islam thrives in China despite tight rein', Reuters, 4 November 1997.

67 See, for example, 'Xinjiang leader mentions "grim situation" in social stability', *Xinjiang Daily (xinjiang ribao)*, 19 October 1997, in BBC, 18 November 1997.

68 " 'Indigenous policies" hamper non-public sector in Xinjiang', *Xinjiang Daily (xinjiang ribao)*, 18 October 1997, in BBC, 17 November 1997.

69 Tenzin Gyatso [the Dalai Lama], *Freedom in Exile* (London: Sphere Books, Ltd., 1991), pp. 276–7. The number of Han Chinese in the Tibetan Autonomous Region is far lower than the number in all of what the Dalai Lama considers to be Tibet, as many of the Chinese live in western regions of what is now Sichuan and eastern regions of what is now Qinghai (including especially the city of Xining).

70 Areas for Xinjiang, Tibet, Qinghai, Inner Mongolia, Ningxia and the PRC as a whole are 1.600; 1.200; 0.720; 1.100; 0.070; and 9.560 million square kilometres respectively. *Atlas of the People's Republic of China [Zhongguo Renmin Gongheguo Dutuji]* (Beijing: Map Publishing House, 1984). This statistic does not include parts of what is now Sichuan which were once claimed by Tibet, nor does it include Manchuria or Yunnan, other areas with distinct nationality groups.

71 Zhang Xia, 'Nation to boost minority economies', *China Daily*, 3 December 1996.

72 Tenzin Gyatso, *Freedom in Exile*, pp. 274–5. See also Dawa Norbu, 'China's dialogue with the Dalai Lama 1978–1990: pre-negotiation stage or dead end?', *Pacific Affairs*, 64(3) (Fall 1991), pp. 351–72.

73 For a very thorough, authoritative source on Tibet's legal claims for statehood, see Michael Van Praag, *The Status of Tibet: History, Rights, and Prospects in International Law* (Boulder, CO: Westview Press, 1987).

4 Post-nationalist Taiwan

Christopher Hughes

Taiwan's geographical, political and economic characteristics could easily justify the claim that it is a distinct nation entitled to the status of an independent state. It is an island of nearly 36,000 square kilometres, located 160 kilometres from the coast of southern China. Taiwan has a population of 21.4 million people, its own government in the capital city of Taipei, powerful armed forces, and a large trading economy which plays an important role in the global market. Even more important is the process of democratisation, which since the mid-1980s has allowed the population of the island to exercise sovereignty through regularly electing representative government bodies, at the local level through to the presidency.

However, instead of this leading to a clear sense of Taiwanese nationalism, the island has a constitution written for the Republic of China. Moreover, despite democratisation, the popularly elected government has not formally claimed independence from China and its policy towards the Chinese mainland does not rule out eventual unification. Although half a century of Chinese nation-building on the island has been challenged by a combination of external and domestic crises, it is clear that there remain strong constraints preventing the rise of a strong sense of Taiwanese nationalism.

One of the strongest constraints is the 'one-China' policy of the People's Republic of China (PRC). According to this, Taiwan is a Chinese province and the Chinese government will break diplomatic relations with any country that recognises it as a state. The number of states that recognise the Republic of China on Taiwan thus hovers between twenty and thirty, and consists of very small and poor countries. Needless to say, with China a permanent member of the UN Security Council, Taiwan is also excluded from international organisations that require statehood for membership. The ultimate negative constraint on the burgeoning of some form of Taiwanese nationalism, however, is China's threat to use force to bring about unification if Taipei makes a formal declaration that Taiwan is not a part of China.

However, as well as these negative constraints imposed by the PRC on Taiwan's room for international manoeuvre, there are also important domestic constraints on the promotion of Taiwanese nationalism. The most significant of these is that there is no broad consensus on what constitutes Taiwanese identity among the population of the island. Instead, the people of Taiwan are divided by complex loyalties to local and national identities. Any definition of individuals in terms of an exclusive concept of 'Taiwaneseness' could thus be highly destabilising, and could lead to ethnic politics which would wreak the kind of havoc that has torn apart societies in newly independent states, such as the Balkans and East Timor. Although demographic and generational change has helped to encourage many residents of Taiwan to identify themselves as 'Taiwanese', and to take part in and enjoy the burgeoning of local culture, this has been accompanied by the maintenance and development of strong economic, kinship and cultural links with the Chinese mainland. Naturally, the PRC has adapted its Taiwan policy to do all it can to encourage such integration with the Chinese mainland.

Rather than the rise of Taiwanese nationalism, then, this complex situation has encouraged political actors to try to redefine the relationship between Taiwan and China in ways that allow more flexibility and creativity than was allowed by the Chinese nationalism imposed on the island after the Second World War. The results make it increasingly possible to talk about the emergence of a Taiwan that has gone beyond the nationalist principle that 'the political and the national unit should be congruent'.[1] Instead, the island can be described as moving towards a 'post-nationalist' political settlement. The key to formulating this political dispensation is to develop a situation within which the special links with China that arise from cultural, kinship and economic ties can thrive, while the island simultaneously maintains control over its own sovereignty through developing democratic politics, all within the constraints of the 'one-China' policy imposed by the PRC.

The Chinese claim to Taiwan

The claim that Taiwan is a part of China has been made by the governments in Taipei and Beijing on historical, ethnic and legal grounds.[2] The island was formally incorporated into the Qing dynasty empire in 1684, and its present population is overwhelmingly composed of descendants of migrants from various parts of the Chinese mainland. Chinese rule was broken when Taiwan was ceded as war booty to Japan by the Treaty of Shimonoseki (1895) after the Qing's defeat in the Sino-Japanese war. This, however, was only an interruption, because the Republic of China (ROC) secured commitments from the Allies during the Second World War for its return to China. The ROC forces thus took the surrender of the island in 1945.[3] Another separation from the Chinese mainland followed in 1949, when the Communists won the civil war and the ROC retreated to Taiwan, but this division is said to be one of civil war between Chinese rather than the creation of an independent Taiwan. Thus, the events of

1945 are still celebrated by the Chinese as a 'glorious retrocession' (*guang fu*), and true unification of the motherland is viewed simply as a matter of waiting for the two sides in the Chinese civil war to find a solution to their differences.

The reasons why the claim that Taiwan is part of China has been upheld for so long in both Taipei and Beijing are closely linked to the legitimacy of the two contestants in the Chinese civil war. Following their establishment as political parties, both the Communists and the Nationalists asked the Chinese population to judge their right to rule according to their ability to defeat imperialism and unite the nation, which had fallen into a state of division among fighting warlords. For the Communists, the retreat of the Kuomintang (KMT) to Taiwan in 1949 meant that the mission to unify China had not been completed and that its own rule would be challenged by the existence of a rival regime with the support of the United States.

For the KMT, the claim that Taiwan is part of China was vital for legitimising the dictatorship which the party imposed when it occupied the island in 1945. This claim became even more important when Taiwan became the only territory to be occupied by the Nationalists following their expulsion from the mainland. As a consequence, the KMT developed a constitutional argument which stated that, although it was an essentially democratic organisation, its mission was to introduce democracy to the whole of China, and not just to Taiwan. The KMT could thus argue that it had proved its democratic credentials by holding elections in the mainland in 1947 and 1948. However, since then, the elected representatives had been forced to flee to Taiwan by the civil war, where they could not be replaced until the mainland was re-conquered and new elections were held in their constituencies. In the meantime, the state of national emergency justified the imposition of martial law on Taiwan, placing all authority in the hands of the president, generalissimo Chiang Kai-shek.

Building the Chinese nation in Taiwan

The prospects for mobilising the population of Taiwan behind Chinese nationalism were not bright in the early years of KMT rule. By the time the ROC forces took the Japanese surrender on behalf of the Allies in 1945, the population of the island had experienced fifty years of 'Niponisation'. Cultural mores had been strongly influenced by the colonial experience and Japanese had been made the official language. Although the government under Japanese control had been harsh, the Taiwanese had appreciated the upholding of law and order and the effective development of the island's economic and social infrastructures. Even the seeds of a democracy movement had been sown by community leaders who formed an association to pressure Tokyo for greater representation for the islanders in the Tokyo Diet. Thus it is not surprising that the Japanese occupation is seen by many of the older residents of the island as something of a 'golden age';

many of the island's men even served with Japanese forces during the Second World War.

A simple sharing of national identity between the islanders and the new arrivals would thus have been hard to achieve in 1945. They had, after all, been on different sides during the war.[4] To make matters worse, the new government was characterised by arrogance, resentment of the native population and general maladminstration. On 28 February 1947, the islanders rose up against the occupiers, only to be crushed by reinforcements from the Chinese mainland.[5] Loyalties to China that might have existed in the minds of the native population were dealt a serious blow by this action. The inculcation of Chinese identity became even more problematic with the massive influx of refugees from the mainland that came when the ROC shifted its resources and personnel to Taiwan. In the late 1940s, the population of the island grew from just under 6 million to just over 8 million. Against the backdrop of the disastrous first two years of ROC administration, the need to provide the basics of accommodation, food and education for the new arrivals did little to reduce tensions between the natives and the in-comers. Subsequently, a basis was established for a dangerous cleavage of society between 'Taiwanese' and 'Mainlanders'.

It is a mistake, however, to understand the politics of identity in Taiwan as determined wholly by this binary division. This is because neither the Taiwanese, nor even many of the Mainlanders, had really consolidated any sense of *national* identity. Loyalties to Taiwan had been eroded by the Japanese occupation. A sense of being 'Taiwanese' was also compromised for the pre-1945 residents by lingering loyalties to old provincial identities, with the majority being able to trace their roots to the Chinese coastal province of Fujian and speaking the Minnan dialect at home. The pre-1945 population was also fragmented by the existence of significant minorities, such as the 'aboriginal' tribes whose ancestors probably came from Austronesia and Indonesia long before any arrivals from the Chinese mainland,[6] and much larger minorities who originated in the province of Guangdong and from the trans-provincial Hakka community.

It is also wrong to impose too much homogeneity on the Mainlanders. They, too, were grouped around provincial networks, and most of them even had difficulty speaking Mandarin (in Chinese, *Guoyu*, or 'national language'). The most notable case was Chiang Kai-shek himself, whose Mandarin was difficult to understand for most people who did not originate from his home town of Ningpo. These diverse loyalties among both pre- and post-1945 residents of Taiwan opened up the possibility for all kinds of alliances to be made and broken, with some important Taiwanese figures being co-opted by the KMT while numerous Mainlander intellectuals joined their indigenous counterparts in pushing for democratisation over the years.

Rather than seeing the ethnic composition of Taiwan society after the 1940s simply in terms of the binary 'Mainlander–Taiwanese' division, then, it is more accurate to understand the situation faced by the KMT in terms of a Chinese nationalist political elite trying to cultivate loyalty to itself from a population with an extremely diverse sense of ethnic identity. In this context, the party set about nation-building in a number of ways. First, it broke down existing local loyalties and power structures through a programme of land reform, which destroyed the rural landlords and created a large owner-cultivator class that looked more favourably on the KMT.[7] It also co-opted members of the island's elite in the context of a radical restructuring of the party and state organisations in the early 1950s. Promising young candidates for co-option were cultivated through military conscription, the representation of the military on campuses, and the establishment of a Chinese Youth Anti-Communist League (CYACL).[8]

However, if this system was to have the 'faith of its investors',[9] the KMT also had to propagate symbols and institutions by which individuals could identify with the 'imagined' Chinese nation. The calendar thus began counting from 1912, the year of the establishment of the ROC. Maps of the national territory included the whole of the Chinese mainland and even Outer Mongolia. Streets were renamed after mainland places, while educational and cultural institutions (such as the National Palace Museum, where much of China's cultural heritage was preserved) were held to be the true successors to their mainland counterparts. Mandarin was made the 'national language' in schools, where children had to perform mind-numbing exercises: for example, memorising the names of all the railway stations in the Chinese mainland as they had existed before 1949, and the thoughts of the 'National Father', Sun Yatsen.[10]

It is unlikely, however, that this project could have succeeded without foreign support, most significantly from the United States. This was vital for two reasons. First, US aid and advice played a major part in developing Taiwan's economy, laying the foundations for a stable and relatively contented society. Equally important, the United States supported the ROC's claim to be the government of China. It was this that ensured Taiwan's security against attack from the PRC, permitted the ROC to occupy the China seat at the UN, and allowed the ROC to maintain diplomatic relations with a significant number of states, including the world's most powerful nations. Although it might have seemed absurd to outsiders, the contrast between an ROC that was widely recognised as the legitimate government of China and a PRC that was isolated and tearing itself apart with Mao's mass movements gave the KMT's nationalism a lease of life that it might not otherwise have been able to enjoy. Yet if US support was one of the key factors that enabled this, it was also the Achilles heel of the KMT.

The crisis of Chinese nationalism

When the ROC retreated to Taiwan in 1949, the US initially signalled that it was not prepared to carry on supporting the regime. This policy changed with the outbreak of the Korean War in June 1950, which made Taiwan an important link in America's Cold War containment policy. The situation changed again, and this time at Taiwan's expense, with the PRC–US rapprochement which began with the visit by Henry Kissinger to Beijing in 1971. The withdrawal of US support for the ROC was a condition for better relations between the two powers. The ROC stood down from the United Nations on 25 October 1971, and a string of states began to switch their official recognition from Taiwan to China. The biggest blow to Taiwan was the normalisation of relations between Beijing and Washington on 1 January 1979.

In these circumstances, the KMT's nationalism began to be a serious liability for Taiwan. As the party could not compromise its claim that the ROC was the government of all China without undermining its own dictatorship at home, diplomatic relations with any state that recognised Beijing had to be broken off. Some comfort was gained from the passing of the Taiwan Relations Act by the US Congress in 1979, which committed the US administration to the security of Taiwan. But the KMT was left in an embarrassing situation as its nationalist ideology tied Taiwan into a future of increasing isolation and dependence on the goodwill of the American public and politicians. No amount of indoctrination could prevent a growing awareness in Taiwan that the KMT would probably never be the government of all China and that it was fast losing control over the destiny of even Taiwan itself.

The rise in living standards that had originally helped the KMT to consolidate its rule now created the conditions of urbanisation, higher levels of education and study overseas that facilitated a greater awareness of the dangers facing the island and the growth of an organised opposition. The KMT's Chinese nationalism began to be eroded by a growing interest in Taiwan's identity, most apparent in the emergence of a new literary trend of 'native literature' (*xiang tu*), which harked back to a 1930s tradition of social-realist writing about Taiwan.[11] A more thorough political deconstruction began to take place in the writings of exiled dissidents, and then increasingly in the opposition magazines that began to spring up from the late 1970s onwards.

In such literature, the individuals who settled in Taiwan under the Qing were portrayed as pioneers fleeing from Qing despotism, with their descendants having about as much reason to live in one Chinese state as do Americans, Australians, British and New Zealanders to live in one Anglo-Saxon state. The Qing dynasty even banned contacts across the Taiwan Strait for long periods, and its belated attempts to assert control over the island and integrate it into the empire pale into insignificance against its cession to Japan. When the islanders proclaimed a Taiwan republic (Asia's first), this was quickly crushed by the Japanese. The ROC only occupied Taiwan in 1945 and then lost control of the Chinese mainland in 1949. This means that the island has been ruled by a state that simultaneously exercised sovereignty over the Chinese mainland for a mere four years.[12]

Therefore, the claim to Taiwan has about as much validity as a claim by contemporary Turkey to the lands of the Ottoman Empire.[13]

Nationalism and democratisation

The options open to the KMT in responding to this crisis of legitimacy were limited. Clamping down on dissent was tried at times, with dissidents imprisoned and opposition magazines banned. This, however, only stimulated public discontent and appeared increasingly unrealistic in the context of the Third Wave democratisations that began to sweep the world in the 1980s. Perhaps most important, such measures threatened to alienate crucial support for Taiwan in the United States. To suddenly abandon Chinese nationalism in favour of some kind of Taiwanese version, on the other hand, would have been unthinkable to party elders and hardly a credible option for a party that was formed for the purpose of achieving Chinese unification. The only viable option left to the KMT was to come up with its own democratising initiatives. The real challenge, however, was to make democratisation in Taiwan compatible with Chinese nationalism.

It was easier for the KMT to stay in power and steer the process of democratisation than it had been for some of the Latin-American and East European governments that were thrown out of office due to major socio-economic crises or external shocks in the 1980s. What the KMT faced was rather a long process of diplomatic de-recognition, accompanied by cumulative social and political mobilisation produced by rapid industrialisation and strong economic growth.[14] This had an important influence on the way in which the ruling party and the opposition responded to the developing crisis of legitimacy. In many ways these responses were determined by political developments in Taiwan going back to the 1950s. High among these was the development of a pseudo-democratic politics which began at the level of local government and slowly spread to the representative chambers of central government.[15]

The reasons why this creeping democratisation began to develop can be found both in the nature of the KMT's ideology and in the party's need to co-opt the native population and invigorate government organisations. One of the merits of the ROC constitution is that it stresses the importance of developing local democracy, which was seen by those who drafted the constitution as a way to tutor China's population in the workings of constitutional politics. Although Taiwan was under martial law, there was no need for *local* elections to conflict with the claim that the island is a part of China. From 1951 onwards it was thus possible to hold elections for county magistrates and city mayors, and from 1954 for the Taiwan Provincial Assembly.

Limited elections also began to be held for the central government chambers, which were endangered by natural attrition among the mainland-elected representatives. Supplementary elections at this level were thus introduced in

1969, and a small number of new seats were created to represent the increased population of Taiwan. The most significant move towards representative government came in 1972, when the regime initiated regular elections for a small number of members to represent Taiwan.

This creeping democratisation presented the KMT with opportunities, but also with challenges. First, in the short term it made it easier to control democratisation in ways that would prevent it from becoming an organised challenge to Chinese nationalism. At the local level, a complex system of factions allowed the party to cultivate loyalty by acting as 'king- maker' between groups competing for control over the allocation of resources and for prestige.[16] At the 'national' level, the number of posts open to election was tiny, and the KMT insisted that representatives were supposed to represent Taiwan only as the 'free area of China'. Despite this, concessions that allowed more representation for the population of Taiwan could be used to take the pressure for fundamental constitutional reform off the KMT, making it easier to maintain a ban on raising the issue of independence and establishing new political parties.

In the long term, however, this did not prevent the rise of individual politicians independent of the KMT, who could survive and develop alliances in the space created by the limited democracy allowed. The seeds of an opposition movement were sown from as early as the late 1950s, when independent politicians began to develop important links with influential reformers among the mainland elite. This movement grew in the context of the international crisis of the 1970s and finally bloomed in the following decade. On 28 September 1986 the opposition Democratic Progressive Party (DPP) was established. Although this act was in defiance of the ban on new parties, the then President, Chiang Ching-kuo, signalled that multi-party politics would be allowed when he did not disband the new organisation.

Loosening the nation-state link

The development of electoral, multi-party politics finally became a constitutional reality when elections were held for a new National Assembly in December 1991. This was followed by elections for other bodies, so that by the time of the presidential election in March 1996, it could be claimed that all of Taiwan's central and local government representative offices were filled by elections held on the island. Yet, quite remarkably, all of this was achieved while still maintaining that Taiwan is a part of China and within the framework of the ROC constitution. How this happened can be understood by looking more closely at the response of the two main parties to electoral politics.

First, the conditions for the KMT to do well in elections had begun to be put in place by a long-term co-option of the island's elite that had become well enough established by the 1990s to dilute opposition charges that the KMT was a

'Mainlander'-only party. The process of 'nativisation' of the party had been accelerated by Chiang Kai-shek's son, Chiang Ching-kuo, in the 1970s when he had taken over the leadership following his father's death in 1975. Before Chiang himself died in January 1988, his boldest move on this front had been to make the Taiwan-born Lee Teng-hui his successor.

In order for Lee to build a wide base of support for the KMT, he had to be careful not to alienate more sectors of the population or his own party than was necessary by making any clear commitment on the issue of Taiwan's identity. A move towards Taiwan independence would have undermined his own support in the upper echelons of the party, which were still dominated by elder Mainlander politicians, as well as the bedrock of KMT support among Mainlander voters. Maintaining the KMT's bald obsession with unifying China, on the other hand, would have played straight into the hands of the opposition and alienated the KMT's grassroots support.

Lee's task was made somewhat easier by the way in which the DPP developed. Originally, it had been a party composed of an alliance of Taiwanese and Mainlander politicians, united by their common call for democracy. However, the former soon dominated the party, especially as pro-independence dissidents returned from exile abroad. As the DPP veered increasingly towards a pro-independence platform, the KMT responded by introducing its own radical reforms. By seizing many of the DPP's pro-democracy and pro-welfare initiatives, but stopping short of its call for independence, the KMT effectively took the wind from the DPP's sails.

Central to this strategy was the development of an ambiguous stance on the issue of Taiwan's relationship with China. This can be seen quite clearly in the development of KMT mainland policy, presented in the *Guidelines for National Unification*, which were drawn up in 1991. The core of this policy is a plan to achieve unification with China in three stages. The real effect of the policy, however, can be seen by the fact that within the short term alone, Beijing is required to make radical changes in the way it governs, for example, allowing freedom of speech and implementing democracy and the rule of law. In the meantime, Taiwan can benefit from relations with the Chinese mainland by developing indirect social and economic ties, while political confidence can be built through holding informal talks.[17] In essence, this is a position of 'unification but not now', which can satisfy the mass of voters who do not particularly want to be politically united with the Chinese mainland or to take the risk of declaring formal independence.

As well as developing this flexible mainland policy, Lee Teng-hui also had to respond to domestic discontent over Taiwan's growing international isolation. This could only be done by developing a much more energetic foreign policy. The foundations for this had already been established when the ROC's international status started to come unstuck in the early 1970s and it had been forced to accept a variety of 'unofficial' ways of maintaining its foreign relations. A model for maintaining links with other states was established in 1971 when Tokyo recognised Beijing but maintained an 'unofficial' representative office in Taipei staffed by officials on leave or retired from government service. Taiwan's growing economic resources also began to be mobilised to develop what came to be called 'substantive' foreign relations in the economic and cultural spheres, which were forged through 'pragmatic diplomacy' (*wushi waijiao*).

When Lee Teng-hui came to power he developed this pragmatic foreign policy with a new vigour that held little respect for nationalist taboos. In the late 1980s the Taiwan press began to quote unnamed government sources as indicating that Taipei would no longer insist on being recognised as the sole legitimate government of China, and the Foreign Ministry floated the possibility that Taipei would no longer 'flatly reject' offers to establish relations with countries that recognised Beijing.[18]

By the time that the KMT was ready to hold genuine island-wide elections for a national representative body in December 1991, Lee Teng-hui had developed an extremely flexible combination of policies that could be seen by voters as both perpetuating the *status quo* of neither unification nor independence in cross-Strait relations, while simultaneously attempting to raise Taiwan's international profile.

National identity in electoral politics

The first test of the KMT's new policy orientation came in the form of the elections for a new National Assembly (upper chamber) on 21 December 1991, the first truly democratic island-wide elections to be held. One of the most notable things about the KMT campaign was the absence of calls for Chinese unification. Instead, the focus was placed on Taiwan's economic and social achievements since 1945. The DPP, on the other hand, entered the contest with a bold commitment to achieving Taiwan independence. The election was thus a crucial test of electoral support for the independence issue, and one that would shape the nature of electoral politics in the future.

The radical independence activists had good reason to be optimistic. They had performed well in recent supplementary elections and were calling for independence in the context of new states emerging from the collapse of the Soviet Union. Yet the DPP suffered a crushing defeat, polling a mere 23 per cent of the vote. This represented an actual fall from the 28 per cent that it had polled in the 1989 supplementaries, and gave the opposition a mere 25 per cent of the seats. The KMT did spectacularly well, winning 71 per cent, an 11 per cent increase from 1989.

This débâcle served to strengthen the voice of moderates in the DPP who had argued that democratisation should not be put at risk by pushing the independence issue too far and too fast. Their appeal for the party to build strong support by concentrating on everyday issues of pressing concern to the Taiwanese people, such as corruption, welfare and the environment, was to prove far more successful in winning votes after 1991. This trend was only reinforced whenever the DPP tried to adopt a more pro-independence stance. Most serious was the mistake of selecting the veteran secessionist Peng Ming-min to be the party's candidate in the presidential election of March 1996. Peng polled 21 per cent of the vote, reflecting the hard-core minority prepared to make the commitment to independence. Lee Teng-hui won a landslide victory with 54 per cent, a solid endorsement of the ambiguous stance of the latter on the unification-independence issue once again. Even the combined votes of the two pro-unification candidates, in total 25 per cent, accounted for more than Peng's share.

Subsequently, Peng set up his own Taiwan Independence Party. The moderate Hsu Hsin-liang took over the chairmanship of the DPP and fought local elections in November 1997 with a strong emphasis on developing good relations with the mainland. This time the opposition actually polled more votes than the ruling party for the first time, winning 43.2 per cent of the vote against the KMT's 42.12, a margin big enough to give the DPP control of 12 out of 23 constituencies. If the trend of Taiwanese electoral politics between 1991 and 1997 tells us anything about the sentiment of voters then, it appears to be that the precondition for winning their confidence is for political parties to accept and develop the compromise between democratisation and nationalism that was built under Lee Teng-hui's leadership. The reasons why this consensus has developed are both external and domestic.

The international compromise

High among the reasons for the voters of Taiwan not to vote for independence is the military threat from the PRC. China has consistently threatened to use force to prevent the creation of an independent Taiwan.[19] The real danger presented by this was illustrated when the PLA undertook large-scale military exercises and missile tests near Taiwan due to fears that the granting of a US visa to Lee Teng-hui in June 1995 might signal a change in Washington's Taiwan policy in the run-up to the island's presidential election. If this did not demonstrate the ability for the mainland to launch an invasion of Taiwan, it certainly showed how easy it is for the PLA to cause serious demoralisation of Taiwan's population and the flight of capital and people from the island. Such measures quickly led to heavy international and domestic pressure for Lee to tone down his rhetorical attacks on the PRC. It was only after this that he went on to win the presidency.[20]

Perhaps the greatest pressure for Lee to moderate his stance at that time came from Taiwan's business community. This is not surprising, because the other side of Beijing's Taiwan policy has been to hold out carrots to draw the people of Taiwan into developing closer relations. Business links have thus been growing strongly since 1987, when Chiang Ching-kuo lifted the ban on indirect travel to the mainland, alongside family, cultural and educational ties. In 1995, total cross-Strait trade amounted to US$22.5 billion.[21] By the end of 1992 Taiwan had overtaken Japan to become the second largest source of foreign direct investment in the mainland after Hong Kong.

It is hardly surprising, then, that the practice of sovereignty by the people of Taiwan and their growing sense of 'Taiwan consciousness' (*Taiwan yishi*) has been balanced by pressure from the business community for politicians not to create insecurity and for them to lift the restrictions that remain on direct transactions with the mainland.[22] Instead of democratisation leading to a rise of Taiwanese nationalism, this has reinforced the need to develop a *status quo* in which the two sides of the Taiwan Strait can exist in a situation of stability and mutual benefit.

The possibilities for doing this have been greatly enhanced by the way other states have adapted to the situation by developing 'unofficial' relations with Taiwan. This is not to say that there is no pressure on leaders in Taiwan to find ways to upgrade Taiwan's international standing. Whenever residents of Taiwan travel abroad and are treated as stateless persons they are painfully reminded that lack of diplomatic recognition is no mere formality. Thus, there have been large campaigns to pressurise the KMT into taking initiatives to raise the island's international profile, the most successful of which forced Taipei to launch a campaign for UN membership for the ROC in 1993.

Given the importance of Beijing's role in international politics and the intransigence of its claim to Taiwan, however, initiatives which demand this kind of recognition seem doomed to failure. The way in which relations between Washington and Beijing have been repaired at the expense of Taiwan, following the set-back caused by Lee Teng-hui's 1995 visit to Cornell, is a testament to this. When President Clinton visited China in June 1998, he verbally announced a 'Three Nos' policy towards Taiwan, of 'No one China, one Taiwan; no Taiwan independence; no Taiwan membership in international organisations requiring statehood'.

In the light of such developments it is understandable that voters in Taiwan are reluctant to encourage any kind of move towards greater international recognition if it shows signs of alienating international support. Most significant of all is that there is even a consensus emerging within the DPP itself that as much stress needs to be put on developing good relations with the PRC as into consolidating Taiwan's own society. This is the message behind the slogan 'strong base, westward advance' (*qiang ben xi jin*) that was produced by a DPP seminar held on 13–15 February 1998 to devise a mainland policy likely not to alienate domestic and international support for Taiwan by presenting the island as an 'international trouble maker'.[23]

The domestic compromise

In addition to the above external constraints, the complex identity of Taiwan's own society provides a compelling enough reason for politicians not to go down the road of advocating any kind of Taiwanese nationalism that is based on an exclusive conception of ethnic identity.[24] This may seem strange, given the understandable resentment generated by a situation in which the minority who came to Taiwan from the Chinese mainland after 1945 monopolised power for nearly fifty years. Yet on the rare occasions that attacks on Mainlanders and their property have occurred at the time of an election, these have been roundly condemned in the letters pages of leading newspapers and by leading figures in the arts and entertainment worlds.[25] It seems as though the threat of instability that might arise from any aggravation of the division between 'Mainlanders' and 'Taiwanese' is enough to make the politics of ethnicity distinctly unpalatable to most people on the island.

Why, after all, should most people welcome attacks on individuals who could easily be their friends or relatives thanks to the natural integration that has occurred across the Mainlander–Taiwanese divide over the years? An independent survey in 1985 calculated that a mere 5.7 per cent of the population of Taiwan had actually been born in mainland China,[26] a figure that must have shrunk considerably since. The children of such people, who tend to be identified as 'second-generation Mainlanders', probably number around 13 per cent of the population. A high rate of intermarriage combined with the socialisation that takes place at school and in the workplace, has eroded the distinctiveness of this group.[27]

None the less, credit must also go to politicians of the opposition in Taiwan who have not tried to upset the process of integration by mobilising resentment against the 'Mainlanders'. It would in fact be difficult to do this when the notion of being 'Taiwanese' is hotly contested itself. The 380,000 aboriginal residents of the island and the large Hakka minority who maintain their distinct dialects and ways of life react indignantly when the majority who trace their origins from the mainland province of Fujian claim a monopoly on what should be seen as 'Taiwanese' in terms of ethnic characteristics.[28]

Aside from this difficulty, the milking of any resentment of Mainlanders has lost much of its possible political value as the KMT has become increasingly dominated by politicians born in Taiwan. At the same time, prominent Mainlander politicians have been making efforts to become more 'Taiwanese'. Most notable of these is the KMT high-flier and Lee Teng-hui's *enfant terrible*, James Soong, who is adept at campaigning in the Minnan dialect. Even many of the leading members of the opposition rose to prominence largely due to the efforts of the KMT to co-opt them. Hsu Hsin-liang, for example, began his career as a disaffected KMT politician. Peng Ming-min was promoted in 1961 to become the youngest professor of law at National Taiwan University as part of the KMT's attempt to cultivate his loyalty.[29] Disillusionment only set in later.

These opposition figures have themselves long been aware of the dangers that ethnic politics would pose for Taiwan. When Peng was searching for an answer to Taiwan's problems, the vision of political community that appealed to him most was the one he found in Renan's *What is a Nation?* This is the idea of the nation as a group that is formed not by race, language or culture, but by a deeply felt sense of being a 'community of shared destiny' (*mingyun gongtong ti*).[30] For Peng, this meant that Chinese nationalism should be replaced in Taiwan by a political community into which anybody would be welcomed, regardless of origins, so long as they were loyal to the island. This need not imply a rejection of pride in the individual's Chinese culture and ancestry, merely a separation of such aspects of identity from one's political and legal status. After all, as Peng points out, Eisenhower could be proud of his German ancestry but did not shirk from leading the Allies against the Germans in the Second World War.[31]

Most indicative of the success of this vision of identity in Taiwan is the fact that it has been adopted by Lee Teng-hui himself. Lee prefers to talk about Taiwan as a 'living community' (*shengming gongtong ti*) and traces this idea to the concept of *Gemeinschaft* found in Goethe and Kant.[32] The similarity of his thinking to Peng's has not been lost on most people, though, especially Lee's Chinese nationalist critics. The most important similarity is that it allows the individual to be identified as both Taiwanese politically, and Chinese in terms of culture and ethnicity, at the same time.[33]

This is particularly useful for Lee because it is compatible with the official KMT mainland policy that Taiwan is a part of some kind of Chinese entity, although not under PRC sovereignty. A vital degree of space is thus created for creative thinking about the relationship between Chinese identity and statehood. For example, although Lee seems relatively inflexible when it comes to accepting anything that might imply Beijing's sovereignty, he is simultaneously President of the National Council for Chinese Cultural Renaissance and speaks in terms of the grand vision of a new Sino-centrism with Taiwan as the focus.[34] This conception of a multi-layered identity, with Taiwan at the core and expanding out into China, is set to become better established as historians and educationalists use it to develop a new history and civics curriculum that is more appropriate than the one inherited from the days of Chinese nationalism, in which Taiwan barely figures at all.

Conclusion

This overview has attempted to show that national identity in Taiwan has been moulded by forces that pull the island in two directions: towards integration with the Chinese mainland and towards independent statehood. None of these has so far proved strong enough to move Taiwan decisively in either direction, leaving it in an intermediate state between the two extremes. This is the underlying condition that is reflected in Taiwan's emergent 'post-nationalist' identity. According to this, Taiwan may be a part of the Chinese nation in terms of special cultural, kinship and economic ties with the Chinese mainland. Yet this does not imply that Taiwan is under the sovereignty of the PRC.

Democratisation in Taiwan makes the island a particularly interesting case for theories of nationalism. On the one hand, electoral politics has allowed sovereignty to be practised by the people of Taiwan. On the other hand, the official policy of the government is that Taiwan is still a part of the Chinese nation. Moreover, rather than leading to a rising tide of Taiwanese nationalism, democratisation appears to have acted as a constraint on politicians who would like to take the risk of pushing Taiwan towards the politics of ethnicity. Instead, what we find is that a lively debate is taking place over the actual meaning of such concepts as 'Taiwan' and 'China'. The resulting vocabulary of Taiwan as a 'living community' and a 'community of shared destiny' is already well established.

Perhaps the fudging of identity that is going on here is best summed up by the official attempt to label Taiwan as a 'political entity' (*zhengzhi shiti*). According to the *ROC Yearbook*, this is an alternative to 'state' or 'government', which allows 'sufficient "creative ambiguity" for each side to live with'.[35] The flexibility that is implied in such terms can be seen as providing an opportunity for building a lasting political settlement that is acceptable to both sides involved in the dispute over Taiwan's status and identity.

However, such 'creative ambiguity' does also present problems. This is particularly so when Taiwan has to present its case in an international society that is structured to deal with the neat entities of states. This was especially clear in 1999 when Taiwan came under pressure from the United States and the PRC to engage in political negotiations for a settlement of the Taiwan issue. The benefit of a political settlement between Beijing and Taipei for Washington is that it may prevent the recurrence of the kind of military crisis that developed during the run-up to the 1996 presidential election. For Taipei, however, entering negotiations under the 'one-China principle' gives the appearance that Taipei has accepted the PRC claim that Taiwan is merely a province of China under Beijing's sovereignty, and is willing to talk about 'one country, two systems'. With this in mind, Lee Teng-hui told the German radio station Deutsche Welle on 9 July 1999, that cross-Strait relations could be defined as 'special state-to-state relations' ('*teshu de guo yu guo de guanxi*').

Thus, the question has been raised as to whether such a position constitutes a declaration of independence. Following Lee's remark, much effort has been spent on both sides of the Taiwan Strait to pin down its true meaning. The official interpretation provided by Taiwan's Mainland Affairs Council, maintains that Lee was merely strengthening Taipei's position before talks with Beijing on political issues could begin, and that the idea of 'special state-to-state relations' does not go beyond the one-China principle.

Perhaps more can be learned about Taiwan's peculiar situation, however, by looking at how the international reaction to Lee's new formula reveals the constraints imposed on the development of Taiwanese nationalism. Predictably angry and threatening statements were made by the PRC. The Taiwan stock market lost an eighth of its value and the Taiwan dollar saw a sharp depreciation. Statements of concern were made by neighbouring states, with the most significant players, the US and Japan, quickly restating their commitment to the 'one-China principle'. Editorials throughout the world, and in Taiwan's own leading newspapers, portrayed Lee Teng-hui as a trouble-maker. Within days the KMT was trying to reassure the world that there had been no fundamental change in policy, and Lee's new definition of cross-Strait relations was repackaged in the formula, 'one nation – two states'.

The seriousness with which the US viewed Lee Teng-hui's new formula was clearly underlined when President Clinton told PRC President Jiang Zemin at the APEC summit in Auckland, New Zealand on 11 September 1999, that it had created even more problems for the PRC and the US. Further, when the UN General Assembly considered whether to put the ROC's bid for membership on the agenda on 15 September 1999, the states opposing the motion were joined for the first time by the United States, the United Kingdom and France, three countries which had previously abstained on the issue.

As for the domestic reaction in Taiwan, it is significant that just as the PRC was tightening the noose around Lee Teng-hui, on 20 September 1999 the DPP candidate for the 2000 presidential election, Chen Shui-bian, revealed how far the opposition had moved from its heady secessionism of the early 1990s when he outlined his policy towards the PRC. The policy included holding negotiations with China, establishing military confidence-building measures across the Strait, examining the limits placed on direct business, transport and investment links, and paying a personal visit to the mainland. The precondition for this, insisted Chen, is the guarantee of Taiwan's security. In terms of Taiwan's international status, Chen repeated that Taiwan had been reborn as a new state when the National Assembly elections had been held in 1991.[36]

So far, then, reactions from Taiwan, the Chinese mainland and international society continue to indicate how any political settlement of the Taiwan issue will be determined not only by the wishes of the population of Taiwan, but also by the constraints imposed by Beijing. In this context, the solution of the Taiwan problem will have to be worked out through the difficult process of negotiating the kind of political institutions that can allow the two sides to co-exist. This is essential if some kind of international regime to contain the security threat posed each time Taiwan holds a presidential election is to be contained.

As the Chinese Communist Party has repeatedly made the unification of Taiwan with the motherland an issue of its own legitimacy to rule, Beijing's room for flexibility has so far been limited to Deng Xiaoping's formula of 'one country, two systems'. Although this makes significant concessions to Taiwan, particularly by allowing the island to keep its own government and armed forces, the people of Taiwan are waiting for a signal that the new generation of leaders in Beijing can take this a step further. Most welcome of all would be some movement towards allowing Taiwan to have a more secure international status and room for manoeuvre. Beijing must be aware of the paradox that, if this is not achieved, increasing its diplomatic stranglehold could fuel the kind of anti-Chinese resentment that would only breath life into a Taiwanese nationalism that has so far not been able to gain mass support. This is an increasingly salient point as young generations come to maturity in Taiwan whose main experience of China is the threat posed by PRC missile tests and military manoeuvres.

Ultimately, any meaningful negotiations between the two sides will reveal the limits of what 'China' can actually imply for Beijing and Taipei. To arrive at an interpretation that would both reflect the *de facto status quo* and be acceptable to broad sections of the populations on both sides of the Taiwan Strait is one of the biggest challenges facing the leaders of both sides. If this can be achieved, then Taiwan's peculiar circumstances will not only have forced a rethinking of the relationship between state and nation in Taiwan, but will have also brought about a fundamental transformation of the discourse of Chinese nationalism in the PRC itself.

Notes

1 Ernest Gellner points out that this is the central principle of nationalism, in *Nations and Nationalism*, (Oxford: Basil Blackwell, 1990), p. 1.

2 For the orthodox ROC version of Taiwan's history, see *The Republic of China Yearbook. 1997*, (Taipei: GIO, 1997), pp 58–69. For the PRC version, see *The Taiwan Question and Reunification of China*, (Taiwan Affairs Office and Information Service, State Council of the People's Republic of China, 1993)

3 The position of Taiwan in international law is not as clear as Chinese nationalists maintain. The population of Taiwan was not consulted about the Cairo and Potsdam commitments. Moreover, although Japan did give up its title to the island, the post-war powers felt it best not to ask Japan to state to whom it was being ceded. For a dispassionate account of this issue, see J. Crawford, *The Creation of States in International Law*, (Oxford: Clarendon Press, 1979), pp. 145–51.

4 Many of Taiwan's business community spent the war years in the Chinese mainland supplying the Japanese occupation forces. Some 204,183 Taiwan natives were conscripted into the Japanese forces, 30,304 of whom became casualties. See Lin Man-hong, 'Liang an wenti xiang guan je ge lishi guan' ['A number of problems relating to the historical view of the cross-Strait problem'], *Lishi yuekan*, July 1996. Chen Liling (ed.), *Taiwan ren riben dang bing de zhanzheng jingyan* [*War Experiences of Taiwanese Soldiers for Japan*], (Taibei: Taibei xian li wenhua zhongxin, 1995).

5   On the February 28 Incident, see George Kerr, *Formosa Betrayed*, (London: Eyre and Spottiswoode, 1966); Chen Zhongguang, Ye Mingqing and Lai Zehan (Lai Tse-han), *Er er ba sihian yanjiu baogao* [*Research Report on the 228 Incident*], (Taibei: Shibao chuban-she, 1994); Lai Tse-han, Raymon Myers and Wei Wou, *A Tragic Beginning: The Taiwan Uprising of February 28, 1947*, (Stanford, CA: Stanford University Press, 1991).

6   Today there remain nine such tribes, numbering a mere 380,000 people.

7   Thomas B. Gold, *State and Society in the Taiwan Miracle*, (Armonk, New York and London: M. E. Sharpe, 1986), p. 66.

8   Tien Hung-mao, *The Great Transition*, pp. 87–8. An account of KMT nation-building in Taiwan is Allen Chun, 'From nationalism to nationalizing: cultural imagination and state formation in postwar Taiwan', in Jonathan Unger (ed.), *Chinese Nationalism*, (New York: M. E. Sharpe, 1996), pp. 126–47.

9   Bendix makes the analogy between political legitimacy and the faith depositors place in a bank. R. Bendix, *Kings of People: Power and the Mandate to Rule*, (Berkeley, CA: University of California Press, 1978), pp. 16–17.

10 R. Wilson, 'Political socialization of children', in J. Hsiung (ed.), *The Taiwan Experience 1950–1980*, (New York: American Association of Chinese Studies, 1983), pp. 95–9.

11 Joseph S. M. Lau, 'Echoes of the May Fourth Movement in Hsiang T'u fiction', in Hung-mao Tien (ed.), *Mainland China, Taiwan and US Policy* (Cambridge, Mass: Oelgeschlager, Gunn and Hain, 1983), pp. 138–47. For a condensed survey of the impact of *xiang tu* on the national identity discourse, see Thomas B. Gold, 'Taiwan's quest for identity in the shadow of China', in Steve Tsang (ed.), *In the Shadow of China* (London: Hurst, 1993), pp. 183–92, and 'Civil society and Taiwan's quest for iden-tity', by the same author in Stevan Harrell and Chun-Chieh Huang (eds), *Cultural Change in Postwar Taiwan* (Boulder, Colorado: Westview Press, 1994), pp. 61–4.

12 These arguments are clearly made by the independence activist Peng Ming-min in exile as early as 1972. See Peng's autobiography, *A Taste of Freedom: Memoirs of a Formosan Independence Leader*, (New York: Holt, Rinehart and Winston, 1972), pp 240–1.

13 Li Ao, *Taidu fenzi kan dalu* [*A Taiwan Independence Advocate Looks at the Mainland*], (Taibei: Quan neng chubanshe, 1987), p. 6.

14 Yun-han Chu and Tse-min Lin, 'The process of democratic consolidation in Taiwan: social cleavage, electoral competition, and the emerging party system', in Hung-mao Tien (ed.), *Taiwan's Electoral Politics and Democratic Transition: Riding the Third Wave*, (New York and London: M. E. Sharpe, 1996), p. 82.

15 For an historical overview of this process, see Hung-mao Tien, 'Elections and Taiwan's democratic development', in Tien (ed.), *Taiwan's Electoral Politics*, pp. 3–26.

16 Joseph Bosco, 'Taiwan factions: *guanxi*, patronage and the state in local politics', *Ethnology*, vol. XXXI, no. 2 (April 1992), pp. 157–83; 'Faction versus ideology: mobilization strategies in Taiwan's elections', *China Quarterly*, 137 (March 1994), pp. 28–62.

17 ROC Executive Yuan, *Guidelines for National Unification* (Taipei: ROC Executive Yuan, 1991).

18 *Lianhe bao* [*United Daily News*], 13 November 1988.

19 On Beijing's Taiwan policy, see Christopher Hughes, 'Democratisation and Beijing's Taiwan policy', in Yunhan Chu and Steve Tsang (eds), *China's Challenge: Democratization in Taiwan: Implications for China* (Basingstoke: Macmillan, 1998).

20 On the change in Lee Teng-hui's stance between July 1995 and March 1996, see Hughes, *Taiwan and Chinese Nationalism*, pp. 93–4.

21 *The Republic of China Yearbook 1997* (Taipei: GIO, 1997), p. 116.

22 One of the most vociferous voices has been that of Wang Yung-ch'ing (Wang Yongqing), president of Formosa Plastics. For a recent outburst by Wang against the restrictions, see 'Wang Yongqing zai mei tong ma jieji yongren' ['Wang Yung-ch'ing in America bitterly criticises no haste-be patient'], UDN (overseas), 22 August 1998, p. 2.

23 The papers presented at the seminar are on the internet at http://taiwan.yam.org.tw/china_policy/.

24 For a thorough survey of the spectrum of views on national identity in Taiwan, see Alan M. Wachman, *Taiwan: National Identity and Democratization* (New York: M. E. Sharpe, 1994).

25 Christopher Hughes, *Taiwan and Chinese Nationalism*, p. 97.

26 Quoted in Hung-mao Tien, *The Great Transition* (Stanford, CA: The Hoover Institution, 1989), p. 36.

27 Wang Fuchang, 'Shengji ronghi benzhi' ['The nature of provincial integration'], paper presented to a conference on provincial and ethnic identity, Taipei, October 1992, published in *Zili wanbao* [*Independence Evening Post*], 10 May 1992.

28 Fu Dawei, 'The words hunter in the jungle of Bai Lang: when Taiwan's aboriginals write in Taiwanese', paper presented to the London-China Seminar, School of Oriental and Asian Studies, University of London, 1993.

29 On Peng's life and ideas, see his autobiographical work, *A Taste of Freedom.*

30 Ibid., p. 26. Peng became fluent in French thanks to an early period of study spent in Canada and Paris.

31 Ibid., p. 245.

32 Lee Teng-hui, 'Regional security and economic cooperation: the case for the Asian-Pacific region', in Lee Teng-hui, *Creating the Future* (Taipei: GIO, 1992), p. 117.

33 Although Lee has never admitted his debt to Peng, it is something that has been claimed by Peng himself, as well by many of Lee's Chinese nationalist critics. On the concept of *Gemeinschaft* in Lee's thinking, see Christopher Hughes, *Taiwan and Chinese Nationalism*, pp. 97–9.

34 In January 1995, Lee coined the slogan 'Manage great Taiwan, establish a new Central Plains' ('*jingying da Taiwan, jianli xin zhongyuan*'). 'Central Plains' is a reference to the loess plains of mainland China, the mythical cradle of Chinese civilisation. See Lee's speech in *Lianhe bao*, 15 January 1995; and Christopher Hughes, *Taiwan and Chinese Nationalism*, p. 161.

35 *ROC Yearbook 1994* (Taipei: GIO), p. 147.

36 *Lianhe bao* (overseas edition), 21 September 1991, p. 1.

5 Nationalism in Japan

Ian Nish

Introduction

There are special historical characteristics underlying Japanese nationalism. It is hard to know how far back nationalism can be traced in Japan's long history. In general, the Japanese are a fairly homogeneous island people with a common language and religion. From 1630 to 1853 they had the unusual experience of living in a closed country (*sakoku*), whereby they were confined by their rulers within their home islands and were forbidden to go overseas. During this period, they had only limited contact with the outside world through the Chinese and the Dutch who occupied their own enclaves. The Japanese have always been conscious of the threat of invasion of their islands from either their mighty continental neighbours or intruders from elsewhere. Yet, despite the perceived threat of external attack, they generally lived in their clan communities and probably had less conception of a nation or nationality than of the class to which they belonged in their feudal society.

Japan's voluntary isolation was broken by the Black Ships of Commodore Perry of the United States in 1853. Despite the official policy of isolation, some Japanese went abroad as representatives of their clans and later of the shogunate. While they were in some cases defying the government of the day, the trips were made not for adventure or tourism but for education which was for the betterment of their own communities. Thereafter even the shogun rulers encouraged their nationals to slip away overseas in greater numbers. In 1868, following a brief civil war, Japan experienced an upheaval which brought the Emperor Meiji to the throne, the so-called Meiji Restoration. Soon after the Emperor's ascension, large numbers of talented young Japanese were sent overseas to learn as representatives of the new government. This followed the injunction laid down in the Charter Oath, published as an edict of the Emperor Meiji in 1868, which stated that citizens should seek knowledge throughout the world in order to strengthen imperial rule. If they were to guard against the naval depredations of foreign powers and make preparations against the penetration of their cities and countryside by foreign merchants, the Japanese could not look inward as they had in the past, they had to look abroad.

The nature of the societies that they encountered around the world in about 1870 were therefore very relevant to Japanese nationalism. One of the Meiji government's early problems was to secure the superiority of central government over the clans, some of which had been influential in bringing about the Restoration. Italy and Germany had both faced, and overcome, not dissimilar problems of unification which was regarded as the supreme attainment of self-determination as a nation. But it was accepted that, if these states were to hold together, they must cultivate nationhood. At this time, nationalism was viewed as a good thing for all modern states. But once these goals had been achieved, nationalism developed in different ways in European countries. Under Chancellor Bismarck who was the outstanding leader of continental Europe, nationalism in Germany became linked with war and expansion. Undoubtedly his achievement and methods attracted many Japanese at the end of the century who were to mould their constitution, parliament and educational and military systems in the image of Germany.

When Japan entered the modern world, there was no question but that it would aspire to become a nation-state on the European model. To illustrate this we can look to the Iwakura mission, an epoch-making event in Japan's history, in which five senior members of the new government visited the US and Europe between December 1871 and September 1873 accompanied by a large entourage of observers. The object of the mission was partly educational and partly promotional. It was educational in that the mission wanted to select from the countries it visited worthwhile elements to incorporate in the new Japanese nation-state. The observers studied bureaucracies, law courts, armies and all types of factories and mines. It was promotional in the sense that Japan felt that the time had come when it ought to make known to the world that it wanted to modernise and Westernise its institutions. Thus the Iwakura mission visited the Vienna Grand Exposition of 1873 at which the Japanese government exhibited some of its wares in the hope of developing trade.

By the 1880s Japan had made demonstrable progress in nationalism, having attained its objectives of creating 'a prosperous country and a strong army'. The distinguished observer, Sir Ernest Satow, who was in Japan as a British diplomat in 1862, was well placed to make a comparative judgement on Japanese nationalism. He was surprisingly positive about the healthy qualities of Japanese nationalism. While posted in Bangkok as minister in the 1880s, he reported that he looked in vain among the Thai people for the same patriotic spirit that he had seen in the Japanese, while the Chinese, he claimed, did not know what patriotism was. By contrast, Japan was full of loyalty and fighting spirit and energy. He even praised Japan for having backbone enough to maintain its independence and expand. Satow, like others of the Victorian era, admired Japan as the country in Asia which exhibited patriotism and efficiency. If the prevailing global philosophy was Darwinism, Japan was seen as the symbol of the survival of the fittest. It was a country that appeared to have the potential for survival in a hostile expansionist world.

The Meiji reforms were on the whole successful. The apparatus of the new state was set up around 1890 with a cabinet, a parliament, a constitution and a modernised educational system. Underlying these reforms was a strong emphasis on Japanese nationalism and that nationalism was identified with the position and ideology of the Emperor, the focus of the new state becoming the emperor system (*kokutai*). The Emperor, who claimed the loyalty of his citizens, held the authority, but not the power. However, he was the commander-in-chief of the armed forces which were a fast growing movement due to fears of outside attack. There is nothing so effective for developing the nationalist spirit as war and Japan emerged on the winning side in four wars: China in 1894–1895 and in 1900; Russia in 1904–5; and in the First World War. Soldiers fought and died for their Emperor.

The reign of the Meiji Emperor's successor, the Emperor Taisho (1912–1926), was relatively peaceful and the nation-state developed many positive aspects: the coming of the first commoner prime minister in 1919; the introduction of universal adult suffrage in 1924; the disarmament proposals; and the so-called 'liberal interlude' when cabinets were formed by political parties in rotation. Nationalism was achieved in the context of social democracy. At the same time, nationalism through the *kokutai* was weakened by the widely known fact that the Emperor Taisho suffered from a chronic illness, preventing him from having any say in political affairs from 1920 until his death in 1926.

World depression hit Japan as strongly as the rest of the world. The economic boom of the 1914–1918 war period had evaporated, and Japan suffered her own minor depression in 1927 which may have been helpful to her when the worldwide catastrophe struck. Depression affected the price of rice and impoverished the peasantry and the country districts. The army who had become disaffected because of the disarmament programmes imposed on them by (as they saw it) money-grubbing and unpatriotic party politicians, sided with the depressed peasantry and used them as allies as they increasingly intervened in politics and influenced government policy-making. The army played on Japan's sense of insecurity in the face of communism in Russia and hostility in China and called for greater national commitment.

What emerged in the 1930s in Japan is not one conception of nationalism but many. In other words, any account of nationalism is complicated by the rivalries among those who professed to be nationalists. First, there was the long-standing rivalry between the army and the navy which each had a different conception of national security. Second, there was the permanent split between, on the one hand, the armed services and their political allies, sometimes described as the ultra-nationalists, and on the other hand, the cautious nationalists, often associated with the Emperor and the court. On the 26 February 1936, the crack guards regiment occupied the heart of the bureaucracy in Kasumigaseki, Tokyo in an attempted *coup d'état*. They proclaimed themselves loyal to the throne, and in their view the Emperor was being misled by the courtiers around him. Since the cabinet ceased to function, the Emperor was left with no alternative but to call on the forces which were not mutinying to quell the rebellion. This intervention in the interest of national unity was an almost unique action on the part of Emperor Hirohito until 1945.

In the tendency towards extreme nationalism and militarism, Japan was, of course, reflecting a trend which was present elsewhere in the world. The collapse of liberalism in many countries was replaced by nationalism, racism and imperialism. In Japan, as elsewhere, nationalism was the obverse of internationalism. It meant going it alone and implied a growth in power and self-confidence. It was not surprising, then, that Japan gave notice in 1933 to leave the League of Nations, of which it had been a pillar in the 1920s, rather than accept a rebuke from that body. Japan stood alone until its increasing alignment with Germany from 1936.

Japan was mobilised for war with China from 1937 and with the United States and Britain from 1941. In so far as these battles were fought on the mainland of Asia, the Japanese found themselves drawn in to making claims to leadership of Asia. Many Japanese thinkers expressed themselves in pan-Asian terms, in terms of hegemony in East Asia. Obviously, Japan's pride in her achievement within a relatively short period of sixty years meant that many Japanese thought of their country as the natural leader of East Asia. And the doctrines of the New Order in East Asia and later the Great East Asia Co-prosperity Sphere – imprecise as they were in many respects – were a natural development of this form of nationalism. It was the notion of Japan as the fulcrum of a family of nations in Asia.

It is also true, of course, that many in Asia looked to Japan for leadership from its defeat of Russia in 1905 onwards, but they did not like it when it came. This turning to Japan had started at the end of the nineteenth century with young radical Chinese and Koreans attending military schools in Japan and returning to take the lead in the Chinese revolution of 1911–1912. Japanese nationalism had its impact on nationalistic movements around Asia during its brief occupation of South-East Asian territories, not least by offering training and financial assistance to anti-colonial Filipinos, Indonesians and no doubt French and British colonial peoples, too.

Post-war Japan

Japanese nationalism was obviously affected by its defeat in war and, even more humbling, by the imposition of unconditional surrender. Japan the nation-state had had a rapid rise and an even more rapid fall. As the Japanese looked around to point the finger of blame, it was often directed at the 'old nationalism', and especially at the Emperor system. Many features of the old nationalism disappeared automatically.

Nationalism was equally affected by the relatively long Allied military occupation of Japan's islands from 1945 to 1952. The attitude of the occupation authorities was strongly reformist and anxious to eliminate the excesses of pre-war nationalism, for which they claimed to have a warrant in the Potsdam Declaration. There was a strong emphasis on democratisation which the Americans regarded as the antithesis of nationalism. Initially, the Allies wanted to destroy the trappings of nationalism (army, navy, state Shintoism) and reduce the power of the police and thought-control mechanisms. They took special care over the education system, especially the teaching of history and thinking about the imperial origins of the state. But the attitude of the Allied occupation authorities became more ambivalent as the Cold War set in.

None the less, some sort of national framework needed to be put in place, and the formula this was based on was a reformed imperial institution. On 1 January 1946, approximately three months after Japan's surrender, Emperor Hirohito issued of his own volition an imperial edict denying his divinity. The institution of the Emperor was preserved. Thus under the new constitution of 1947 the Emperor is no longer described as the head of state; he is the symbol of state, the servant of an elected cabinet (Article 1). He has authority without power. Following the Emperor's edict, the occupation on 5 July 1948 removed Kigensetsu (the anniversary of the foundation of the Japanese state) from the list of national commemoration days. As one scholar has noted, 'the aim of the authorities was evidently to reduce the atmosphere of extreme reverence that surrounded the Emperor' (Falt 1996: 233).

After the occupation ended in 1952, the Japanese recovered sovereignty. They acknowledged the faults of pre-war nationalism, patriotism, militarism and expansion. There existed, of course, a sense of patriotism which expressed itself in a fierce determination for improvement and recovery, but how far this was for the state and how far for the individual and the family and the company is a moot point. Militarism, too, fell out of the equation. In reaction to the war, there was a broadly pacifist spirit among the Japanese. Its military operations are limited by Article 9 of its new constitution. The self-defence forces which were set up in the 1950s, found it hard to attract recruits. Its dependence on the US for defence meant that Japan took a low posture in foreign affairs, and was more conscious of contraction than of expansion.

For two decades Japan was unsure of itself as a country. Was there scope for such a thing as a 'new nationalism'? There developed an ongoing political battle over the revival of nationalism. It was fought on minor issues: the national flag; the national anthem; imposition of moral teaching in the school curriculum.

Little by little, the national arguments prevailed. The most overt manifestation of the struggle occurred over the visits of politicians in August each year to Yasukuni Shrine, the main war memorial in Tokyo; the debate revolved around whether they should take place at all and whether they should be 'official' or 'personal'. The right wing argued that these gestures were essential to the restoration of national pride; the left, meanwhile, argued that it was a retreat into the symbols of the past. A consensus seemed to arise that some gradual revival of nationalism would be beneficial and 'wholesome' for Japanese society (Yoshino 1992).

Japan experienced an uninterrupted period of conservative rule by the Liberal-Democratic party from 1955 to 1993. In about 1972, there was an awareness that Japan had become a prosperous country and a trading giant on the world stage. It was therefore felt appropriate for Japan to have a greater say in global affairs. This coincided with pressure from the United States for Japan to take its share in world affairs, particularly by assuming an increased role for the armed forces overseas. However, Japan is still constrained by Article 9 of the constitution, which for reasons of parliamentary arithmetic, it finds impossible to amend. It has, therefore, taken only faltering steps towards some role in international defence and is still vigilant about calling for a permanent seat in the United Nations Security Council.

Modern Japan

Allowing for the fact that Japanese nationalism has tended in the past to be defined by the position of the Emperor, much significance was attached to the illness of the Emperor Hirohito in 1988, which ended in his death in 1989. The question is, does this event offer any clues to the state of nationalism among the modern Japanese? The people who gathered outside the gates of the Imperial Palace in Tokyo, often in inclement conditions, in acknowledgement of the Emperor's illness, saw him as the focus of a benign nationalism which was not unhealthy. Somewhat to the surprise of commentators, the numbers were very large and, while the majority of well-wishers were elderly, a significant number were teenagers, mainly girls. It would appear that much of the earlier respect for the imperial institution still survives, even if the political and legal authority of the throne has been much reduced. However, there was equally vocal (though less conspicuous) opposition in various quarters (see, for example, Field 1991).

Nationalism affects one's view of history. On this point several controversies have surfaced in Japan in the 1990s. They relate to the philosophy underlying the education system, the curricula and the textbooks used in Japanese classrooms. The problem in the Japanese education system is the fear on the part of the bureaucracy of teachers and teachers' unions – who are suspected of being left wing, and even Marxist – and a desire to protect schoolchildren from an overly negative view of Japan's past. To that end, the ministry of education in Japan exercises control over all textbooks in schools. In effect, it influences by strict inspection the text and the language used in such a way as to preserve a certain view of Japanese society and government action in the past. The issue of textbooks in Japanese schools has had international repercussions. China, Korea and the Philippines (among others) have all protested against what they see as the biased slant of Japanese history textbooks. This has brought out into the open the defenders and opponents of this practice.

Nationalism underlies the great political debate over apologies for the war and expansion, which naturally came to the fore during the fiftieth anniversary celebrations to mark the end of the war in 1995. Japan has apologised for its actions in the war through its ministers and diplomats, most notably Prime Minister Murayama. However, some countries feel that the apology should come from the Emperor himself. The current Heisei Emperor was 10 years old at the time of Pearl Harbour. The right wing in the Liberal-Democratic party will not allow the Emperor, as a symbol of the state, to be drawn into this political minefield. Thus the issue is stalled between the Japanese and foreign governments.

Seen in this context, it is scarcely surprising that there are those in Japan who carry the counter-attack to foreign countries. For example, the criticisms made of the United States by Ishihara Shintaro in *Iie to ieru Nihon* (*The Japan that Can Say No*, 1989). The title is a play on words: the Japanese have a way of answering a question with 'Yes', whether they mean 'Yes' or 'No'. Ishihara argues that Japan has been too nice to its allies in the past and should throw off its politeness and be more frank in its approach. There is no doubt that frankness is a sign of an adult relationship between powers. But, if there is a strong case for frank speaking, there is an equally strong case for sensitive listening.

Conclusion

Has Japan learnt the lessons of the extremes of nationalism in the past? It is, of course, difficult for anyone (most of all a non-Japanese) to give an authoritative answer to this question. The Japanese themselves are polarised in their attitudes to nationalism. There are the right-wing Japanese who take seriously issues like the Japanese national flag and the national anthem. But they are a small minority, even if a prominent and vocal one. In general, Japanese nationalism is not fundamentally different from that of other countries and is not unhealthy. On balance, it is more restrained than that of some of its neighbours. (Indeed, can there be such a thing as Asian nationalism or even East-Asian nationalism?) Japan has developed a mature nationalism. There are good aspects to this nationalism: an example is the country's pride in its sporting achievements. The 1989 Nagano Winter Olympics is a case in point. It was a strident, effervescent and – doubtless – xenophobic affair. But it was also good-humoured and unobjectionable, and served in marked contrast to the examples of bad nationalism which litter Japan's history. The creation of a national image is important to any state.

One difficulty is to predict the attitudes of today's youth as they reach maturity. There exists a generation gap over the issue of nationalism. Older Japanese who have experienced the hardship of war, question whether the younger generation have a sense of nationalism. They speak of them as 'the affluent generation' who have been pampered by their parents. One is conscious of competing concepts of nationalism and of the strain which lurks under the surface. But the young are more internationalist than their parents and should to that extent be less introverted and nationalistic. Nationalism, by which I mean pursuing one's national interests without considering the rights and sensitivities of others, is likely to be less sinister than it was in the past.

The young are disenchanted with many aspects of Japan the nation. Since the Lockheed scandal of the 1960s, Japan has seen an uninterrupted series of scandals of various sorts, culminating in the general collapse in the Japanese financial market in 1997. It is little wonder, then, that the young are disillusioned with the society created by their elders (in the same way that an earlier generation were disillusioned with the Japan of the post-war years). Although the younger generation appear disinterested in politics, it does not follow that they will still be disaffected at the age of 30 when they are 'sararimen' ('salarymen') who no longer can look ahead to a guarantee of life-time employment. But this is a hypothetical situation which we cannot predict.

References

Brown, Delmer (1995) *Nationalism in Japan: An Introductory Analysis*, Berkeley: University of California Press.

Falt, Olavi K. (1996) 'The image of the Emperor Showa as a symbol of national aspirations', in Ian Neary (ed.), *Leaders and Leadership in Japan*, Folkestone: Japan Library, pp. 232–42.

Field, Norma (1991) *In the Realm of a Dying Emperor*, New York: Pantheon.

Gellner, Ernest (1996) *Nationalism*, London: Weidenfeld and Nicholson.

Ishihara, Shintaro (1989) *The Japan That Can Say No*, trans, Frank Baldwin, New York: Simon and Schuster.

Kersten, Rikki (1996) *Democracy in Postwar Japan: Maruyama and the Search for Autonomy*, London: Routledge.

Lamont-Brown, R. (1998) *Kempeitai*, Stroud: Sutton Publishing.

Large, Stephen S. (1992) *Emperor Hirohito and Showa Japan*, London: Routledge.

Morris, Ivan (1960) *Nationalism and the Right Wing in Japan*, Oxford: Oxford University Press.

Nish, Ian (1993) 'Nationality, patriotism and nationalism in Japan', in Roger Michener, *Nationality, Patriotism and Nationalism in Liberal Democratic Societies*, St Paul, Minnesota: Paragon.

—— (ed.) (1998) *The Iwakura Mission in America and Europe*, Richmond: Japan Library.

Richardson, Bradley (1997) *Japanese Democracy: Power, Coordination and Performance*, Newhaven: Yale University Press.

Takeda, Kiyoko (1988) *The Dual Image of the Japanese Emperor*, London: Macmillan.

Tipton, Elise K. (ed.) (1997) *Society and the State in Interwar Japan*, London: Routledge.

Yoshino, Kosaku (1992) *Cultural Nationalism in Contemporary Japan*, London: Routledge/ London School of Economics.

6   Communalism, secularism and the dilemma of Indian nationhood

Meghnad Desai

Introduction

'Communalism' is a word that has special connotations with regard to events in South Asia. The term was used in both India and Ceylon (as it then was) in colonial times. Community/communitarian are words with a good image in British life, but community/communalism have a particular imperial connotation of how the British saw communities as forces for damage in the Indian empire. Communalism signifies riots – between Hindus and Muslims in India, and Buddhists and Christians in Sri Lanka – which are always called 'communal' riots. Riots between Sikhs and Hindus or upper-caste Hindus and the Dalits are not called communal riots. In this sense, then, communalism is any ideology, attitude or behaviour that is likely to incite or lead to a Hindu–Muslim riot.[1] (It is interesting to note that in the UK the 'troubles' in Ulster are called sectarian, and the bloody war in the former Yugoslavia led to the term 'ethnic cleansing'. These are similar phenomena, but each deserves its own treatment.)

In the year preceding independence/partition on 15 August 1947, India experienced a continuous stream of Hindu–Muslim riots across the country. It was a civil war in a not very civil society. The war climaxed in the partition of Indica into India and Pakistan.[2] The partition, an event which was unforeseen as late as the end of 1946, was hastily decided upon within weeks of the arrival of Mountbatten as the last British Viceroy in March 1947. In the aftermath of partition and the flood of fleeing families – Hindus, Muslims and Sikhs who managed to cross the recently drawn borders alive – there followed even more riots. Nehru was appalled at these events (see Gopal 1979, chapter 1), and so too was Gandhi, who eventually died trying to stop Hindu–Muslim violence. Communal riots and the forces that may eventuate in them – communalism – have been for ever the nightmare of the Indian polity.

Since independence/partition, India has managed a miracle. It has chosen parliamentary democracy, universal adult franchise, a multi-party system and a free press. Over a period of approximately fifty years, the number of voters has trebled to around 600 million. India's position as a multilingual, multi-religious, multi-ethnic polity is unique. Apart from the fourteen languages listed in its constitution, there are a further 700 languages spoken throughout the country, not including dialects. The majority of the 950 million people are Hindu, although that term covers a wide variety of beliefs.[3] There are 110 million Muslims, making India the third largest country after Indonesia and Pakistan in terms of Muslim population, larger, paradoxically, than Pakistan. In addition, there are Sikhs, Christians, Jews, Zoroastrians, Buddhists, Jains, as well as many tribal religions.

The partition of Indica was a sudden, traumatic event. No one in the early 1930s took seriously the talk by some Cambridge students about Pakistan as a separate nation for the Muslims.[4] However, by 1940 this idea had become the official policy of the Muslim League. Even so, it is not obvious that Mohammad Ali Jinnah, the leader of the Muslim League, envisaged a separate nation-state. He argued that there were two nations in Indica. But the question is were there two nation-states? The majority of Muslims in 1940 lived in provinces where they were in a minority. The Muslim-majority provinces were, relatively speaking, sparsely populated. In only two provinces – Punjab and Bengal – was there a large Muslim population in a state of precarious majority. These provinces were divided in the partition and were the scenes of bloody massacres.

In contrast to Pakistan which was set up as an Islamic republic, India chose to be a non-religious, non-theocratic democratic republic.[5] The Indian state's neutrality with regard to religion was partly a rejection of, and a reaction to, the two-nations theory which had led in the view of the Congress Party to the partition. The Congress Party had been the principal negotiator of Indica's independence (although it was ultimately pipped at the post by the Muslim League), and it had taken the view that all of Indica represented a single nation and a single people, though professing different religions and speaking different languages. However, the British denied the label of nation to Indica as vehemently as the Congress asserted it.

Another reason for the state's stance on religion was the Congress Party's claim that it was the direct successor, rather than a joint inheritor along with Pakistan, of British power, and the fact that the outgoing colonial state was secular (that the Mother country was one where the monarch was also the Head of the Church of England was of little consequence).[6] This had been the case since the East India Company which was the *bête noire* of Christian missionaries. The Christian church in any of its many sectarian forms was not allowed undue importance in India under British rule. At the same time, of course, both Hindus and Muslims complained that the British favoured one group over the other. It was therefore logical that an independent India would choose to be secular in her constitution. However, this was not stated officially in the original constitution, which declared India a 'sovereign democratic republic'. In 1976, while the 'democratic' bit was under some strain, the then prime minister Mrs Indira Gandhi added the words 'secular socialist' to the constitution. Since then, if anything, the secularism of the Indian union has been more in question than ever.

Secularism, as an ideology, was propagated by Nehru as the cement to hold together the newly independent India and to act as a counter to the communal riots and the communalism of the Hindu Mahasabha and the Rashtriya Swayan-sevak Sangh (RSS) movements. Nehru was a modernist and an atheist who tried to inculcate secularist habits of thought and behaviour into India's public political life. By contrast, most of Nehru's Congress colleagues were religious and held orthodox social views. This meant that Nehru had to fight a constant battle with his own party members – Patel, Pant, Prasad, Tandon, Kripalani – in the first decade after 1947 to assert secularism as a positive philosophy and as a code of behaviour in public life.

For a period of about twenty-five years following independence, communalism was held back and communal riots were infrequent, isolated events quickly put down by the Indian state. Indeed, during the 1950s and 1960s other fissures especially linguistic divisions, as well as the possible alienation of the south – were much more feared as possible causes of the Balkanisation of India. The reorgani-sation of the states along linguistic lines and the agitation in the south demanding the recognition of Hindi as the sole national language caused more street violence than did communal riots. The unrest in the Telangana region in the immediate aftermath of independence and in the Naxalbari region from the mid-1960s to the present day, were also 'secular' challenges faced by the Indian state.

The concern about Balkanisation was not misplaced. After all, Pakistan which was created as a mono-religious nation split between West and East Pakistan, creating Bangladesh in 1971. This showed that the spectre of multinationality haunted both the countries into which Indica was partitioned. In Pakistan's case, the nationality of the East Pakistanis was defined by a different language, as well as the homogeneous territory which they occupied at some distance from West Pakistan. Religion, language and territory have proved to be a potent combina-tion, threatening the stability of both India and Pakistan.

The Khalistan movement in Punjab and the riots in Assam during the 1970s and 1980s, plus the continual problem in Kashmir, have all taken their toll in terms of violence against the Indian state and individuals. Further, in the north-east, the Mizo and the Naga nationalisms have resulted in constant state surveillance and the suppression of disorder, showing that the Indian state is capable of deploying formidable force when its existence is even slightly at risk. Pakistan, too, has experienced nationality problems, with the Baluchis, Pakhtoons, Sindhis and Mohajirs. But while Pakistan's nationality problems are based on language and territory, India has to cope with religion as the sole divisive element within its society. This is why communalism can be considered a peculiarly Indian problem. (That said, there are of course the Shi'a/Sunni divisions within the Muslim religion, and the persecution of minor Muslim sects such as the Ahmadiyas in Pakistan.)

Communalism, however, is not confined to particular regions or states within India: although more virulent in the north than in the south, it is the central problem of the Indian polity as a whole. This is because what is communalism to some is an alternative basis for defining India's nationhood – *Hindutva* – to others, the latter view expressed by the Bharatiya Janata Party (BJP). Since 1990, the BJP has gained increasing public support: from 1992 it was the principal opposition party in parliament; in the 1996 election it was the largest single party; and in 1998, after forming a majority coalition with various parties, it came to power. Interestingly, as the party's appeal has broadened, it has soft-pedalled over the issue of *Hindutva*, especially after the demolition of the Babri Masjid temple on 6 December 1992 by large mobs of Hindu communalists.

Since 1989, India has not had a single party majority in power – and often not even a coalition in a majority. Between 1947 and 1989, India saw six prime ministers come and go, and the same number again between 1989 and 2000. The Congress Party has in the meantime lost support across the country: it has split at least twice and shows little sign of winning office. The Party was meant to be the guardian of secularism, a role it fulfilled in the first thirty years of its rule, 1947–1977. However, in the 1980s, although still officially adhering to the principle of secularism, it began to adopt a more compromising attitude towards the communalists. On the issue of secularism, the Congress Party has always relied on the support of left-wing parties – including the Communist Party India (CPI), the Communist Party Marxist (CPM) and some socialist parties. In the past, the left and the Congress Party seldom questioned the meaning of secularism. If anything, it meant simply not siding with the Hindu communalists who had been part of the sorry episodes of violence at the time of independence/partition; it meant being against a party which under one name or another – Hindu Mahasabha, Jan Sangh, BJP – represented the Hindu communalist alternative.

As a footnote to the glorious *temps perdu*, I should mention that for the Indian left, religion and caste were seen as a diversion from the main issue: that of the class struggle. The heated debates that took place on the left were mainly about the strategy which would take India from the bourgeois revolution to a socialist one. The issues of caste and religion were generally considered irrelevant – the USSR–China divide mattered more than the communal question. The left is still a formidable presence in Indian politics, and it has taken up the issue of secularism much more seriously since the 1992 Babri Masjid incident (and as the prospect of a socialist revolution has dimmed).

The urgency of the political challenge raised by the prospect of the BJP coming to power, as well as the shock of the Babri Masjid incident, has led to much writing on the subject of communalism in India.[7] Although this literature is important, any discussion of communalism and secularism must take, in my opinion, a broader view. For example, there is the centrality of Gandhi, the relative economic failure of Nehru's strategy which led to stagnation in employment and output growth (and its eventual abandonment in 1991), the worldwide resurgence of religion in politics, the prospering diaspora and the phenomenon of globalisation and its instant communication technology. The aim of this chapter is to weave these themes into a wider critique of secularism and communalism in India.

The background to communalism

There is no one appropriate point at which to start a discussion of the history of communalism. Religious clashes are not unknown in India, and Hindu–Muslim riots have some record in pre-colonial times. But communalism is a special kind of ideological problem since it is about nationality as sought to be defined in terms of *religious identity*. Thus, neither Shi'a–Sunni riots nor Hindu–Sikh riots have attracted the same attention as have Hindu Muslim clashes, and this is because of the way in which nationality was defined under British colonial rule. (One exception is the anti-Sikh riots in Delhi in 1984, following Indira Gandhi's assassination. But Khalistan was mixed up with this event in a very vital way. This does not, of course, excuse the shocking delay in bringing the culprits to justice.)

The question we must ask is: was Indica a nation? The British rulers always denied that it was. This was based on the fact that, since before the arrival of the Westerners in Indica in 1498, there had not been a single government across the country. Indeed, while the idea of Indica was well known as a cultural entity, its boundaries were never clear. Did they extend beyond the Khyber Pass into what was later Afghanistan, where Kanishka and later Mughal kings ruled? How far in the East did they extend – as far as Burma? And what was the line in the Himalayas where Indica stopped and Tibet began? These issues were the cause of a lot of conflict later on, but they were up in the air in the early part of the nineteenth century, by which time the East India Company had acquired territory in more than one region of Indica.

No single king had ruled over this territory, even vaguely defined. We can perhaps look to the one hundred-year period from around the middle of Akbar's reign in approximately 1580 to the ebbing away of Aurangzeb's strength in approximately 1680, as the one point when there was a single powerful government which ruled over much of what later came to be occupied jointly by India and Pakistan. Thus, *administratively*, India's boundaries were defined by the British Raj some time in the late nineteenth century, after Sind had been captured and Afghanistan proved difficult to conquer.

But if Indica could not be defined territorially without colonial help, could it be defined culturally – as an imagined community? This is where the battlefield was pitched in colonial times, mainly by Indians who had received a Western-style education. Through the Bengal renaissance of the first half of the nineteenth century to Western Indian reform movements of the latter half of that same century, the three sea ports – Calcutta, Bombay and Madras, by and large all colonial cities – became the centres where a national consciousness was forged. This consciousness had to be forged in reaction to the criticisms of the ruling power, using the tools of the British but deployed in a different way. Thus, the professed liberalism and parliamentary constitutionalism, as well as the much-vaunted tradition of a free press, of the imperial country were all harnessed by the subjects of British India to build up an ideology of nationhood.

In the first phase of establishing a sense of nationhood, Muslims played a very minor role. This was because the British had singled them out as the hostile people in the early nineteenth century and blamed them for the events of 1857. In addition, the Muslim community did not take to Western education with the same alacrity as did Hindus and Parsees. The reformist debates were very much Hindu-centred if they related to social and religious life or Hindu- and Parsee-centred when concerned with civic matters in Bombay. It was not until the late nineteenth century that the Muslims, under the leadership of Saiyad Ahmad Khan, embraced Western education. It is of some significance that Saiyad's appeal had to be made in terms of the nation-wide Muslim community, and opposition to him was from orthodox Muslim quarters. For Hindus, Western education came at different paces in different provinces, and different communities took to it at varying speeds. Brahmins and upper castes were the first groups to benefit, but they could not prevent other (lower) castes from gaining access to education as successfully as they had done in the past, thus ending their monopoly on education.

National consciousness in Indica, as against the sense of Hindu or Muslim identity and the need to reform society, has its roots in the final quarter of the nineteenth century. It is necessary to retell this familiar tale because national consciousness was defined very much in the context of a likely concession by the rulers, of the granting of some legislative presence to the native community. With their knowledge of the British parliamentary system, the native elite was rightly excited by this prospect. Here it is important to point out the differentiation on the side of the colonial rulers as well, as political events at that time in Britain were very relevant to the changing fortunes of constitutional reform in British India, with the nationalist movement experiencing waves of reform or repression depending on who was in power. The imperialists may have divided and ruled, but they were divided at home as well, and some of their divisions were not just for show. Thus, the Liberal ascendancy under Gladstone – while it lasted – did better for Indica compared to when Salisbury and the Tories were in power. It was for a good reason, then, that the early Indian nationalists were Liberals.

Thus it was with the debates around the Ilbert Bill in 1883 that the first organised nationalist agitations began and the Congress Party was formed.

However, it was Viceroy Curzon, a Tory, who gave the best fillip to the nationalist movement by partitioning Bengal. The partition inflamed nationalist sentiments, but it also exposed the fissures within the nationalist movement and within Indica itself. The Congress Party was split between the moderates and the extremists. Divisions appeared between the Hindu landlords and Bhadralok of Bengal and their tenant Muslim peasants who lived in East Bengal. The Nawabs of Dacca led the upper- and middle-class Muslims of Bengal who were the principal beneficiaries of the partition. The Western liberal rhetoric employed by the Congress Party was challenged by a Hindu rhetoric in Bengal by Bankim Chandra, in Punjab by Lala Lajpat Rai, and in Maharashtra by Tilak. There was thus already emerging a diversity in the construction of Indian nationhood.

Varieties of Indian nationhood

What was the notion of nationhood in, say, 1900? I would argue that it was constructed around the liberal concept of loyal subjects aspiring to be granted some self-rule, for example the right of Indians to take part in the Civil Service. This developed into an economic argument in favour of protectionism following the placing of duties on cotton yarn, imposed at Manchester's request, on Indian cotton mills, and the disquiet about the exchange rate for the rupee. But apart from that, we can see by referring to the works of Dadabhai Naoroji or R. C. Dutt (Naoroji 1901; Dutt 1908) that the case against the British was economic rather than political. Independence, or even some sort of autonomy was not on the cards. Nor for that matter was the situation all that different in the white parts of the British Empire, as the war in South Africa or the land agitation in Ireland were demonstrating.

Apart from this theory of the Westernised Indian elite about loyal subjects demanding the end of 'un-British' behaviour from the rulers, were there any other theories of nationhood? I believe there was the same theory naturalised, but with two variants. Thus people were loyal subjects, but not of the British Empire; rather, they looked to a bygone one of their own which had to be revived. Two theories had been mooted in 1857, but had lost out. None the less, they simmered. One was the revival of the Hindu *Pata Padshahi* that the Maratha Empire had aspired to and even briefly enjoyed before its loss at Panipat in 1761. This remained a shining ideal for the Maharashtrians and many others. (The strength of Marathi-speaking thinkers in the later construction of *Hindutva* is not unrelated to this ideal.) The Maratha's was the most recent of the Hindu kingdoms that tried to establish an all Indica hegemony (for another example, one would need to go back a thousand years). The second and alternative movement was the revival of the Moghul Empire, which was not formally dissolved until 1857 and constituted a rallying point for some groups at that time. Indeed, it was this experience and the bitterness surrounding 1857 that made the British suspicious of the Muslims right up until the end of the nineteenth century. There was also a Bengali version of Hindu nationalism which appealed to some hoary past when Hindus ruled. Bankim Chandra's *Anand Math* belongs to this vision, though attempts have been made subsequently to secularise him. This strain of Bengali-Hindu nationalism waned during the 1930s and 1940s. The Punjabi variant was based on the *Arya Samajist* movement, which remained powerful throughout the 1920s before fading away.

Thus, there were three subjecthoods on offer in 1900: the British Empire, the Maratha Empire and the Moghul Empire. Of these, only the British version was modern, though colonial, and only it had the force of progress behind it – something which Gandhi recognised during his time spent in South Africa. Gandhi believed that subjecthood of the British Empire, especially given the Proclamation of the Queen in 1858, was a very good deal. The Proclamation had promised equal treatment of all British subjects regardless of race or religion, and Gandhi tried to leverage that promise in his fight with the powers in South Africa. He joined loyally on the British side, albeit in the medical corps, in the Boer War, the Zulu War and the First World War, precisely because of his belief in these principles of equality for all. Although Gandhi's attitude may appear shocking in the context of contemporary notions of racism and imperialism, we have to remember the historical context in which he was fighting for justice.

The Morely-Minto reforms and the Muslim League

The 1909 Morley-Minto reforms offered the next step in this progressive British subjecthood, recognising the need for constitutional reform in British India. However, faced with the prospect of granting the universal franchise, the British had to decide on what basis. One should recall that the adult franchise had not yet been granted in Britain – women and poor people were excluded from the right to vote. As well, Britain saw itself as a Protestant nation: Catholic emancipation had been achieved in 1829, but Oxbridge colleges restricted fellowships to practising Anglicans late into the nineteenth century, and Jews were discriminated against in society (even though Disraeli had been the leader of the Conservative Party). Little surprise then, that Indica was primarily seen in religious terms – as a patchwork of religious communities – and that the notion of a liberal democracy with individual voters was alien. In British India, the Muslims were on the whole poorer than the Hindus, and numerically in a minority at whatever level the property qualifications for the franchise could be pitched.

The Morley-Minto decision to have separate electorates for Muslims is believed by many to have sown the seeds of the subsequent partition. Fenner Brockway, for example, has described the issue of separate electorates as 'a small cloud on the horizon, an anticipation of a later fatal division' (1971: 82). I believe this view is too teleological, however. The Congress was Hindu-dominated; who else could it be dominated by? Of course, there were prominent Parsees, Anglo-Indians and Muslims – Jinnah, for instance – in the Congress. But the Bengal partition movement had played on Hindu symbols and disregarded the interests of the East Bengal Muslim peasantry. Congress extremists were led by Tilak who mobilised people by using Hindu symbolism. From 1909, the movement was split between loyal British Empire subjects petitioning for more rights and a nationalist movement which evoked the Maratha Empire and Hindu symbolism.

It is a staple of Indian historiography that once the Muslim League was established, the pro-Muslim bias of the Raj became transparent, as seen in the Morley-Minto decision to establish separate electorates for Hindus and Muslims. However, it was not long before the Muslims were complaining about the ending of Bengal partition in 1911 and the lack of official support for making Aligarh – which was intended to bring Western education to Muslims – a full-scale university (Nanda 1989). Thus hindsight, especially of Indian nationalist historiography, can be misleading. Britain was neither consistently pro nor consistently anti Hindu or Muslim. This was partly because there was no single British view on the matter; and even if there had been one, the British genius is not in tight conceptualisation but in a common-sense muddling through. Thus, the British view on nationalities in Indica was at best fuzzy.

The powers at Westminster, including even the Liberal Party, saw Indica as made up of different religious and social groups. In this regard, India was not unique within the British Empire: Ireland, the major headache for the Liberals, was also divided along religious lines, and South Africa, too, had two Christian churches. So it was not entirely scheming and far-sighted of the British to concede to the demand by the Aga Khan and the Muslim League for separate Muslim electorates. Mushirul Hasan (1997) dates the formation of Muslim national consciousness from this point in history. I would argue that the prospect of electoral representation also sharpened Hindu national identity. Questions such as whether the untouchables were Hindus took on a new importance since numbers were about to become a vital source of political strength. The 1911 Census went into much greater detail about the 'caste system' and received petitions from many Jatis about upgrading their varna status. Indeed, casteism could be said to be a product of the ballot box. Once group identification was used as a marker for franchise, then group solidarity became a political asset.

The result was that both groups, Hindus and Muslims, began to crystallise their nationalities much more strongly once the possibility of even limited representation had been presented to British India. From 1909 onwards, despite the Nehru Report which in 1928 ruled out communal electorates in an independent India, Congress also operated on the system that was on offer, for example in the 1922 elections in which the Swarajists took part and, later, in the 1937 elections. The Congress may have been ecumenical but it did not, and could not, challenge the theory of political membership on offer. This is why the 1916

Lucknow Pact makes so much sense. It was by combining across the separate electorates that Jinnah was trying to forge a vision of a united India. Jinnah hailed the Lucknow Pact as 'the birth of United India' (Brockway 1971: 87).

The Lucknow Pact was perhaps the climax of old-style nationalist politics in India, with its exclusive reliance on subjecthoods. The Great War transformed the nature of nationalism across the world. There was rampant inflation for the first time in India on a sustained long-term basis after falling prices during much of the nineteenth century. India had begun to enjoy some freedom on tariffs and the Industrial Commission of 1916 had pointed out the potential for limited guided industrialisation. But just as the demands of economic nationalism were about to be accommodated, the emphasis shifted to political nationalism.

Gandhi and the new Indian nationalism

The entire map of the Indian struggle for self-rule changed after the Jalianwala Bagh incident of 13 April 1919. Gandhi had returned to India and begun his own style of politics in Champaran, Ahemdabad and Kheda. But the Rowlatt Act and the firing on unarmed crowds at Jalianwala Bagh shattered for ever the illusion that 'un-British' behaviour was exceptional. Gandhi, who had up to this point been loyal to the British Empire, concluded that this was an evil with which he could not co-operate. Subjecthood was no longer an adequate ideal. Despite the official reprimand that Dyer received, the militant wing of the Congress did not believe the British could be trusted.

Thus despite the Montagu-Chelmsford reforms of 1917 and the inclusion of an Indian – Sir Satyendra Sinha (later to become Lord Sinha) – into the Imperial War Cabinet, constitutionalism was put on the defensive and the constitutional wing of the Congress lost its dominance. But in fashioning the weapon of mass mobilisation, Gandhi also deployed the religious card. Hinduism guided his life and he therefore assumed that religion guided everyone's life. The choice of Khilafat – the movement to re-establish the Caliph as head of the Muslims – as an issue on which to recruit Muslims into the non-cooperation movement was perhaps even more significant than the sectional electorates set up by the Morley-Minto reforms. It recognised the Muslims as a separate estate to be recruited into the independence struggle not on *national* issues but on *religious* ones. Gandhi thus legitimised the vote-bank that the Morley-Minto reforms had created. After this there was no question of an Indian nationhood: there was always a Muslim agenda and a Sikh agenda and, by default, the all-India agenda that remained was a Hindu agenda.

Gandhi's sudden and idiosyncratic suspension of the non-cooperation movement after the violence in the village of Chauri Chaura in 1922 bitterly disappointed the Muslims (Khaliquzzaman 1961). Of course, Atatürk had already devalued the Khilafat demand as being contrary to modernity for the Muslims of

Turkey. He had opted for Turkey to be a secular state while Gandhi was encouraging the mullahs to consolidate their stranglehold on Muslims. Modernists such as Abul Kalam Azad were treated on a par with the more orthodox Ali brothers. Disappointed with Gandhi and the Congress after Chauri Chaura, the Muslims began to think that an alliance with the Congress was a risky option (Khaliquzzman 1961; Nanda 1989; Samad 1995).

It would seem that neither Gandhi nor the Congress appreciated the deep wounds that the suspension of the non-cooperation movement inflicted on the Muslim community. Accounts of the formation of Pakistan highlight the Khilafat episode and the cavalier way in which Gandhi abandoned the movement as crucial breaking points for the Muslims, who had just ventured for the first time *en masse* to throw in their lot with the wider nationalist movement. There was never again a Hindu–Muslim joint platform; there were Congress Muslims and Muslim League Muslims, but no single, broad movement (Samad 1995).

After 1921 the Congress began to presume that it was the sole all-Indian nationalist movement. While its leadership remained overwhelmingly Hindu – and upper-caste Hindu at that – it began to project a nationalism based not on subjecthood but on citizenship. While the Sawarajists who took part in the 1922 dyarchy elections still adhered to the loyal subjecthood idea, albeit with stiffer demands, the Congress for the first time during the 1920s espoused a nationhood based on the possibility of dominion status. This was later changed to a demand for independence after the Lahore Congress in 1930, where Jawaharlal Nehru was president. The 1928 Nehru Report that had preceded the Lahore Congress, and which had been the response of the Congress to the Simon Commission Report of 1929, ruled out any Muslim electorates. Jinnah tried desperately through the 1920s to propose various *modi vivendi* going beyond the Morley-Minto reforms which would trade separate Muslim electorates for some protected rights for Muslims, but the Congress did not agree to any of the suggestions (Samad 1995; Nanda 1989).

The sidelining of the Congress after the Simon Commission Report and the Round Table conferences (at which a federal solution for British India and the native states began to be formulated) resulted in Gandhi launching the Dandi Satyagraha (or Dandi March). This led to the Gandhi–Irwin pact; the first time that His Imperial Majesty's Viceroy had signed a document on equal terms with a private subject. However, it only managed to get the Congress to the second Round Table conference, and even then Ramsay MacDonald stuck with a separate electorate scheme. Thus the Congress gained little from the Dandi March.

Significantly, however, Gandhi's fast in Yeravada prison on the issue of separate electorates for the untouchables reinforced his religious view of politics. His insistence that the untouchables should be counted as Hindu rather than be given separate electorates vindicated the Morley-Minto view of religious nationalities. Had Gandhi not objected to the separate electorates for the untouchables, these arrangements could have been seen as *minority protection* – a mixture of religion and deprived status – rather than as *religious separation*. Indeed, additional separate electorates could have been encouraged, diluting the religious principle and emphasising the secular one of minority rights. By his protest to remove the small amount of protection won for the untouchables by Ambedkar at the Round Table conferences, Gandhi cemented the religious principle in politics. Although this was consistent with his world view, it was a fatal step for Indian independence. Ambedkar never forgave Gandhi for helping to take away from the untouchables a small amount of hard-won political clout. The failure in post-independence India to raise the status of the untouchables – as evidenced by their dissatisfaction, first in neo-Buddhist conversions and later in the Dalit movement – shows that the Congress and Gandhi were unable to resist the religious principle. And in so doing, they deprived the downtrodden the power of self-emancipation through the political process.[8]

A federal India?

By the beginning of the 1930s, theories of subjecthood had taken a back seat. While there were loyalists still willing to take part in various elections to provincial councils, dominion status had been put on the table by Irwin. Neither a revived Muslim kingdom nor a Hindu one were attracting any support. The proposed models of nationhood were based around the size and structure of franchise, the power of the provinces versus Delhi, and native states versus Delhi. The Government of India Act 1935, was the culmination of a long process that had begun with the Simon Commission (itself a review of the workings of the Montagu-Chelmsford reforms) the Round Table conferences and the various parliamentary commissions following on from the conferences, and the debating and enacting of the longest piece of legislation to be seen at that time in Westminster.

From the point of view of British politics, the Act was a remarkable piece of all-party co-operation. The Simon Commission had been appointed by F. E. Smith (Lord Birkenhead) during the 1924–1929 government. The Commission's report had come during a Labour government (1929–1931), and Wedgewood Benn conspired with Irwin and Baldwin to set it aside and to hold the Round Table conferences. (It was this as much as his dislike for Baldwin that made Churchill resign from the Shadow Cabinet and join the backbenches as a stalwart on India.) The British government kept up the pace after 1931. Except for Churchill and his fifty supporters, there was no opposition to the passage of the Act. Thus, by 1935 some form of eventual self-government for Indica was a fixture of British politics.[9]

In terms of subjecthood, the 1927–1935 process moved the debate about Indica's future towards the possibility of dominion status akin to such countries as

New Zealand and Australia. The date at which such status was to be given was not made clear but, the Congress Party apart, the participants in the Round Table conferences saw the Montagu-Chelmsford promises delivered in the 1927–1935 process. The people of Indica were to be absorbed within a single federation – native states and British India – as subjects of the Crown, capable of self-government. The concept of a single nationhood was not defined in this proposal. That was the rival model put forward by the Nehru-led wing of the Congress which forced the pace to adopt the Lahore Resolution asking for full independence in 1930.

There were three rival models of nationhood. First, the Congress vision was of an independent Indica with the Party representing the nation of undifferentiated Indians (at least as far as Nehru was concerned) who in their private lives could remain Hindus, Muslims, Sikhs, etc. The second was Gandhi's model which was not as secular as Nehru's vision but was equally inclusive of all people of Indica. Gandhi had formed his model during his time in South Africa where he had organised the immigrant Indian community to fight for its rights as a single undifferentiated group contrasted to the whites and the blacks. The third model was a 'federalist' one that emerged out of the 1927–1935 process. This was based on a view of Indica as a multinational polity. Provinces were, in this view, nations with their own language (usually) and history. Punjab, Bengal, Sind were already such single-language provinces. The native states, at least the larger ones – Hyderabad, Mysore, Gwalior – had pretensions to autonomy. By emphasising the local nationality, the federalists did not deny an Indian super-identity: one could be Bengali *and* Indian or Punjabi *and* Indian.

Again, it is necessary to avoid hindsight. In 1935, proposals for Pakistan were dismissed as nonsense by sober Muslim leaders like Zafrullah Khan. And Jinnah refused to push them on the subject. What was on offer was a large extension of democracy at the provincial level and some arrangement – in the event, never implemented – to bring British India and the native states into a federation. This was the Act which shaped the contours of the partition of Indica. Elections in 1937 and 1946 were conducted on this basis. Its treatment of minorities – untouchables and tribals – has become part of the constitution of India via its Schedules, hence Scheduled castes and tribes. Its division of powers between the centre and the provinces has survived the test of time in the Indian constitution. It was a map for the eventual dominion status for Indica; it could have been the blueprint for an undivided Indica.

War and the coming of partition

An undivided Indica was not the eventual outcome, however. I would argue that there are at least two reasons for this. The first was, of course, the outbreak of the Second World War and the revival of Churchill's career. But the second and more contentious reason was the behaviour of the Congress in power between 1937 and 1939 and, further, its decision to resign and go into exile/prison for five years from 1939 to 1944.

Churchill had spent the 1930s in exile on the Tory backbenches. His quarrel with Baldwin had started over the issue of India and the treatment of the Simon Commission's report by the two front benches. By the end of the decade, he had begun to campaign for the need to arm against the threat of a hostile Germany. The leadership of the Conservative Party was against him on both issues – India and armament. The outbreak of war in September 1939 returned Churchill to the Cabinet as First Lord of the Admiralty, the same position he had held in the previous war. He began immediately to make his views felt on India but was restrained by Chamberlain and his Secretary of State for India, Zetland. Churchill's main concern when he eventually became prime minister was winning the war. Nevertheless, he continued to have his say on India, and appointed Leo Amery as his Secretary of State for India. Churchill understood the importance of retaining India at the heart of the British Empire. His father, Lord Randolph Churchill, had been Secretary of State for India, and Churchill himself had been stationed there. Nevertheless, his knowledge of India was sparse and peculiar, and he hated Indians, especially educated, middle-class ones. Churchill's accession to power transformed the Indian negotiations.

The decision by the Congress to contest the elections at the provincial level to implement part of the 1935 Act led to, and coincided with, the emergence of Nehru as the undisputed leader of the Congress after Gandhi. Nehru headed the electoral wing of the Congress while Patel, as Chairman of the Congress Parliamentary Board, undertook the organisational role. Nehru's theories about citizenship and democracy were far more radical than Gandhi's. A liberal democrat who advocated a left-wing economic programme, Nehru was also an atheist who believed religion had no role to play in India's political life. He viewed voters as atomistic individual citizens whose religious, caste or regional affiliations were a sign of backwardness which would melt away once economic progress was achieved. In his writing, he frequently attributes communalism to lack of employment. His was a simple majoritarian view of democratic politics without any religious distraction. He also had a fairly well formulated (though not Comintern) view of class: backwardness and poverty were due to economic forces and religion/caste/regionality were part of the superstructure that needed to be removed from politics. Nehru's views formed the classic formulation of secularism in post-independence India.

Nehru was always unhappy with Gandhi's religiosity, and some of this anger can be seen in his autobiography (Nehru 1936). He made peace with Gandhi following that outburst, but a sense of unease remained between the two men until the end. Nehru's anti-communalism was anti-religious *in toto* as opposed to Gandhi's ecumenical view. Nehru's conduct as the leader of the electoral wing of the Congress was crucial for the elections of 1937 and what the party did after that. But before turning to the elections, we need to look at the background to the 1935 Act which led to them.

The long process of negotiations about India's future status, which started with the appointment of the Simon Commission in 1927 and ended with the passage of the Government of India Act in 1935, was carried out without the full participation of the Congress. Congress joined in only one of the three Round Table conferences, sending Gandhi as their sole delegate. He chose to speak last and took the stance that Congress was the *only* party with which the government should negotiate. But the Round Table conference process had brought together a variety of political interests – princes of native states, representative delegations of provincial governments, leaders of Muslims, Sikhs, Hindus and untouchables. It was during the first Round Table conference that the Maharaja of Bikaner had proposed a federal arrangement for the future government of India. What he meant by 'federation' was a confederation, with considerable local autonomy for native states and provinces. The representatives of Punjab and Bengal agreed with this demand for autonomy. Congress, and indeed Jinnah, also preferred a strong centre and weak provinces. The Congress believed that a weak centre would Balkanise India. Jinnah consented, but wanted solid guarantees for the largest single minority. However, his problem was that Muslim politicians preferred provincial autonomy – in Punjab, Bengal and Sind – and they did not want to come under a single Muslim League umbrella (Samad 1995; Jalal 1985).

The Muslim League did not have much success in the 1937 elections. Despite his best efforts, Jinnah could not persuade Muslim candidates to fight under the aegis of the Muslim League Parliamentary Board. But Congress, too, had very few Muslim members and those who were Congress Muslims (for example, Ansari and Azad) were told to fight not as Muslims but as Congressmen. By contrast, the orthodox Hindus in the Congress – Jayakar, Rajendra Prasad, Gobind Ballabh Pant – were not limited in the same way. As the majority community, they did not have to fight as Hindus, but merely had to strengthen the anti-modernist forces that Gandhi represented and which frustrated Nehru (Nehru 1936).

Although the Congress Party won seven out of eleven provinces and the Muslim League managed to form a coalition government in only one province – Bengal – neither party represented the Muslims. Hence the drive to recruit Muslims for the Congress that Nehru encouraged in Uttar Pradesh (UP). This was after negotiations between the Congress and the Muslim League for power sharing in UP had broken down. Nehru did not want to encourage the League; indeed, he thought all sectarian parties – Muslim League or Hindu Mahasabha – should be driven out of politics. Needless to say, Nehru's views were in a minority. Many Congress leaders sympathised with the Hindu Mahasabha, whose leader, Pandit Madan Mohan Malaviya, held a higher place than Jinnah in the affections of the Congress, although both men represented sectarian parties.

The Congress drive to recruit Muslims was not terribly successful in its aim but it did finally end any hope of an accommodation with the Muslim League, either at the UP level or at the national level. Jinnah realised that he could not succeed in his plans to negotiate a trade-off with the Congress in return for giving up separate Muslim seats. After 1937, Jinnah became more inclined to accept the Pakistan proposal which hitherto he and other secular Muslim leaders such as Zafarullah Khan had dismissed. He too had to recruit more Muslims to the banner of the Muslim League to prove his credibility.

Jinnah's hand was strengthened by the outbreak of the war. The behaviour of the Congress Party at the time was presumptuous, parochial and, ultimately, counterproductive. Linlithgow, the Viceroy and Governor-General, was a Tory, and Zetland, the Secretary of State for India, was no friend of the Congress. Together they discouraged the native states from fulfilling the 1935 Act's provisions which would have brought about a Central Legislature, no matter how reactionary in its composition. But when war broke out, there was no directly elected majority on the Central Legislature and no elected representation on the Viceroy's Council. That was the constitutional position in which the Congress had connived, by taking part in the 1937 election.

The presumption of the Congress Party to act as the sole representative of the people of India was rather far-fetched, even considering its victory in seven out of eleven states. Six of the seven states were in what is now India (with the exception of the Northwest Frontier Province). But while the Congress controlled a majority of the seats in the general electorate, it did not represent Muslims, nor had it won over the untouchables and anti-Brahmin forces in the south. Ramaswamy Naicker, the Periyar, was willing to share an anti-Congress platform with the Muslim League. Ambedkar was also very suspicious of a Congress government in any eventual post-British India (Ambedkar 1940).

The declaration of war by Britain committed the British Empire as a whole. There had been no consultation with Australia, Canada or New Zealand over the matter, so although India may have commanded special attention, the Congress could not claim primacy. The high point of the Gandhi–Irwin pact was past. Labour was no longer in power and Linlithgow was far less liberal than Irwin. But more than that, the Congress Party failed to understand the seriousness of the war for Britain. The resignations of provincial Congress governments over the lack of consultation over entry into the war were precipitate. But as a bargaining ploy, it failed. In Britain, Parliamentary elections due by 1940 were suspended. The British were not about to take the Congress Party seriously on this issue, especially once Churchill was prime minister.

The episode of the 1937 governments, especially Congress's drive for Muslim recruitment and, most important, the declaration of war and the resignation of the Congress governments, gave credence to a third and rival theory of nationality – Jinnah's theory of dual nationality. The paradox is that Jinnah was an atheist and a modernist in the same mould as Nehru. He also had a unitary — as opposed to a federalist — view of how independent Indica should constitute itself. The view of Jalal (1985) and others, that Jinnah used Pakistan as a bargaining ploy for securing the rights of the Muslim minority in post-independence Indica, is convincing. But the important thing is that apart from the Hindu Mahasabha, a religious view of nationhood had been avoided by *all* parties. The League represented Muslims as a constituency not as a separate nation. Muslims, of course, were asserted to be a nation but they shared neither a common language (unlike Punjabis, Bengalis or Sindhis, for example) nor a common territory. Nor for that matter did the Hindus or Christians. (The Sikhs were the only community that had a religion, a language and a territory which they could call their own. Before 1947, this was in separate pockets in West Punjab in the canal zone and in East Punjab. After the partition, the Sikhs were concentrated in Indian Punjab. This was to cause a lot of trouble forty years later with Khalistan.)

Thus, by 1940, three models of nationhood were being advanced. First, the Congress model was of all Indians, undifferentiated by religion, region or language, forming one nation; cultural diversity was acknowledged and the Congress gave linguistic regions a recognition that supplemented the provincial boundaries of British India. This was a unitarian, centralist model ever worried about Balkanisation. Second, the federal model made region (province/nation-state) the primary basis for defining nationhood with the overarching India as a supra-nation. The centre would have a small number of portfolios but would remain powerful, and the provinces would have many portfolios and a lot of autonomy. Finally, the Pakistan model argued for two nations in Indica — Hindus and Muslims. In 1940, its territorial ambitions were not well articulated and indeed over the next seven years were variable.

A good way to illustrate the three models is to take the example of someone from Bengal. To the Congress, he was an Indian who belonged to the Bengal province; to the federalists, he was a Bengali whose province would federate to India; and to the Muslim League, he was a citizen of a Muslim-majority province which was part of Pakistan. To begin with, the Muslim League was not concerned about differences of religion since it wanted all of Bengal, Hindus and Muslims. Pakistan, as an exclusively Muslim nation-state, was not to emerge in public until after 1946. Before 1946, the idea was that the Hindu minority in the future Pakistan would be a hostage for the Muslim minority in Hindu-majority provinces.

An illustrative account of the issues at stake at this time is given in Ambedkar's book on Pakistan, *Pakistan or the Partition of India* (1940). Relying on his reading of the formation of new nation-states after the First World War, Ambedkar raised the question about the transfer of populations. He was quite clear that no one on either side of the Pakistan debate had any idea what the demand for a separate state really involved. As of 1940, the demand for a Muslim nation was an alternative federal model with groupings of Muslim majority provinces. However, the list of such provinces was not precise.

I want to leave the story of the partition to another essay. But suffice to say that between 1940 and 1945, Congress lost a considerable amount of time, influence and bargaining power *vis-à-vis* the British and Jinnah. Burdened by the war, Britain appreciated any help it could get, whether from Jinnah or the communists. It became irritated by Gandhi and the Congress, mainly due to Gandhi's stand on non-violence and on an independent India's attitude in the event of Japanese invasion. This gave Churchill a propaganda weapon to represent Gandhi to the Americans as a collaborator of the Japanese. The high command of the Congress Party was forced to distance itself from Gandhi for a time during 1940–1941, only to go running back to him when even without Gandhi the British would not negotiate on anywhere near the terms laid down by the Congress. US entry into the war put pressure on Churchill, but he was able to fend this off by sending Stafford Cripps on a mission in 1942 with an offer for post-war settlement, which he then sabotaged.[10] Frustrated by the failure of the quiet, principled and individual protest that he had led, Gandhi turned again, after the failure of the Cripps mission, to his old tactics of mass mobilisation, leading the Quit India campaign. He hoped that this show of power would bring the Viceroy to the negotiating table. But what had worked with Dandi and Irwin did not work with Quit India and Linlithgow. The government made a pre-emptive arrest of the Congress leadership. The unguided and spontaneous struggle that broke out after 8 August 1942 was brutally handled by the government. Subversion in the middle of a war, especially a war that had come to India's borders, was not tolerated. Thus Gandhi's Quit India gamble failed. Of course, this is not the view taken by Indian nationalist historiography.

Luckily for the Congress, the Allies won the war and, more important, the Labour Party won the 1945 General Election.[11] The Viceroy Field Marshal Wavell who replaced Linlithgow was as suspicious as his predecessor had been of Gandhi, but he realised the urgent need for talks between the two sides. However, the long and complex negotiations about India's independence – which had in some sense gone on since the Gandhi–Irwin pact, if not earlier with the Round Table conferences – came to a sudden and unexpected end within less than two years of Labour coming to power. Within that time, a scheme for a compromise between the three models of nationhood – the federal model, the Muslim League model and the Congress model – was put forward by the 1946 Cabinet Mission, but the eventual agreement reached did not stick. Jinnah's resort to mass mobilisation on 16 August 1946, declaring it a 'black day', was to inaugurate a year-long bloody communal war.

There were no further negotiations after August 1946 with British Parliamentary parties. By March 1947, and following the experience of the interim government, partition had become unavoidable. Despite the denials of the

Congress, Jinnah's theory of nationality had won – at least as far as Pakistan was concerned. Even after 12 June 1947, when it had agreed to the partition, the Congress denied that this was the case, insisting instead that its own theory of nationhood had won. The federal model ostensibly lost out. The native states were bundled into each of the two post-partition states. Here again, the status of the native states in independent India/Pakistan was not decided until July 1947. Had Mountbatten stuck to the Attlee timetable of independence by June 1948, this problem might have been contained. As it was, all but three complied. Two out of the three – Junagadh and Hyderabad – were dealt with firmly by India under the newly inherited doctrine of paramountcy. Only one – Kashmir – on the border of both India and Pakistan, and large enough to have dreamed of autonomy – dithered over which country to sign up with. In the event, efforts by Pakistan to force the Maharaja's hand by launching an agitation (a tactic the Congress successfully tried in Junagadh, though with unarmed civilians led by Shamaldas Gandhi) faltered resulting in Kashmir's accession to India. The problem that festers to this day in this area is a vivid illustration of the irreconcilable theories on which the partition of India occurred.

Gandhi and the partition

The Congress agreed to the partition while at the same time denying the two-nations theory. The contradiction in this position is irresolvable and is one aspect at the heart of the problem of communalism. But Gandhi's attitude in the three years following his release from prison was equally inconsistent. He refused Jinnah's demand to acknowledge Pakistan but opened negotiations with him in 1944, based on a formula of the province of Rajagopalachari which accommodated the two-nations theory. At various times during the talks, Gandhi offered peculiar solutions – such as proposing the handing of all power to the Muslim League to save Indica as a single entity.

Considering that he had negotiated one to one with Jinnah (and had conferred upon him the title of 'Qaid-e-Azam'), it is difficult to understand Gandhi's shock at the partition and the communal riots. Indeed, Gandhi never understood or accepted the riotous behaviour of the mobs, either in 1921, in 1942 or in 1946–1947. Seeking to find an answer for the eruption in violence, he blamed imperfections in his own character and thought that only his personal suffering would atone for the violence (Parekh 1989). But neither his suffering nor his pilgrimage through Bengal and Bihar during the civil war made a difference. The killing continued, albeit less in the east than in the west, and partition went ahead.

Gandhi's theory of nationhood was, of course, not the same as Nehru's, but like Nehru's it was inclusive. He regarded religion as the prime identifier of an individual, and his politics were guided by his own religious beliefs which were a form of Christianised-Hinduism (Parekh 1989). As such, he was a religious nationalist; but he was also ecumenical which meant he did not understand communalism. For Gandhi, the Indian nation consisted of the main religious communities – Hindus, Muslims, Sikhs – living side by side. This view stemmed directly from his experiences in South Africa where he had seen Gujarati Hindus and Gujarati Muslims living in peace. And it was this ideal vision that he projected on to Indica.

Gandhi's denial of Jinnah's theory of nationality thus appeared strained but was perhaps very subtle and impractical. His belief in the primacy of religion but the denial of it in politics as a basis for defining nationality are not irreconcilable views; however, it is easier to establish this position in principle than it is in practice. It is also an obstacle if you want to base a secular state on the liberal-democratic principle that individuals are citizens in their public life and only Hindus or Muslims in their private life. Hence, the discomfort of Nehru with Gandhi. Gandhi used religion as a mobilising factor in the independence movement. His entry into the Congress Party alienated constitutional modernists such as Jinnah and C. R. Das, though he won over many others, especially Nehru and his supporters. In mixing up non-cooperation with Khilafat, Gandhi helped to mobilise Muslims on a Muslim issue, rather than on an Indian one. In abandoning non-cooperation unilaterally before the Khilafat issue was resolved, he alienated Muslims and never fully regained their confidence. His Yeravada fast on the issue of the separate electorate for untouchables showed his conservative Hindu electoral concerns. He did not contemplate a similar fast on the issue of Muslim electorates, though that could be due to the fact that it was a *fait accompli* from 1909. Gandhi may have helped to win India's independence, but he arguably also bequeathed it partition and its associated problems.

Thus, at its birth, India was not the nation that the Congress Party wanted, one which corresponded to its theory of nationhood – an undivided Indica – nor was Pakistan what Jinnah wanted. Punjab had lost its battle to stay united and autonomous as had Bengal. But unlike China and its view of Taiwan, India did not treat Pakistan as a breakaway 'province' which needed to be brought under control. If the partition was legitimate, then what was needed was a new model of Indian nationhood. Why was India, as opposed to Indica, a nation? Was it not a large fragment of Indica and hence an incomplete nation? Or was it the coming together of many regional nationalities based on language and territory, but not religion?

Constructing Indian nationhood

In 1947, an independent India emerged out of Indica, which was divided into three parts and two nation-states. However, the year-long civil war and the increasingly fanatical behaviour of the Muslim League led to an unanticipated outcome. Rather than becoming a nation-state with a Muslim majority, Pakistan, with a few exceptions, became a totally Muslim state. This was due to a late and large-scale transfer of population caused by decentralised but severe violence in the border areas. Sind, Punjab and Bengal were the main sites of population transfer. The outgoing colonial power lost all control of the partitioned territories (French 1997). This left the independent nation-states with a huge problem of resettlement as well as the more serious problem of reconciliation. In the fifty years since independence, the fragments of Indica have been at war with each other three times, dividing from two nation-states into three (East Pakistan gained independence in 1971 to become Bangladesh). Today, India and Pakistan are engaged in a constant state of military confrontation in the northern region around Kashmir and Punjab. To add to the tension, both countries have nuclear weapons.

Ironically, the political situation that emerged in 1971 – three separate political units – was foreseen in the proposals of the 1946 Cabinet Mission. In first accepting then rejecting these proposals, the politicians of pre-independence wasted twenty-five years in futile conflicts. This 'international' context cannot be ignored when looking at the problem of communalism in India. But the appropriate way of examining the communalism issue is to see it as a problem of constructing a theory of nationhood for India. All the writings before independence argued that Indica *was* a nation against the British denial. Events after independence in part vindicated the British argument, and even blaming them for the trouble was only a partial answer. The question that remained was: is India a nation or a part-nation, that is an incomplete nation (as in the case of China and its claim over Hong Kong, Macao and Taiwan)? Was the history of Indica also the history of India? Pakistan, of course, had a more serious problem when it came to writing its history. For example, should the Indus Valley civilisation found in the Mohanjo Daro be included as part of Pakistan's history, or did the country's history begin with the invasion of Mahmud of Gaznavi, or did it date from the establishment of the Muslim League (Desai 1993)?

Ultimately, it was Nehru who recognised the need for the construction of a form of Indian nationhood. Before partition, he had argued in his book *Discovery of India* (Nehru 1946) that Indica was a nation. Following partition, he was faced with a new challenge of establishing India's nationhood. During his seventeen years in power, Nehru set about using available institutions and creating new ones which contributed to this construction of nationhood. His vision had to counter both the two-nations theory by emphasising secularism of the new nation-state and the multinational theory of the federalists by creating a sense of 'unity in diversity'. I have dealt with the latter point elsewhere (Desai 1993), so I shall concentrate on the former: the construction of a secular state.

Secularism was badly dented by the partition. The right-wing Congress leadership was Hindu and took a religious view of nationhood. This manifested itself in several ways against the Muslims. Doubts were cast over the loyalty of the

Muslims who remained in India, and whether they were entitled to enjoy equal rights with the Hindu-majority community. For Patel, Prasad, Kripalani and Pant, the two-nations theory was the cause of partition. They did not agree with it nor of course did the Hindu Mahasabha which wanted an undivided India. But once partition was agreed they held that it had to be implemented in India as well. There were discussions immediately after independence that advocated the merging of the Hindu Mahasabha and the RSS into the Congress Party (Jaffrelot 1997), and had it not been for Gandhi's assassination, this would have come to fruition.

Nehru used Gandhi's name and his ecumenical vision of Indian nationhood to counter the pro-Hindu vision of the Congress right. However, he encountered strong opposition from many of his Congress colleagues over the issue of the treatment of Muslims – their right to stay in India, to leave India, and/or to return to India at a later date. Nehru had Azad, Kidwai and the Congress Socialists on his side, but little else.

Nehru's struggle against the Hindu revivalists

Between 1947 and 1951, Nehru battled against the pro-Hindu faction. They managed to defeat him at first by electing Tandon to the Congress presidency. But once Patel passed away in December 1950, Nehru had Tandon thrown out. This was a tough battle, and Nehru had to summon up all his reserves in the Congress high command to win. But by 1951, Nehru was in total command of the Congress. This resulted in Kripalani leaving to found the Kisan Mazdoor Praja Party, and the successful containment of Pant and Prasad (Jaffrelot 1997; Gopal 1979). But Nehru was not entirely victorious. During 1947–1951, he accepted a shoddy compromise over the issue of Babri Masjid. Pant and Patel had made only half-hearted gestures to prevent the installation of the idols of Ram in the periphery of the Masjid, and Nehru did not insist on their removal – a decision which would come back to haunt India in 1992.

Even with Nehru in control of the Congress, the battle over secularism was not over. This continued in a number of ways, three of which are worth highlighting:

1   The Sanskritisation of Hindi and the downgrading of Hindustani and Urdu was one area in which organised forces worked against secularism. (Indeed, the only thing that saved India from Sanskritised Hindi was the Hindi film industry.)
2   The forces of Hindu revivalism had financial support from Hindu merchants and industrialists. The rebuilding of the Somanath temple was initiated by K. M. Munshi whose Bharatiya Vidya Bhavan party became a leading movement in Hindu revivalism.

3   A major battle was fought over the question of India's history. Nehru mobilised academics and intellectuals on the side of constructing a secularist and ecumenical history. In this respect, Pannikar's *Survey of Indian History* was seen as an important text. Support came from the left, around the CPI, as well as from the various Socialist Party formations and from left-wing historians who held hegemonic positions in universities. A rival project was commissioned by the Bharatiya Vidya Bhavan, but this multi-volume history failed to attain the national standing of the secular vision. The secularists found a much more engaging enemy in 'neo-imperialist' history (as they called it) which emerged from Cambridge University in the UK and, increasingly, from US functionalist accounts.

In the 1980s and 1990s, Indian history was once again an issue for debate with Romila Thapar taking up cudgels on behalf of a secularist history. It is a mark of the success of the Nehru programme as secularist historiography that the Hindu version of history did not seriously challenge it for nearly forty years.

Secularism in practice

Due to partition and the Congress Party's confused attitude over the two-nations theory – which involved an ideological/rhetorical rejection of the theory but a pragmatic/operational acceptance of it – policy aimed at Hindus and Muslims developed along different lines. Nehru pleaded with his colleagues and the country at large to treat the Muslims in India with greater and asymmetric tolerance as compared to the majority Hindu community. To aid in this, the reform of Hindu family law became part of Nehru's modernising agenda, and he pursued this through the attempt to codify Hindu law. The Hindu Code Bill had a stormy passage, with President Rajendra Prasad unhappy with its progress. In the end, Nehru was forced to compromise by breaking up the large portmanteau Bill into several separate legislations. There was no parallel attempt to codify and/or modernise Muslim law. Indeed, as with the Shah Bano case in the 1980s, the Congress always took a reactionary stance on the reform of Muslim law.

Secularism, then, meant state neutrality towards religion but not symmetry when it came to the interrelationship between religion and social practice between the majority and the minority communities. This could have been justified in terms of protection of minority rights. However, although positive discrimination was constitutionally possible with respect to Scheduled castes and Scheduled tribes, Muslims were not classified as a 'Scheduled' minority. Thus there was no attempt to give them special constitutional protection.

Despite these caveats, while Nehru was prime minister, especially between 1951–1964, a secular state flourished in India. Nehru's construction of nationhood involved making India 'special': this meant non-alignment, rapid economic development with a strong public sector role and planning (the socialist pattern of society), and the establishment of a secular democracy. Republic Day festivals were used to demonstrate the diversity of India's many cultures, but also the underlying unity which joined them. The Ministry of Information and Broadcasting utilised its control of All India Radio and Films Division to disseminate a positive image of the Indian nation. The weekly *Film News Reel* was shown in cinemas across the country and All India Radio promoted classical Indian music and broadcast the news in local languages and in English. In addition, the various academies encouraged the teaching of syncretic Indian culture (for a further discussion on this, see Desai 1993).

The result was a very low incidence of communal riots during this period (see Figure 1). Although there was a sharp upsurge in rioting in 1964, India experienced a period of relative stability – except for the 500-plus riots that took place in 1969 and again in 1970 – which lasted through the 1970s. The average number of riots in the 1970s was around 220 per year. But in 1979 this figure rose to 304, the highest since 1971. In the mid-1980s, the average number of riots per year was 700, and in the early 1990s it was 1,000. The freak rise in communal riots in 1964 coincided eerily with the death of Nehru, the one person who embodied the secularist ideal. And, although the numbers dropped after 1964, they never returned to the low levels of 1954–1963. Thus we can hypothesise that the increase in riots was in part due to the collapse of Nehru's programme of reform; or perhaps it was Nehru's personality and commanding reputation that managed to keep the number down.

Nehru's reputation was severely dented towards the end of his life due to the India–China border war. In the confusion that prevailed in Delhi after the first setback on the borders, there was an unseemly rush by India into the arms of the Western powers for military help. India regained its nerve when the Chinese unilaterally withdrew and declared a cease-fire, but India's policy of non-alignment, as well as its pride in the Indian army, was seriously harmed by this incident. On the economic front, the early 1960s saw a severe fall in the rate of growth in income – well below the set targets outlined in the government's third 'Five-year Plan'. Although the economy showed some signs of recovery after 1962, it failed to meet the targets on time. This was followed by two severe droughts in 1965 and 1966. Economic plans based on Nehruvian lines were sufficiently discredited for the new prime minister – Lal Bahadur Shastri – to declare a suspension of the fourth 'Five-year Plan', and shift to annual plans. Neither the dent to the national pride in the Indian army nor the check to Nehruvian economic plans lasted long, however. India won the war with Pakistan in 1965 thus restoring the army's prestige. However, the war also revealed the first signs of a fundamental change in post-Nehru India. Throughout the three-month war, Muslims in India had been regarded with suspicion and many of their leaders incarcerated. Although Prime Minister Shastri was not on the right wing

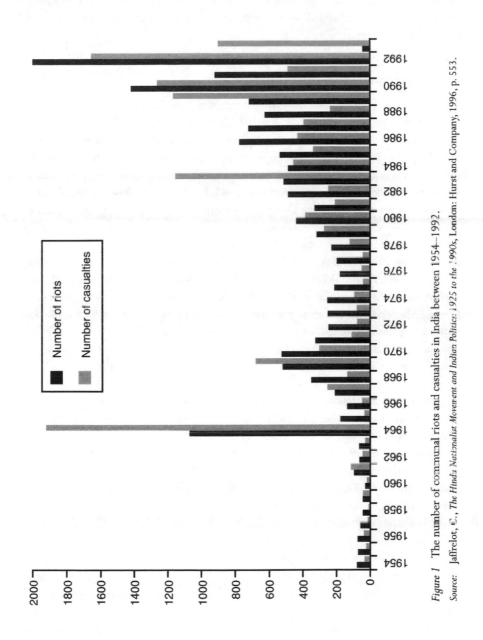

Figure 1 The number of communal riots and casualties in India between 1954–1992.

Source: Jaffrelot, C., *The Hindu Nationalist Movement and Indian Politics: 1925 to the 1990s*, London: Hurst and Company, 1996, p. 553.

of the Congress, nor was he a Hindu revivalist, the loss of neutrality between Hindus and Muslims signalled to both communities that the Nehru era of secularism was over.[12]

Indira Gandhi and the crisis of secularism

The effects of slow economic growth and the two famines were felt in the decision to devalue the rupee taken by the new prime minister, Indira Gandhi, in 1966. However, the promised relief from Western donors as a reward for devaluing the rupee did not materialise, mainly because the US wanted to punish India for its stance on the Vietnam War. As a result, the Congress Party lost many of its seats in the 1967 election and was lucky to survive in power at the centre. One contributing factor to the Congress downturn was the erosion of the Muslim vote following the war with Pakistan.

Indira Gandhi nationalised the commercial banks in the summer of 1969, a move which split the Congress Party. For the first time since the defeat of the Telangana rebellion in 1949, a Maoist rebellion broke out in West Bengal and spread to Andhra Pradesh. It was against this background of unrest that Indira Gandhi changed the political rhetoric: under her leadership, India's sense of nationhood became based on its territorial integrity, established by the war to liberate East Pakistan in 1971. Henceforth, armed strength was given pride of place. Nehru's socialist vision took on a populist hue led by the government slogan, '*Garibi Hatao*' ('Remove Poverty'). The government's policy of non-alignment was also reconsidered, with India moving towards friendly relations with the Soviet Union. Secularism, the third plank of Nehru's vision, was for the first time used as a blatant bid for the Muslim vote.

Throughout the 1970s, the rhetoric of poverty removal and socialism grew louder but the economy's growth rate failed to improve to any significant degree. This led to an acceleration of social conflict, but these were 'secular' struggles against inflation and against government repression. The tight economic and social situation resulted in a battle between various groups over funds. This took a political form, with linguistic, regional and casteist forces all taking part. By the end of the 1970s the 'Hindu rate of growth' – a low 3.5 per cent per annum – looked permanent. It was during this period that Lokayan was established – the grass-roots movements of Dalits and tribals against the state. By the 1970s, then, the illusion of a Nehruvian state as the champion of the poor had gone, despite India's now official status as a secular socialist state.

A more alarming feature of Indira Gandhi's leadership was her government's doctrine of popular sovereignty. The constitution of India can be amended much more easily than that of many other countries, and Gandhi amended it whenever her legislation was successfully challenged in the courts. Two amendments that she made include the modification of property rights and the declaration of India as a secular socialist state. This attitude towards the constitution – that the people through their elected representatives had the right to amend it – is not unique to Gandhi; indeed, it was part of the left's programme that also embraced secularism. But it is a majoritarian doctrine. Minority rights cannot be guaranteed if the majority can change fundamental law at its whim. In the debates before independence, it was majoritarianism, albeit defined along religious lines, that had haunted Jinnah. Further moves in favour of the power of the elected majority against the civil service, the judiciary and the police were also encouraged at both the state level and the central level during the 1970s and 1980s. Again, while a popular mandate was the argument put forward to defend such practices, the elimination of politically neutral places in the state meant that whoever was in power could wield it arbitrarily.

Losing power in 1977, and regaining it in 1980, taught Indira Gandhi one thing: it was not enough to be populist. Her success depended on the majority community – the Hindus. The populist doctrine enunciated by her was practised by the Janata government as well. But to reclaim power, she had to make a passionate bid for the Hindu vote. Henceforth, she saw all religious groups as separate vote-banks to be placated depending on their size and degree of support.

During the Gandhi family period of rule, from 1980–1989, the strains of Indian nationhood became clearer. In the early 1980s, the Sikhs suffered a similar situation to that of the Muslims in 1965, experiencing suspicion and discrimination because of India's battle against the Khalistan movement. Kashmir and the north-east became more troublesome and violent, and many 'secular' struggles – involving the Dalits, the tribals, and women – continued. The civil war in Sri Lanka washed on to India's shores and claimed the life of Rajiv Gandhi.

The decline of secularism and the rise of the Bharatiya Janata Party

After 1989 and the defeat of the Congress Party, India experienced a decade of coalition governments. The 1990s was the decade in which the BJP strengthened its power base. The Nehru version of nationhood had long ago become hollow, and the end of the Cold War had made India's policy of non-alignment redundant. The advent of globalisation and India's own economic crisis in 1991 meant that Nehruvian planning was considered a handicap to progress. In addition, secularism had been compromised and weakened by the two Gandhis throughout the 1980s.

It was within this context that the BJP was able to offer *Hindutva* as an alternative positive theory of Indian nationhood. Tracing the argument back to Savarkar against Gandhi in the early part of the twentieth century, the BJP merely codified the hidden agenda of the right wing of the Congress Party and the actual practice of Lal Bahadur Shastri and the two Gandhis which favoured the Hindus and marginalised the Muslims. In the next three elections (1989, 1991 and 1996), the

BJP increased its representation in the Lok Sabha, becoming the largest single party in office. The prospect of a BJP government was finally realised in March 1998. The increasing strength of the BJP is not merely electoral. The party, along with the RSS and the Vishwa Hindu Parishad (VHP), has been waging a *Kulturkampf* against the theory of secularism, as well as its contradictory practice. The evasions of the Congress about the two-nations theory, the neutral but asymmetric treatment of Hindu and Muslim communities, the blatant playing – opportunistically and erratically – of both the Hindu card and the Muslim card by the Congress under the two Gandhis, all served to strengthen the BJP. Against this threadbare secularism, asserted rather than understood or argued, the BJP and its intellectuals posed the view that India is a nation because it is a Hindu country with a Hindu religious majority and a Hindu society, that is all but encompassing even of the minorities. The BJP constructed a monist but popular version of Hinduism around the figure of Ram and, in a parody of the Mahatma, tried to mobilise the Indian masses around religious symbols. The possibility of bricklaying for a temple on the site of the Babri Mosque in Ayodhya was the BJP equivalent of the Dandi Salt Satyagraha – a highly inflammatory gesture.

In the event, the destruction of the Babri Masjid in 1992 initiated the first serious discussion of the meaning of secularism in India. The BJP had overplayed its hand, though even then its Lok Sabha representation increased in 1996 but fell short of a majority. Temporarily at least, the BJP was thwarted from power. An alternative coalition built around the divisive but democratic forces of caste, region and religious politics came to power. This coalition harked back to the vision expressed in the Round Table conferences of India, of a multinational polity with nationality defined along the lines of region, language and religion. But neither the vision nor the coalition government was sustainable. It lost power in 1997 and new elections were held in early 1998 which brought a coalition led by the BJP to office. In another election, in September 1999, the BJP was re-elected along with its coalition partners to a majority in the Lok Sabha.

Nationhoods on offer

At the dawn of the twenty-first century, then, there are several competing theories of Indian nationhood. The first is a vision of Indian nationhood based on an inclusive but single nationality that Nehru tried to articulate. This vision has been badly tarnished but is still capable of a fresh reformulation.[13] The leading alternative is a notion of India as a Hindu nation with ostensible and formal guarantees for the Muslims. This puts forward the idea of India as a state built around the religious beliefs of the majority. The practice of previous 'secular' governments regarding legalities and constitutional guarantees renders any promises of minority rights fragile and incredible.

The third vision has come about through the grass-roots struggle of the 1970s against the failure of the Nehruvian economic programme to deliver growth or equity. Backward castes, Dalits, Muslims and women – overlapping groups often at odds with one another but united by their exclusion from the privileged elite which has enjoyed power and patronage – have formed a loose and shifting coalition of national and regional parties. Although they do not offer a coherent theory of nationhood, inasmuch as these coalitions have arisen from the vigorous practice of electoral democratic politics, they embody a realistic practice of Indian nationhood. It is a multinational vision of nationhood – in which region, language, social status are combined (along with an anti-religious streak among the Dalits), and one which offers the Muslims a haven. It is not a secular vision as such, but it is anti-elitist and anti-centralist, and it is trying precariously to hold the tide against the BJP and its pro-Hindu stance.

One of the main arguments in Indian political life since the Babri Masjid incident concerns secularism versus the BJP. In their narrow anti-BJP focus, the secularists display much the same asymmetry as was shown in the past towards the Hindus and the Muslims. Inasmuch as the proponents are left oriented, they adopt the Nehruvian theory of nationhood along with the economic programme as well. But the decline and drift in the Congress has weakened the secularists. Its arguments against the BJP's theory of *Hindutva* are based on a rejection of religion as the basis for defining nationhood; as well, they object to the BJP's monistic version of Hinduism, preferring instead a pluralist and heterogeneous version (see Vanaik 1997).

The BJP has always nominally denied that it is an exclusively Hindu party. Its *parivar* (literally meaning 'family', and comprising of parallel political formations such as the RSS, Vishwa Hindu Parishad, Bajrang Dal, Rashtriya Jagaran Morcha, etc.) is another matter. The Babri Masjid episode was an embarrassment for the BJP because its nationalist colours were exposed as exclusively Hindu and aggressively anti-Muslim. As a party, the BJP has sought to use Hindu religious symbolism to mobilise the masses almost in a parody of Gandhi, but without his ecumenism.

The intellectual arguments against the BJP's version of Hinduism are, in my opinion, less potent than the Ambedkarite root and branch antagonism to Hinduism displayed by the Dalits. Added to this has been the practical political mobilisation around the Mandal Commission, which recommended the reservation of government jobs for lower castes and untouchables. Ideologically, it exposes Hinduism not as a seamless whole, as some upper-caste intellectuals have tried to demonstrate since Raja Ram Mohan Roy, but as a kaleidoscope mosaic of little traditions and multiple sects. Politically, it has shown that while Hindu religious symbols may have helped Gandhi mobilise people (though even here after Khilafat, the Muslim support for the Congress Party diminished), in post-colonial democratic India it is the fissures in Hindu society which shape party politics at regional, local and national levels. There is no single Hindu vote-bank.

Yet a BJP-led coalition with regional and caste parties came to power in 1998. In October 1999, a coalition of the BJP with a large collection of regional and 'backward class' parties won the election with a convincing majority. I believe that this reaffirmation of the winning formula vindicates my argument in this chapter. The coalition shows that to construct a majority in government in India today, one has to encompass at least two of the three nationhoods on offer. In the 1999 elections, the Congress Party, under Sonia Gandhi, tried to win a majority and lost. This means that the BJP is now the new ruling party. The question this poses is, why is there fear concerning the BJP and its rise to power? The answer, in my view, has to do not with communalism but with constitutionalism.

Communalism or constitutionalism

The issue of the constitution is now the central difficulty facing the secularist programme. There is a serious prospect that a majoritarian government in India may be openly non-secular. Since in practice, if not in theory, an elected government can abridge the authority of the civil service and the police as it likes, the fragility of minority rights is all too clear. The left is used to thinking that it will be perennially in the majority in government. If the balance of power in India were to shift to the right (and as of 2000, this had not yet been the case), then the left would wake up to the value of the old-fashioned virtues of a neutral civil service and a constitution beyond the reach of easy manipulation by a government.[14] I would argue that there is a need to look at the fragility of the present constitutional arrangements in India, which in turn implies a reconsideration of the nature and purpose of secularism; that is, its instrumentality in terms of minority rights rather than its ideology *vis-à-vis* religion.[15] Nehruvian secularism has also been asymmetrically more anti-Hindu religiosity and obscurantism, more anti-BJP (and the Sangh Parivar) than against all religious obscurantism. Thus, the modernist, secular forces in the Muslim community have not had much support from the Nehruvian secular forces. I would maintain that secularism needs to be a philosophy of secularisation and modernisation for *all* religious communities (Vanaik 1997; Hasan 1997).

Secularism within the Indian political context has also been an elite philosophy that has been fiercely defended by the leadership of certain left-oriented parties, though it has not had mass support. Until the end of the 1970s, one could have said that the large support for the Congress Party was a sign of support for secularism. But during the 1980s, this ceased to be the case. As the Congress Party played the Hindu card and the Muslim card simultaneously, it was obvious that the Muslims were thought of as a special vote-bank, as they had been in 1909 with the Morley-Minto reforms. The Congress Party now pays slightly greater lip-service to secularism because it wishes to recapture the Muslim vote which it lost in the 1996 elections, but it is difficult to take its professions seriously.

The connection of secularism with the dirigisme of the Nehruvian economic policy is, in my view, also unfortunate. Achin Vanaik (1997) argues passionately, but wrongly in my opinion, that liberal economic reform will strengthen the forces of Hindu fundamentalism and that a return to socialist economic policy is the only guarantee for secularism. I believe it is the economic stagnation, wastage and corruption of the old policies, as seen clearly in the 1980s, that have discredited secularism (Desai 1995). India's economic failure was compounded by a failure to act decisively on literacy, health and social projects such as clean water. It also gave the state, and of course whichever party controlled the government, enormous and arbitrary powers. The case for secularism has, therefore, to be argued independently of the dirigiste economics which have become part of the problem facing India today.

Finally, secularism must be separated from majoritarianism. No matter who is in power, certain fundamental rights must be guaranteed – by the police, the judiciary and the civil service. Thus, secularism must be part and parcel of a civil libertarian philosophy, in which civil society plays a vigilant role. Civil rights should not depend on who is in power. As a consequence of these considerations, a movement to restore the neutrality of the civil service, the judiciary and the police, in short to restore the rule of law, is imperative. Institutions that were inherited from the British and strengthened in the 1950s, and new institutions created in the 1950s and 1960s to implement a rule of law, have eroded alarmingly over the past three decades. Secularism must be dissociated from government and indeed from religion. What is required is the expansion of a neutral, government-free space in civil society. It is not just a question of Hindu–Muslim riots or of the validity of a Hindu fundamentalist reading of Indian history as against Islamic fundamentalism and its defensiveness of its family law. The caste Hindu–Dalit riots, the Hindu–Sikh riots, the Shi'a–Sunni riots, and the many violent attacks on women in all the social orders by the orthodox patriarchy, are all signs that the rule of law has broken down in India. Religious beliefs are a private matter. Naturally, there are times when religion will spill over into politics (and this has been the case since the days of Tilak and Gandhi). But a space needs to be created and expanded which is outside the domain of the government in office, which gives hope that the many and excellent fundamental rights guaranteed by the Indian constitution are actually enjoyed by all citizens, no matter what their religion, sex or caste or which region they are from.

Conclusion

The decision by Morley and Minto to create separate electorates crystallised nationalism in India around electoral politics. As two further episodes of franchise expansion and relatively greater self-government occurred in 1917 and 1935, the contention of various groups within Indica to have a formal representation became insistent. In contrast to this was the vision of a single nation defined either in terms of a harmonious collection of religious communities (as espoused by Gandhi) or as a liberal-democratic community of citizens who in their public life were neutral, or at least unmindful of their own and others' religion (as advocated by Nehru). Fears of the rights of a minority in the face of a majoritarian interpretation of democracy led to the articulation of a two-nations theory (by Jinnah). In the hurried and messy negotiations for India's independence between 1944 and 1947, the two-nations theory won and secured the partition of India. All the various parties to the negotiation connived in this state of affairs and were responsible for partition.

Partition created a challenge of defining a nationhood for India. Nehru consciously, and for a while successfully, accomplished this based on a vision of a secular, non-aligned country engaged in planned economic development. However, this model has in recent years come under considerable strain. Since 1975 a number of social and political movements have contested the hegemonic vision of the Congress, causing the party under the weight of electoral pressure to abandon Nehru's secular vision for India. Communalism in this sense is just one of many opposition movements. Its danger lies in the fact that the subversion of a neutral political space by the Congress following a majoritarian logic exposed India to the possibility of a non-secular party coming to power and oppressing the Muslim minority. With the BJP's victory in the 1998 and 1999 elections, this possibility became a reality, although the BJP-led coalition did not disavow secularism which is enshrined in the constitution. India needs to restore the neutral space from majoritarian political predations as a guarantee of human rights for all minorities. The partners of the BJP in the present coalition (created in the 1999 election) represent the grass-roots and anti-elite elements of society. Perhaps they can ensure the establishment of a neutral political space. India's future will be hopeful if they do so.

Notes

I am grateful to the following for their helpful comments with regard to this chapter: Philip Oldenburg, Yunas Samad, Katharine Adeney, as well as members of the Asian Nationalism seminar and its Chairman, Professor Michael Leifer.

1 I shall concentrate on the Indian subcontinent in this chapter, although Sri Lanka offers an interesting parallel. For Sri Lanka, see Jayawardene (1986).

2 At the risk of appearing pretentious, I shall use the term 'Indica' for India before the partition and India for after the partition. British India, of course, refers to pre-1947. I have used this term once before in Desai (1990).

3 Hinduism is a portmanteau word for the variety of sects and paths which constitute the religion of the majority people. It is somewhat peculiar that there is no name for this religion in any of the original languages. Hindu is a Persian word but religion is not adequate to describe the *sanatan dharma*. There is no single book, no single prophet or martyr or founder, no single God or even a fixed hierarchy of gods. There is no Church and no parallel to clergy or ulema. I shall return to this below.

4 Chaudhury Rehmat Ali (who was a Cambridge student) and Khwaja Abdur Rahim (a civil servant) are credited with this name. A recent account of the origins of Pakistan as a concept is in K. Ahmed (1998). The poet Iqbal had spoken of Pakistan at a private meeting as early as 1930.

5 Pakistan's founder, Mohammad Ali Jinnah, had a broad ecumenical view of Pakistan which he spoke of in a speech given on 14 August 1947. That speech was subsequently suppressed as it contradicted the more Islamist view of his successors.

6 Lord Curzon when Viceroy, in an argument with the Bishop of Calcutta (Weldon) who wanted to proselytise, said: 'The policy of the government was not to interfere with the religious views of the inhabitants of the sub-continent' (Churchill 1964: 325).

7 For example, Achin Vanaik's *The Furies of Indian Communalism* (1997), and Mushirul Hasan's *Legacy of a Divided Nation* (1997) about India's Muslims. For work on the formation of communalism in the north, see Gyan Pandey (1990); for an account of the pre-history of Pakistan see Yunas Samad (1995).

8 The recent election of Narayanan as president does not significantly change this conclusion, just as the election of Muslims to positions of power has been no guarantee of the protection of Muslim rights.

9 Two caveats need noting. Churchill deserves a detailed treatment of his own. Surprisingly, given his demonic status in India, there no major work has been done on Churchill and India. I hope to write an essay on this topic as a companion to this chapter. Also, the Labour Party suffered a severe defeat in 1931 and was not a major force. And even after 1935 it was still politically weak. It was only its inclusion in the War Cabinet after Churchill became prime minister that allowed it a say in negotiations over India. Even then, Cripps and Attlee were not as one on India during the war (for background history on this, see Gilbert 1976; French 1997).

10 For a pro-Indian account of the American–British negotiations on India, see M. S. Venkataraman and B. S. Srivastara, *Roosevelt, Gandhi, Churchill: America and the Last Phase of India's Freedom Struggle* (Sangam Books: London, 1983).

11 Again, teleology has to be avoided. In retrospect, Labour's 1945 victory looks obvious and independence/partition follows in 1947. But the Labour Party is also often accused of being no different to the Tories. However, Indian independence was a manifesto promise of the Labour Party in the run-up to the 1945 election. Had the Conservatives won, Winston Churchill would have been prime minister. No matter how exhausted Britain might have been after the war, Churchill would not have been so quick to negotiate towards independence as Attlee was. After all, France and Holland despite their wartime experiences resisted (for a time) independence movements in Vietnam and Indonesia. Had Churchill come to power, native states would not have been forced to integrate into an Indian Union at the very least. The

final shape of India would have been quite different, and partition might have been avoided.

12 I am grateful to M. J. Akbar for reminding me of this crucial episode.

13 Vanaik (1997) is one such attempt. Hasan (1997) argues for a modernist, secular programme for Muslims.

14 This happened to the British left when Margaret Thatcher was prime minister. This led to formations such as Charter 88 advocating electoral reform to avoid a repetition of what Lord Hailsham labelled 'an elective dictatorship'.

15 See M. Desai (Gresham Lecture), 'India: end of the first republic?', *Times Higher Educational Supplement*, November 1997.

References

Ambedkar, B. R. (1940; 2nd edn 1945) *Pakistan or the Partition of India*, Bombay: Thacker and Co.

Ahmed, Khaled (1998) 'Karakalpakistan', *HIMAL* (February), 11(2).

Brockway, F. (1973) *The Colonial Revolution*, London: Hart-Davis McGibbon.

Charmley, J. (1993) *Churchill: The End of Glory: A Political Biography*, London: Hodder and Stoughton.

Churchill, R. (1964) *Churchill, Volume 1*, London: Heineman.

Desai, M. (1990) 'Birth and death of nation states: speculations about Germany and India', in M. Mann, F. Halliday and J. Hobson (eds) *Rise and Decline of the Nation State*, Oxford: Blackwell.

—— (1993) 'Constructing nationality in a multinational democracy: the case of India', in R. Michener (ed.) *Economics, Culture and Education*, St. Paul Minnesota: Professors for World Peace Academy, pp. 225–41.

—— (1995) 'Economic reform: stalled by politics', in P. Oldenburg, *India Briefing*, New York/London: M. E. Sharpe, pp. 75–95.

—— (1997) 'End of the first republic?', *Times Higher Educational Supplement*, November 1997.

Dutt, R. C. (1908) *The Economic History of India Under Early British Rule*, London: K. Paul, Trench, Trubner and Co. Ltd.

French, P. (1997) *Liberty or Death?: India's Journey to Independence and Division*, London: HarperCollins.

Gilbert, M. (1976) *Churchill. Volume 5: 1922–1939*, London: Heinemann.

Gopal, S. (1975) *Jawaharhal Nehru: A Biography. Volume 1: 1889–1947*, London: Jonathan Cape.

—— (1979) *Jawaharhal Nehru: A Biography. Volume 2: 1947–1956*, London: Jonathan Cape.

—— (1984) *Jawaharhal Nehru: A Biography. Volume 3: 1956–1964*, London: Jonathan Cape.

Hasan, M. (1997) *Legacy of a Divided Nation; India's Muslims Since Independence*, London: Hurst and Co.

Jaffrelot, C. (1997) *The Hindu Nationalist Movement and Indian Politics, 1925 to 1990s*, London: Hurst and Co.

Jalal, A. (1985) *The Sole Spokesman: Jinnah, the Muslim League and the Demand for Pakistan*, Cambridge: Cambridge University Press.

Jayawardene, K. (1986) *Ethnic and Class Conflicts in Sri Lanka: Some Aspects of Sinhala Buddhist Consciousness Over the Past 100 years*, Colombo: Centre for Social Analysis.

Khaliquzzman, C. (1961) *Pathway to Pakistan*, Lahore: Longmans.

Naoroji, D. (1901) *Poverty and UnBritish Rule in India*, London: S. Sonnenschein.

Nanda, B. R. (1989) *Gandhi: Pan-Islamism, Imperialism and Nationalism in India*, Bombay: Oxford University Press.

Nehru, J. (1936) *Autobiography*, London: Bodley Head.

—— (1946) *The Discovery of India*, London: Bodley Head.

Pandey, G. (1990) *The Construction of Communalism in North India*, New Delhi, Oxford University Press.

Parekh, B. (1989) *Colonialism, Tradition and Reform; An Analysis of Gandhi's Political Discourse*, New Delhi: Sage.

Samad, Y. (1995) *A Nation in Turmoil: Nationalism and Ethnicity in Pakistan, 1937–1958*, New Delhi: Sage.

Vanaik, A. (1997) *The Furies of Indian Communalism: Religion, Modernity and Secularisation*, London: Verso.

7   Peregrinations of Pakistani nationalism

Athar Hussain

Introduction

A swath cutting across the north-western border of India, Pakistan is a recent artefact with a short and tumultuous history. It was hastily created in 1947 by combining together provinces and parts of the Punjab and Bengal with a Muslim majority. For the first twenty-four years, it was a freak state made up of two wings separated by around 1,000 miles of hostile India, which were as distant culturally as they were physically. Bar religion, East Pakistan had little in common with West Pakistan. Driven by a mixture of a distinct ethnic identity and a heavy-handed military rule from the Western wing, East Pakistan prised itself loose in 1971 to become an independent state. The addition of the third successor state to British India put an end to the territorial oddity, which Lord Mountbatten (the last Viceroy of India) had referred to as 'moth-eaten'.

Two premises underlie my discussion in this chapter: first, the appropriate starting point for a discussion of Pakistani nationalism is the state and the territory rather than the common features of the population. Not that there are no such features, but their pertinence to a discussion of Pakistani nationalism ultimately derives from the fact of citizenship. Second, the history of emergence of Pakistan, which continues to weigh heavily, is crucial to an understanding of the process of nation formation that is still unfolding. Before going into details of nation formation, it is useful to note three salient features that Pakistan shares in varying degrees with a number of post-colonial states:

* historical contingency;
* coincidence of nation formation and the consolidation of the state;
* importance of an external adversary in the creation of national identity.

Historical contingency

The binary partition in 1947 of the Indian subcontinent into Pakistan and India was a contingent event. Rather than an inevitable outcome, it was one of several possible outcomes of polymorphous politics that preceded the end of British rule: a united India with a strong centre was one such proposal and, schematically, the other was a Balkanised subcontinent consisting of several states either independent or linked under a loose federation (Bose and Jalal 1997). The latter alternative was proposed by the Cabinet Mission in 1946 and was a more likely alternative to the binary partition than a united India was (Samad 1995). With independent Bangladesh, India and Pakistan, the current pattern in the subcontinent is closer to the second alternative than to the binary pattern created in 1947. We have to remind ourselves that in culture and history the subcontinent was, and still is, no less diverse than Europe. Besides, British India was not a seamless political unit but a mosaic of regions under direct colonial rule and 565 princely states subordinated to the British crown under the doctrine of paramountcy. Independent India and Pakistan would later use this doctrine to annex princely states, including Kashmir, to create an integrated state. Dominated by the religious divide, the cataclysm of the partition overshadowed scores of fault-lines that ran wide and deep across Indian society. These began to emerge out of the shadows soon after. One of the most important of these, ethnic division, has been the abiding feature of India and Pakistan and is crucial to an understanding of nation formation in both, an issue which is discussed below. Although the separation of Bangladesh was triggered by internal Pakistani politics (Choudhury 1993), its antecedents reach back to the shaky foundations of Pakistan as created in 1947 and its slim chances of surviving intact. It may be argued that separation of Bangladesh was the final act of the partition with a delay of twenty-four years.

Coincidence of the nation and the state

As do many other post-colonial states, Pakistan exemplifies a population which is marked out by an internationally recognised territory rather than by common features which pre-date Pakistan. Pakistanis have in some measure the attributes of a nation, such as a well-defined territory, psychological identification with Pakistan and a common history, albeit brief (Miller 1997). But on scrutiny these all flow from the history of the creation of Pakistan and its survival since. Aphoristically stated, Pakistan is not a nation-state; rather, Pakistanis are a state nation, or to use a German term, *staatnation* (Habermas 1996). This inversion draws on Gellner's shift of focus away from 'what a nation is' to 'how a nation is formed' (Gellner 1996), a shift which is particularly fecund in the analysis of nationalism in post-colonial states. Commonly with short histories and contingent state boundaries, these states do not represent nations with an air of permanence but still unfolding processes of the transformation of a disparate population into a nation. These processes are polymorphous and not necessarily state-centred, and may, it has to be emphasised, fail. This polymorphism fits ill with the binary opposition between modernity and tradition that Gellner deploys. Pakistan and also Bangladesh and India have some attributes of modernity but lack some key ones. One of these is universal literacy, a key attribute of a modern state for Gellner, which is notable not only by its absence but, more important, by the low priority accorded to it in South Asia. The other is a safe distance between the state and religion. Not only in Pakistan but also in Bangladesh, India and Sri Lanka, political discourses are increasingly permeated with religious idiom, a phenomenon which defies comprehension in terms of the opposition 'modern and traditional' (van der Veer 1994).

Returning to the main point, the history of Pakistani nationalism is the obverse of the history of the emergence and consolidation of the state, which is short – stretching no further back than the 1930s. The territory constituting Pakistan, especially the Indus valley, has a long history stretching back several millennia and so too the Muslims of the Indian subcontinent, in whose name Pakistan was fought for and founded. The history of the Indus valley is no more a history of Pakistan than of India's. Here it is relevant to note that the *Bharat Mata* (Mother India) of Hindu nationalists spans the land between the Indus to the Bay of Bengal. Following the separation of Bangladesh in the 1970s, there was a movement to reposition Pakistan's history around the Indus valley by emphasising language and culture indigenous to the area (see, for example, Ahsan 1996). That movement did lead to a flowering of vernacular languages in literature, broadcasting and cinema, but did not succeed in its wider aim of providing Pakistan with a past to fit in with its present. The history of the Indian Muslims covers the whole of the subcontinent, even further afield. The formation of Pakistan is simply a chapter of this history that does not lend itself to appropriation as the history of Pakistan, which, after the separation of Bangladesh, is home to only a minority of the Muslim population of the subcontinent (Hasan 1997).

Role of an external adversary

Forged in the crucible of antagonistic communal politics, the Pakistani state and nationalism are permeated with rivalry with India. As we shall see, the political mobilisation in favour of the creation of Pakistan drew succour from the anxiety on the part of the Indian Muslims that in a united India an assertive Hindu majority would swamp them. Dating back no earlier than the last quarter of the nineteenth century, this fear arose out of competition for economic resources and rivalry to secure a place in the political arena opened up by the piecemeal constitutional reforms from the beginning of the twentieth century (Brown 1994). Instead of being a shared sentiment of all Muslims of British India, this fear varied widely in depth and form across regions and classes. Nevertheless, as British colonial rule drew to a close this fear managed to galvanise a substantial proportion of the Muslims of the subcontinent behind the rejection of a united India. Instead of surpassing it as past history, the creation of Pakistan has reified this fear into a permanent antagonism with India. Underlying all nations and states, there is a grid delineating 'us' and 'them'; but adversarial relations between India and Pakistan go deeper. As it were, Pakistan still needs an antagonist India to define its distinctiveness and maintain internal cohesion. The antagonism with India does not lend itself to a full explanation in terms of the territorial dispute over Kashmir, which is discussed below. The two countries have since 1947 fought three wars and remain ready for the next. Their mutual antagonism has lately taken an ominous turn with the tit-for-tat nuclear tests. Rivalry with India not only casts a long shadow on Pakistan's internal politics but also dominates its external relations, much of which have been dominated by the aim of building a network of alliances to secure its position *vis-à-vis* India and to keep the Kashmir issue alive.

The reasons that make Kashmir a chronic cause of friction between India and Pakistan illuminate the nature of their mutual rivalry. During British rule, Kashmir (rather Jammu and Kashmir) was a princely state with a Hindu ruler and a majority Muslim population. The dichotomy between the religion of the rulers and of the ruled majority, which assumed importance because of communal politics, was not particular to Kashmir but a feature of a number of princely states, such as Hyderabad in southern India. But of these Kashmir has been the only one to pose a problem because, India or Pakistan depending, the majority religion absorbed the rest. Kashmir has a small population and no natural resources of note, aside from the beauty of its valleys and mountains. Perched on the periphery of India and Pakistan, it poses no special strategic significance for either country. It is a *causus belli* simply because of what its Muslim majority respectively represents for the two countries. For India, Kashmir, being the only territorial unit with a large Muslim majority, is the emblem of its claim as a multi-denominational state. For Pakistan, Kashmir ought to be a part of it by virtue of its Muslim majority and geographical contiguity to the Muslim majority districts of the Punjab, reiterating the principle used in the partition (see Wirsing 1998, for details).

Thus in their dispute over Kashmir, India and Pakistan continue to relive the bloody conflict that attended their birth, at a massive cost in lives and resources and without any regard for the wishes and welfare of the local population. They have fought two wars over Kashmir and engaged in endless skirmishes. They continue to wage a positional war on the icy wastes of the Siachen glacier in the north of Kashmir, a futile war in which frostbite claims more casualties than does enemy gunfire. Here it is instructive to point out that while Kashmir remains a live issue, Pakistan came to terms with the separation of its eastern region into

Bangladesh remarkably quickly. The fact that Bangladesh was the majority part of Pakistan for almost half of its life has been relegated to the register of, as Renan put it, 'shared amnesia and collective forgetfulness'.

The formation of Pakistan

The founding ideology of Pakistan, which is crucial to an understanding of the conjoint processes of state formation and nation-building, is formed by the confluence of two discrepant strands. One refers to the territory spanned by a potential Muslim state in British India and its name. The other concerns the political mobilisation of Muslims on communal lines. The two are discrepant both in space and time. The potential state 'Pakistan', which roughly corresponds to the present-day Pakistan plus Kashmir but not the one that existed between 1947 and 1971, housed only a small minority of Muslims of the subcontinent. Further, the territory thus delineated was not the spawning ground of the movement that would eventually lead to the partition of India. That movement first emerged and developed in parts of northern India, in particular Uttar Pradesh (UP), where Hindus formed a large majority. This glaring incongruity between the territory and the cradle of the political movement would later have far-reaching implications for nation formation in the realised Pakistan. Thus the carving out of parts of British India to form Pakistan in 1947 does not fit in with the usual format of secession in which the two coincide, an example of which is Bangladesh.

The notion of a separate Muslim state within the territorial confines of British India crystallised relatively late, two to three decades after the emergence of social and political organisations representing Muslims. This temporal discrepancy underscores the disjunction between the partition of India and communalist politics, taken in the broad sense of activities in the public domain ranging from religious and cultural to competition for power. Communalist politics was perfectly compatible with a united India, as evidenced by communalist politics in present-day India. The notion of such a state is attributed to a speech in 1930 by Iqbal, who would later be elevated to the status of national poet. The name 'Pakistan' was an acronym of four provinces that make up the present-day Pakistan, and also Kashmir, which is disputed and only partially under Pakistani control. The territory had two features satisfying the elementary conditions of statehood: it was contiguous and a majority of its inhabitants were Muslims. The Pakistan thus defined raised the crucial question of its relation to a large majority of the Muslim population of the subcontinent settled outside its confines, a question to which neither the movement for the creation of Pakistan nor Pakistani government ever had a clear answer. Here it is interesting to note that Pakistan as originally conceived excluded the present-day Bangladesh which until 1971 would form Pakistan's eastern appendage, but with a majority of its population. Pakistan means 'land of the pure', which is ironic given the venality of its politicians, officials and soldiers. The notion of Pakistan on its own had no political appeal. It assumed importance only because of social and political organisations representing Muslims that struck roots in areas which could never be a part of a Muslim majority state.

Religion and ethnicity, being two principal co-ordinates of personal identity in the subcontinent, provided the backdrop for economic competition and political rivalry among communities in British India. For the most part, economic class mattered when it coalesced with either religious (including caste) or ethnic divisions. The emergence at the turn of the twentieth century of political organisations representing Muslims was a part of a broader movement of politics overlaid with communal and ethnic divisions. This was as true of Hindus and Sikhs as of Muslims and was as much a characteristic of colonial administration as it was of indigenous political movements. In fact, it could not be otherwise in a population overlaid with a web of similarities and differences. Indian nationalism, which is an *ex-post*-historical reconstruction, comprised disparate and conflicting strands, reflecting diverse concerns arising out of scores of fault-lines running through Indian society. One strand was secular nationalist which, in its dominant version, accepted the diversity of India as a given and sought to locate Indian identity at an all-inclusive plane. 'Syncretic' rather than 'secular' is a more appropriate description of the stance (for a discussion of notions of secularism, see Taylor 1998). But most were 'exclusive', confined to particular religious and ethnic communities and given over to parochial interests. But the secular strand and exclusive movements were not in opposition; rather, the relations between them were fluid and unstable. Secularism in the sense of being above religious and ethnic ties represented a small minority. For the most part, the secular strand as represented by; for example, the Indian National Congress was a loose coalition of exclusive movements, including some strands of Muslim fundamentalism. Though the Muslim League was confined to Muslims, in its aims and functioning it was, arguably, no more wedded to Islam than the Congress was to Hinduism.

The later part of the nineteenth century saw a proliferation of movements of Hindu revivalism and reform, or blends of the two. Broadly, their purpose was a reconstruction of Hindu identity through a variable mixture of a rediscovery of India's Sanskritic past and adaptation to the changing environment. Coeval to these, there was a parallel proliferation of organisations devoted in various ways to the protection of Muslim culture and interests. Mirroring the ones among Hindus, these covered the broad range from religious purification to adaptation to a changing world. Embedded in their activities was the inchoate projection of Indian Muslims as a distinctive community with its own history, culture and interests. This would in the 1930s crystallise as the 'two-nations theory' which formed one of the two pillars of the ideology of Pakistan. What was new about communal movements, whether of Hindus or Muslims, was the fabrication of, to use Benedict Anderson's phrase 'imagined communities' which would serve as a basis for political mobilisation and social transformation (Anderson 1996). The notions of Indian Muslims and Indian Hindus, that would become a common currency of politics in the twentieth century, were not primordial but arose during competitive communalist politics spawned by socio-economic changes in British India. Three qualifications are necessary here to guard against a simplification. First, there always existed differences between Muslims and Hindus varying between mutual accommodation and antagonism. But it was only from the last quarter of the nineteenth century that these began to serve as bases for a political and social demarcation of populations on the all-India plane. Second, the notions of Muslims and Hindus rather than being internally coherent were collages of disparate and even contradictory elements. Third, though communal movements talked in terms of India, their appeal varied widely across localities and population strata (Brown 1994).

The foundation in 1906 of the All India Muslim League, the organisation, which would later spearhead the movement for Pakistan, was directed towards mundane not spiritual matters. Its aim was not to align the lives of Muslims with the dictates of religion, *Shari'a*. There were Islamic fundamentalist movements devoted to such ends, but these were indifferent to the worldly preoccupations of the League and its precursor organisations, if not hostile. Their relation to the Muslim communalist political movement remained ambivalent. The epithet 'All India' in its title 'All India Muslim League' represented an aspiration not the reality, in the same way as 'Indian' did in the case of the Indian National Congress. At its foundations and for decades to come the League was in no sense the representative of clusters of Muslim populations that were dispersed across the length and breadth of India and occupied with local issues. The historical irony is that until the 1940s the League commanded little interest or support in the regions which would form the present-day Pakistan and that it was founded in Dhakka which would be the capital of Bangladesh. It drew support mainly from the gentry and nascent Western-educated elite from parts of northern India, especially UP, where Muslims were a minority and reflected their particular concerns. The demand for political representation on communal lines surfaced with the first instalment of constitutional reforms in British India (the 1909 Morely-Minto reforms), which in time led to the division of electorates on communal lines. Schematically, the demand had two components. First, minority communities should have protected representations and, second, they should be allocated more representatives than warranted by their share of the population. The demand was aimed at safeguarding the interest of minority communities and premised on the assumption of the coexistence of different religious communities, albeit rival ones. It did not provide a basis for the assignment of territories to communities for the simple reason that in most of India different religious communities lived cheek by jowl in, ranging from, peace to antagonism.

Through a retrospective rendition of history, we can now trace a filiation between the demand for separate political representation of Muslims at the beginning of the twentieth century and the partition of the subcontinent in 1947. But the causal chain from the former to the latter was far from direct. Political developments in the intervening years played a determining role in tipping the balance of probabilities away from one India. In this respect, of special importance was the experience of the elected provincial governments from the late 1930s provided by piecemeal constitutional reforms by the British. The projection of a separate Indian Muslim identity, which began to take shape around the turn of the twentieth century, solidified in the 1930s as the two-nations theory. Jinnah, who played a determining role in the formation of Pakistan, demarcated Indian Muslims in the following terms:

> distinctive culture and civilisation, language and literature, art and architecture, names and nomenclature, sense of values and proportion, legal laws and moral codes, customs and calendar, history and tradition, aptitude and ambition.

(Quoted in Ziring 1997: 21)

It is worth dwelling on this pronouncement because it brings into relief the genealogy of Pakistani nationalism. The principal addressees of the 'theory' were Muslims and its purpose was to mobilise them under the banner of the Muslim League. It is interesting to note that Islam plays a tangential role in the demarcation. As an empirical proposition, the theory rests on shaky evidence. Dotted in clusters across the subcontinent, Indian Muslims were as heterogeneous as other religious communities, and they still are. They were ethnically diverse: spoke different dialects and languages and were embedded in regional cultures that transcended religious communities. Their genealogies as Muslims were also different. Some were close or distant descendants of invaders or migrants from the north-west and central Asia or the Arab Middle East; a large majority were converts who retained elements of indigenous culture. Though nominally they all subscribed to the same faith, they were divided into sects such as Shi'as, Sunnis or Ahmadis (see Madan 1997). Sectarian divisions among Muslims could be as antagonistic as that between Muslims and Hindus or Sikhs. For example, in Lucknow, a centre of high Muslim culture, conflict between Shi'as and Sunnis (the two principal sects) was more common than that between Hindus and Muslims (Hasan 1997). Intra-Islam sectarian disputes, rather than abating, have risen in virulence. The fissures running through Muslims of the subcontinent are not a past history but survive in India, Pakistan and Bangladesh. Ethnic differences among Muslims have proved to be tenacious. As discussed below, Muslim migrants from India to Pakistan (*muhajirs*) and their offspring have refused to assimilate with the local population.

However, a critique of the two-nations theory in terms of the internal differentiation of Muslims and their similarities to the non-Muslim population misses the point. Any grouping of the population of the subcontinent, whether by religion – such as Hindus and Sikhs – or by ethnicity – such as Punjabis or Bengalis – is open to the same objections that can be levelled against the projection of Muslims as a distinct group (see, for example, Chaterjee 1994). To treat the two-nations theory as an empirical proposition to be pitted against evidence is to miss its political purpose and to beg the question of its undoubted success in mobilising a large part of Indian Muslims under the banner of the Muslim League, albeit only in the latter part of the 1940s. The Muslim population as portrayed by the theory is an idealised community and a reification of high Muslim culture that applied to a minority only. Nevertheless, it provided an archetype with which a large majority of Muslims would eventually identify themselves in some respect, thereby recognising each other as members of a community with particular interests. Archetype is used here not in the sense of primordial but of an assumed ideal pattern. Here it is important to distinguish between identity referring to common attributes shared by a group and identification (Hardin 1995). Such identification was not particular to Muslims but a common feature of all ethnic and religious groups represented in the political arena in British India. For example, there is a family resemblance between Muslims as painted by the two-nations theory and the notion of *Hindutva* (Hinduness) proposed by, among others, the Hindu nationalist leader V. D. Savarkar in the 1920s (van der Veer 1994; Frynkenberg 1993). Indeed all mobilisations of an internally differentiated population, such as that of the subcontinent, as a group involve identification with an archetype (Andersen 1993). A polar case of this is the construction of the Jewish nation of Israel in recent times (Tamir 1993). In fact, all identities that individuals carry rest on some process of identification. It is important to emphasise that all instances of identification are partial, one out of several such as that with a religious or an ethnic community or with a state. Thus the interesting issue is not one of the verity of the archetypal Muslims of the two-nations theory but social and political forces which led Muslims to identify with it at a particular historical conjuncture.

At the mundane political level, the two-nations theory served two purposes: first, to establish the credentials of the All India Muslim League as the sole representative of Muslims in competition with the syncretic Indian National Congress. The second and no less important purpose was to override ethnic divisions, thereby dislodging regional nationalist organisations. Here it is important to point out that in the referenda held prior to the partition in 1947 the biggest challenge to the Muslim League came not from the Congress but from the regional nationalist parties in the Punjab and the Northwest Frontier. It was only in the last days of British India that the Muslim League managed to win over these two provinces (Samad 1995). The historical irony is that the Punjab is the bedrock of Pakistan and the Northwest Frontier Province forms its western boundary. A narrow focus on the syncretism of the Congress and the parochialism of the Muslim League overshadows the common features between them. Both fought against centrifugal forces of regionalism. Both drew succour from each other in their success in emasculating ethnic or regional nationalisms.

In both India and Pakistan, regional-cum-ethnic cleavages were overshadowed by the drama of the partition. But these resurfaced with a vengeance after independence. The political history of Pakistan, and also of India, is in large measure a history of how ethnic differences played out in the political arena. In both countries, regional political parties have been important actors in national politics. Thanks to democracy, India has succeeded in accommodating regional differences without fragmentation, but, in contrast, Pakistan did not succeed in accommodating its eastern wing within the confines of one state. To revert to the theme at the beginning of this section, the two-nations theory as such did not provide for the division of India, for the simple reason that the 'imagined Muslim' community was dispersed throughout British India intermixed with a non-Muslim population. Muslims of the subcontinent could not be mapped on to a territory that satisfied two elementary requirements of a viable state: contiguity and a Muslim majority. Once the accommodation of the Muslim League as the sole representative of Muslims was ruled out as incompatible with united India, the demand for separate political representation turned into the demand for Muslim majority states. Here it is interesting to note that the 1940 resolution of the Muslim League, which is widely regarded as the first tangible step towards Pakistan, demanded two Muslim majority states, one in the north-west and the other in the north-east of India. As it happened, the demand was realised with the separation in 1971 of Bangladesh. But the resolution neither specified the territorial boundaries of the two states nor even mentioned the word Pakistan (Bose and Jalal 1998). It was at the same 1940 meeting of the Muslim League that Jinnah came up with the famous formulation of the two-nations theory. It was only a few months before the actual partition that Jinnah accepted the offer of only one state comprised of Muslim majority provinces in the north-west of India with East Bengal, the present-day Bangladesh, tagged on to it. That state was to be called Pakistan.

Nation-building

Nation-building is used here to refer to the disparate processes of evolution of identities affecting relations of Pakistanis to each other and to the Pakistani state. Among these, I focus on, first, mutual accommodation and rivalries between ethnic groupings and, second, the role of Islam. Except for occasional references to Bangladesh (erstwhile East Pakistan), my discussion is confined to the present-day Pakistan. I use the term ethnicity to denote features that mark out a group in the eyes of both its members and outsiders. Aside from descent, identification with a region and a distinctive language (including dialects) are among the most obvious of such features. Islam is taken here to include doctrines, rituals and institutions, and my concern is with the relation between the state and Islam.

The 137 million or so Pakistanis have multiple personae, of which the most important are ethnicity, religion and nationality. The process of nation-building concerns relations between these multiple identities. What makes the process complex is that these are neither ranked in order of hierarchy, nor is the relationship between them stable. At times ethnic grievances in a head-on conflict with national identity have veered towards territorial secession. A special case of which was the splitting of East Pakistan in 1971, which until the downfall of communism in the ex-Soviet Union and Eastern Europe was perhaps the only instance of successful secession. Except the Punjab, each of the provinces of West (or present-day) Pakistan has seen secessionist ethnic movements. But the government has been able to contain them through a mixture of concessions and brute force. It is important to add that the ethnic divisions in Pakistan are not 'givens'. Each of the principal ethnic groups is internally differentiated and the self-perceived ethnic identities are contextual and susceptible to shifts. An ethnic group may identify with the dominant ethnic group in the context of, for example, national politics but differentiate itself in local politics.

In a marked contrast to their ethnic diversity (which I discuss below), Pakistanis are almost homogeneous in terms of religion. Prior to the partition, there were substantial minorities of Hindus and Sikhs in areas that make up Pakistan, especially in the Punjab. Most of them fled to India under the threat of generic massacres that ushered independent Pakistan and India. Among non-Muslim minorities that still remain, the principal ones are Christians and Hindus, and, formally, also a Muslim sect (Ahamdis) which by law is a non-Muslim minority. Due to religious cleansing in the wake of the partition and the separation of East Pakistan with a substantial non-Muslim population, around 97 per cent of the present-day Pakistanis are Muslims. This means that Pakistan's Muslim population stands at around 133 million, which is still substantially lower than the combined Muslim population of Bangladesh and India of over 210 million. Thus Pakistan, initially purported to be the homeland of the Muslim population of the subcontinent, houses around 39 per cent of them. A vast majority being Muslim, religion is the principal common denominator of the Pakistani population, which has not been sufficient to guarantee religious peace or ensure social cohesion.

Ethnic diversity, migration and language

Taking territorial locus and language as emblems of ethnicity, we focus on two issues that bring into relief multiple facets of ethnic rivalry and accommodation in Pakistan. One is population migration and the other is the relative status of principal languages. In so far as migration involves movement across ethnic boundaries, it has implications for the relation between territories and their historic ethnic identities (Weiner 1995). The language issue, which has been particularly intense in Pakistan and India compared to most post-colonial states, encapsulates various dimensions of nation formation in ethnically diverse societies. Large-scale population migration (international as well as national) has been a running thread of Pakistani history. Since its formation Pakistan has been swept by two waves of refugees from neighbouring countries, initially from India following the partition and later in the 1980s from Afghanistan. Created by strife, religious in the case of those from India and civil in the case of those from Afghanistan, these refugees have, in turn, been a source of ethnic friction in Pakistan. Besides an influx of refugees, there has also been a steady stream of internal migration across provincial boundaries driven by economic factors, which too raises issues of accommodation and friction between ethnic groups.

Ethnic diversity and migration

Turning to ethnic taxonomy, Pakistan is made up of four provinces and miscellaneous territories that cover the tribal area bordering Afghanistan and the part of Kashmir under Pakistani control. With each province identified with a dominant ethnic group, there are four principal ethnic groups: Baluchis, Punjabis, Pashtuns and Sindhis. The ethnic map of Pakistan differs from that of India in that one ethnic group and correlatively one province far outweighs the rest. Over much of (the present-day) Pakistan's history, the Punjabis and the Punjab have accounted for a majority of the population. There are scores of minor ethnic groups – some sizeable in numbers – which are regarded as separate or just a variant of one of the four principal ethnic groups, depending on the context. The mapping between provinces and principal ethnic groups is partial rather than total. All provinces are ethnically diverse and the influx of refugees and internal migration has added to diversity. Yet the provincial boundaries are exactly the same as drawn under British rule. Not that they represent an appropriate territorial division in terms of ethnicity or governance, but that any alteration that changes the inter-provincial balance would encounter a major opposition. Stitched together on the basis of Muslim majority, the territory that made up West Pakistan in 1947 (the present-day Pakistan) was not a natural unit in terms of population movement or cultural links. The Pakistani Punjab's links tended to run more towards the east across the partition line and less towards the south to Sindh. For example, the tracts of land opened up in the Punjab by the extensive network of canals constructed around the turn of the twentieth century were for the most part settled by migrants from what is now Indian Punjab and Haryana. Being a part of Bombay Presidency until 1931, Sindh, especially its coastal belt, was linked to western India and Bombay (now Mumbai). The iron curtain that descended with the partition firmly barred all historically established routes of commerce and population that straddled the India–Pakistan boundary, except as an emergency exit by refugees.

This has had both short- and long-term consequences. The short-term consequence was a severe economic dislocation. The long-term consequences flowed from the forced re-routing of commerce and population movement along the north–south axis confined to Pakistan. In terms of ethnic composition, the province most affected by the changed pattern has been Sindh for two reasons. First, it housed Karachi, the only modern port assigned to Pakistan, and, second, it had large tracts of sparsely populated but cultivable land. The creation of Pakistan transformed Karachi from a small city on the periphery of the subcontinent to an economic and commercial centre and a magnet for refugees from India and internal migrants. Its population more than doubled within the first three years of the partition. Sindh has also witnessed an influx of refugees and migrants to its other cities and rural areas. This influx of 'outsiders' threatening to reduce Sindhis to a minority in their homeland has served to consolidate and sharpen Sindhi ethnicity. A similar change has also taken place in Baluchistan, which in the 1980s became a receptacle for refugees from Afghanistan tipping the ethnic balance in the province towards Pashtuns. This has prompted Baluchi elite to demand a redrawing of the boundaries of Baluchistan so as to maintain its traditional ethnic identity, a demand that is unlikely to be accepted.

Refugees from India provide an illuminating case study of ethnic assimilation and friction in Pakistan. The vivisection of communities, which the partition was especially in the Punjab, unleashed a massive two-way flight of religious minorities between Pakistan and India. Not counting several hundreds of thousands who never made it, the total figure was between 14 to 15 million persons, which makes it the biggest episode in forced migration ever. The inflow of refugees into (the present-day) Pakistan exceeded the outflow to India. The two-way flight of religious minorities, all bearing a particular ethnic identity, has had a much larger impact on Pakistan than on India, given the former's much smaller population. More pertinent for the present discussion, the impact on ethnic make-up has been different on different provinces of Pakistan. In the Northwest Frontier Province (NWFP), the outflow exceeded the inflow and the net effect was an almost total disappearance of non-Muslim minority and, correlatively, a reduction in ethnic diversity. In contrast, the inflow into the Punjab and Sindh exceeded the outflow. Though the Punjab received 80 per cent of the total inflow, its ethnic composition was only marginally affected by the refugees, who were mostly from parts of the then Punjab allocated to India (see Ahmad 1998). Facilitated by a shared culture, refugees in the Punjab assimilated quickly with the native population. They do not stand out as a distinct group. In comparison, refugees who settled in Sindh were an alien graft, different in culture and language from the native population, albeit not in faith. In a stark contrast to their counterparts in the Punjab, refugees to Sindh have retained their identity and are, fifty years later, still called *muhajirs* (refugees). Drawn from parts of India with a greater exposure to Western education and capitalism than Sindh, they soon became the economically dominant class. This sowed the seeds of an ethnic friction, which became antagonistic from the 1970s, escalating periodically into a murderous strife (see Tambiah 1996).

The relation of *muhajirs* to Pakistan brings into focus a problem of nation formation in Pakistan arising from the ethnic mismatch between the territory that makes up Pakistan and the cradle of the movement that led to the creation of Pakistan. In the 1980s, the newly established Muttahida Quomi Mahaz (MQM, or the United National Front), popularly known as Muhajir Quomi Mahaz (Muhajir National Front) emerged as the dominant representative of the *muhajirs* in Sindh and demanded official recognition as the fifth ethnic group. With this demand, the history of Pakistan completed a full circle of irony. In 1940 Jinnah demanded Pakistan by claiming that Muslims of the subcontinent were a separate nation; just over forty years later the group which identified most closely with the archetypal Muslim painted by the two nations theory demanded recognition as a minority nationality in Pakistan. The contrasting experience with refugees in the Punjab and Sindh leads on to the salient aspect of the relation between religion and ethnicity, not only in Pakistan but also in the subcontinent. Common language and culture cannot overcome the barrier of religious difference, and common religion alone is inadequate to bridge ethnic differences. But, given common religion, ethnic proximity is a powerful force for assimilation.

An instance of the long shadow of ethnic and provincial rivalries on public administration is the fact that Pakistan went without a population census for seventeen years; the one due for 1991 was finally conducted in 1998. The delay was not caused by want of requisite administrative capacity but by political significance vested in demographic data (Ahmad 1998). Following on from the long-established practice under the British rule, decennial population censuses have until this episode been an established routine. Despite the upheaval in the wake of the partition, Pakistan managed to conduct one in 1951. The political significance of censuses arises from the political and economic implications of the distribution of the population by provinces, mother tongue and the administrative status of localities (urban or rural). Though ethnic membership does not appear as a category on the census form, its close correlate mother tongue or 'language spoken at home' does. For example, the distribution of population between provinces influences the competing claim for resources, the allocation of government jobs and also parliamentary seats when democracy is functioning. There are two major currents in internal migration in Pakistan, one is rural to urban migration and the other is a steady north to south flow from the NWFP and the Punjab to Sindh. These overlap but do not coincide. A part of rural to urban migration has been intra-provincial, and rural to rural has been a significant component of the Punjab to Sindh migration. Over time, internal migration has given rise to three trends, each with political implications: first, an increasing share of the urban population, second, a falling share of the Punjab in the national population and, third, a declining percentage of Sindhis (the indigenous population) in Sindh's population. Each is a source of anxiety in some quarters: the first among the elite with a rural base, the second in the Punjab, given its pre-eminence, and the third among Sindhi nationalists.

As the cumulative effect of these trends began to dawn, multiple anxieties about what a new population census would reveal created a coalition in favour of its postponement. Given the crucial importance of demographic data for the functioning of government, the census was finally conducted in 1998 under army protection, which ensured its conduct but not the reliability of its returns. Though held after seventeen years of substantial rural to urban and inter-provincial migration, the 1998 census shows little change in the distribution of population since 1981. Thus·the census changed from a data source to an instrument for validating an obsolete ethnic-territorial division of population. The crucial point of this episode is not that demographic changes have economic and political implications, which is a commonplace, but that public administration is open to capture by parochial interests.

The issue of language

Mirroring its ethnic diversity, the Pakistani population has numerous mother tongues, which raises two issues related to nation-building. One concerns the media of communication between citizens and between them and the government at various tiers. The other concerns language as a marker of group identities, both ethnic and national. Another salient feature of the Pakistani population is that 63 per cent of adults are illiterate; and the percentage of those unable to use written language is even higher. This automatically bars a large majority from access to written language. One consequence of mass illiteracy in the subcontinent is the elevated role of films, television and radio broadcasting as principal media of distant communication. As we shall see below, the division between illiterate masses and the literate few has implications for the relation between English and vernacular languages.

With regard to linguistic topography, there are five major languages and a host of minor languages and dialects. The total number depends on the criterion of classification and its fineness (Masica 1991). The percentage distribution of the population by principal mother tongues, or 'language spoken at home', is as follows: Punjabi and Saraiki, 58 per cent; Pashtu, 13 per cent; Sindhi, 12 per cent; Urdu, 8 per cent; and Baluchi, 3 per cent (Rahman 1996). Except Urdu, each is identified with a particular province. The linguistic topography of Pakistan presents two anomalies from the perspective of nation-building: first, Urdu, which is either a second or an unfamiliar language for a vast majority, is the national language and, second, English, a foreign language, continues to be the official language. As the figures show, Urdu is the mother tongue of a very small minority (8 per cent), predominantly *muhajirs*, refugees from India. There is a similarity between the status of Urdu in Pakistan and that of Hebrew in Israel, both adopted as national languages on the grounds of their symbolic significance not their wide usage. The symbolic significance of Urdu resides in being the language of high Muslim culture in the subcontinent and, associated with this, its rich literary heritage. Taken together, Punjabi and Siraiki, which are mutually intelligible, is the majority mother tongue. Counting the number of entries in the Directory of Publications for Pakistan, except Sindhi and Urdu, all indigenous languages remain largely spoken with comparatively little literature or none at all. In particular, there are few publications in the majority mother tongue Punjabi and Saraiki (taken together). Thus, for all practical purposes, there are numerous oral languages, but only three written languages, English included. As in India, English remains the official language at the higher echelons of the state and is also the language of higher education and of elite schools, which marks them off from schools for the masses. Urdu is relegated to lower levels of administration, and is used as the medium of instruction in non-elite schools even at the primary level in Baluchistan, NWFP and the Punjab. Thus a child may receive his/her first lesson in a language completely alien to her/him (for a similar case of France, see Weber 1995). This undoubtedly retards learning, whether this promotes nation-building is questionable. The interesting feature is that, rather than being imposed from above, it is in a sense chosen. For it is open to provinces to use a local language as the medium of local administration and of schooling. The example is Sindh where both Sindhi and Urdu are used in tandem.

However, there is an abiding attachment to mother tongues as emblems of ethnicity and non-written languages continue to be used widely at home and between fellow members of ethnic groups. From the 1970s, these, especially Punjabi, are also widely used in films. Nevertheless, Urdu is generally accepted as the rightful national language. In a marked contrast to India, in the present-day Pakistan there has been no strong movement for the recognition of a number of languages as national languages. But the status of Urdu as the sole national language has not always been uncontroversial in Pakistan; it was a major bone of contention between West and East Pakistan (present-day Bangladesh). Soon after the partition, Jinnah declared Urdu as the sole national language so as to mark out newly created Pakistan's distinctive identity. This act of nation-building by decree went largely unchallenged in West Pakistan but sparked widespread riots in the then East Pakistan, which, in retrospect, represented the first major entry in the list of grievances that led to the break-up of Pakistan. This raises the question of the reasons for the difference in the responses of East and West Pakistan to the institution of Urdu as the sole national language. Urdu was more widely used in the West than in the East and closer to vernacular languages in the West than to Bengali. But these were no more than contributory factors. The principal reason lay in the marked contrast between the two parts in their ethnic and linguistic physiognomy. While East Pakistanis were ethnically homogeneous and monolingual, with Bengali as the common mother tongue, West Pakistanis were ethnically diverse and multi-lingual. Moreover, the dominant ethnic group in West Pakistan, the Punjabis, long accepted Urdu as their literary language. Prior to the partition, the relation between Punjabi and Urdu was mediated though religion. Muslim Punjabis, although they spoke Punjabi, identified written Punjabi with its *Gurmukhi* script (fashioned by the second Sikh Guru) with Sikhs and never took to it (see Masica 1991; and Rahman 1996). Instead, they used Urdu as their literary language. Iqbal, a towering figure in Urdu literature and the national poet of Pakistan was a Punjabi. In contrast, Bengali was both the quotidian and literary language and Urdu an alien language in East Pakistan. Here it is interesting to note that political and social cleavage between Muslims and Hindus in Bengal, which historically has been as deep as that in the Punjab, did not carry through to language and literature. Unlike in the Punjab, the literary language of Muslim Bengalis, bar a small elite, was not Urdu but Bengali. As a result, while the opposition to the imposition of Urdu was united in East Pakistan, that in West Pakistan, if expressed at all, was confined to minority ethnic groups and sporadic. Faced with riots, the Pakistani government soon retreated by making Bengali the second national language of Pakistan. With the separation of Bangladesh, Bengali also seceded leaving Urdu as the sole national language. Soon after the secession of Bangladesh, there was a demand in the 1970s to make Sindhi a national language which after a while fizzled out, in large part due to the opposition of the then prime minister Zulfikar Ali Bhutto, himself a Sindhi.

Aside from the language controversy in Sindh in the early 1970s (Rahman 1996), language has not been a site of inter-ethnic friction in the present-day Pakistan. The reason is not the weakness of ethnic attachments but the peripheral role of mother tongues in the projection of ethnic identities in the present-day Pakistan. The major exception is Sindhi. The assertion of Sindhi ethnicity in politics and culture has taken the form of the promotion of Sindhi as the medium of education and provincial governance and also of literary expression. In contrast, the promotion of Pashtu has played a marginal role in the demarcation and projection of Pashtun ethnicity in culture and politics. There has been little or no political pressure in the NWFP for the use of Pashtu as the medium of education or local government. The reason is not that Pashtu speakers are fewer than Sindhi speakers; on the contrary, as shown above, Pashtu speakers slightly outnumber Sindhi speakers. Nor is the reason that the Pashtuns have been less assertive of their ethnic distinctiveness than the Sindhis. The explanation for the contrast lies in the fact that the arena for the promotion of mother tongue is the home province not the whole of Pakistan. The respective position of Sindhis and Pashtuns in their homeland has been very different. Sindh, in particular Karachi, has since the formation of Pakistan seen a huge influx of non-Sindhis, first, refugees from India (*muhajirs*) and then a steady stream of internal migrants from NWFP and the Punjab. Karachi, the capital of Sindh, is the largest Pashtun- and Urdu-speaking city. In comparison, the NWFP has mostly been the source not the destination of migrants, except for the influx in the 1980s of Afghan refugees, most of whom are Pashtuns. In contrast to Sindhis, Pashtuns have been securely dominant in their home province NWFP. While the assertion of Sindhi ethnicity has been a defensive response to the changing ethnic mix in Sindh, Pashtun nationalism, which began to assert itself with the formation of Pakistan, has been directed towards consolidating the political position of the NWFP *vis-à-vis* other provinces, in particular the Punjab.

A feature of Bangladesh, India and Pakistan needing an explanation is the absence of a concerted policy to dislodge English with national languages as the medium of governance. Its symbolic association with the colonial past aside, English remains an alien tongue for a vast majority and creates a chasm between citizens and the government. This feature stands in a marked contrast to a number of countries where the national language has been the fulcrum of nation-building, such as Turkey, Israel and Indonesia. To dispose of two arguments, the survival of English has not been due to the absence of vernacular languages with a rich legacy of written literature. In a technical sense, there are a number that can function as official languages, these include, among others, Bengali, Hindi and Urdu. Though English facilitates communication with the world at large, reliance on a vernacular language as a vehicle of government and internal communication has neither been a barrier to modernisation nor does it preclude learning English as a foreign language. Measured in terms of the growth of per capita income or improvement in various welfare indicators, the modernisation record of South Asia with English as the official language has been distinctly poorer than that of East and South-East Asia, which generally use vernacular languages as official languages.

Indifference to issues concerning language would not seem to be the reason for the survival of English either. Language has long been a live political battlefield in the subcontinent (see Jalal 1995). The later part of the nineteenth century saw a proliferation of movements of renewal of vernacular languages, which strengthened ethnic bonds and in the process also sharpened the lines of demarcation between 'fellow members' and outsiders. Where aspects of language, such as script, overlapped with religious divisions, language movements also took on communal colourings. An important example of this is the proposal in the latter half of the nineteenth century to replace the then widely used Perso-Arabic script for *Hindustani* (covering both Hindi and Urdu) with the Sanskrit script (*devnagri*), which sparked a conflict between Hindus and Muslims in the UP. The leagues and

Anjumans (societies) set up to defend Urdu (written in the Perso-Arabic script) furnished the foundation for the establishment of the Muslim League at the turn of the twentieth century. Though entwined, two aspects of language have been at stake in numerous language conflicts in the subcontinent: the functional and the cultural. The functional aspect concerns competition for jobs in the sense that the currency of a particular language as the medium of government and of business and commerce puts its native speakers at an advantage in the labour market, especially for government jobs. This appears to have been the dominant issue in the Hindi–Urdu controversy, though the cultural associations of the two scripts were also implicated. The changeover from Perso-Arabic to the *Devnagri* script would have handicapped Muslims and also *Kayaisth* Hindus who tended to dominate government jobs open to Indians. It is interesting to note that *Kayaisth* Hindus sided with Muslims in the controversy, which brings into relief the economic stake. The cultural aspect refers to language as a marker of the identity of a community (ethnic or national) and its difference with others. This would seem to have been the principal issue in the Urdu–Bengali riots in East Pakistan. There is an important difference between the functional and the cultural aspect of language. While the former impinges mostly on the literate, generally a minority in the subcontinent, the latter concerns all speakers, the literate and illiterate alike. Given the division between the illiterate majority and literate minority, a language movement can assume a mass character only when the cultural identity of a community is perceived to be at stake.

Thus, the reason for the continued survival of English as the official language in the subcontinent lies in the nature of language battles, vested economic interests and mass illiteracy. Language battles in the subcontinent have been almost entirely confined to vernacular languages and did not concern English. Rather than a generalised warfare, these battles have been highly selective, bilateral and confined to communities living cheek-by-jowl and in competition, cultural or economic. Examples include controversies between Hindi and Urdu in the nineteenth century UP in British India, between Sindhi and Urdu in the 1970s in Pakistan and between Hindi and Punjabi and between Gujrati and Marathi in India (see Brass 1991). Though distributed unevenly, proficiency in English has not been the preserve of particular ethnic communities. Economic competition has tended to prompt the learning of English instead of provoking protests against its use. There are two factors that explain the continuation of English. First, rivalries between vernacular languages have pre-empted consensus on the candidate for the replacement for English, the sharper the rivalries the more difficult it has been to achieve a consensus. This would appear to be the reason for the currency of English in India where there are a number of national languages. But this does not seem to be sufficient because English also continues as the official language in Bangladesh and Pakistan with only one national language. It is here that the second factor, the socio-economic context of a move to replace

English, becomes relevant. Schematically, those proficient in English have, for the most part, no economic incentive to support the change as that would devalue their economic advantage. A majority, but not all, of those who are not proficient in English are also illiterate and therefore have no stake in the change. There is a close relation between the continuation of English as the official language and mass illiteracy. Arguably, the spread of mass literacy, which has to be in a vernacular language, would bring about a crucial change in the balance of forces for and against substituting English. For that would raise the numbers of those proficient in a vernacular language but not in English. Given the advantage proficiency in English confers in the labour market, English is now more widely used as a medium of education and business in Bangladesh, India and Pakistan than during the British rule.

Islam and Pakistani nationalism

One of numerous Muslim majority states, Pakistan is unique amongst them in that it was created on the basis of a division between Muslims and non-Muslims. Pakistan's Islamic identity is writ large, in its flag, title (Islamic Republic), state rituals, laws and international relations. All state rituals begin with a recital from the *Qur'an*, as do all journeys with the Pakistan International Airlines. The prefix 'Islamic Republic' was introduced in the 1956 constitution, excised in the 1960s under the military regime of Ayub Khan, and then restored in the 1973 constitution. Transgressions of Islamic commandments such as consensual sexual relations outside marriage and alcohol consumption are deemed criminal offences. Nominally, no temporal laws repugnant to the *Shari'a* (the corpus of Islamic precepts) may be passed, a constitutional provision in a number of Muslim majority states though its purchase on legislative and judicial processes varies widely from country to country (see Kennedy 1996). With 97 per cent of Pakistanis Muslim, Islam would seem to be the cement that holds Pakistan together. But if Islam unites Pakistanis, it also divides them; and Islam's role in nation-building and the consolidation of the state in Pakistan has been complex. The purpose of this section is to bring out this complexity beginning with the relation between Pakistani citizenship and Islam.

In his address to the first meeting of the Pakistan Constituent Assembly on 11 August 1947, Jinnah proclaimed to the would-be citizens of Pakistan three days later:

> You are free to go to your temples, you are free to go to your mosques or to any other place of worship in this state of Pakistan. ... You may belong to any religion, caste or creed – that has nothing to do with the business of the State.

> (Quoted in Bose and Jalal 1997: 194)

However, the religion of Pakistanis has for some time been an important business of the state. Non-Muslim Pakistanis, including excommunicated heretic Muslims are subalterns. They are barred from being the head of the state, which in isolation is as inconsequential as the convention that the British monarch should be an Anglican. But in practice this bar is extended to include any key position in the government. For example, the Army Chief of Staff between 1996–1998, Jahangir Karamat, faced a clamour for his dismissal on the suspicion of being an Ahmadi (a certified heretic). He was only able to continue in the post after a public declaration that he was not an Ahmadi, though his father was. Non-Muslims are also liable to criminal prosecution for acts and words that Muslims may construe as blasphemous, which carried to its logical conclusion makes subscription to any religious belief other than Islam untenable. Besides, in certain legal contexts women are treated as lesser citizens compared to men. For example, in execution of contracts, a female witness counts as half of a male witness, which, although trivial in isolation, legitimates the inferior status of women in daily life. However, women are allowed to hold high offices of the state, including the position of prime minister, contrary to religious counsel. The precedence accorded to religious identity over citizenship goes against the thrust of modern democracy (Taylor 1998). This is a feature that Pakistan shares in common with a wide variety of states where religion is accorded a central place, such as a number of Muslim states and Israel.

However, the primacy of Islam in Pakistan does not erase its national identity. Pakistan is not a pan-Islamic state. Its pan-Islamism does not go beyond empathy with Muslim states and close relations with some of them. Being a Muslim, even that of the subcontinent, does not entitle a person to Pakistani citizenship, as, for example, being Jewish does for Israeli. Though purported to be the homeland for Muslims of the subcontinent, except for a few years following the partition, migration from India and later on from Bangladesh has been strictly controlled. Citizenship is largely restricted to descendants or spouses of Pakistani citizens, as it is in most countries bar a few (see, for example, Brubaker 1992). Progeny and marital ties rather than faith define Pakistani citizenship. In Pakistan, as in other Muslim states, Islam effaces neither national frontiers nor internal ethnic differences. It proved to be too fragile a bond to hold East and West Pakistan together. But it is interesting to note that ethnic nationalism in Bangladesh has not overshadowed its Islamic identity. Islam occupies as central a place in Bangladeshi politics as it does in Pakistan's. Islamic identity is enduring but it coexists and competes with national and ethnic identities. In this respect, Islam is no different from other religions such as Hinduism or Christianity, notwithstanding the emphasis it places on the *umma* (the community of the faithful).

Taken as a complex of beliefs and practices, Islam of the *umma*, notwithstanding its enduring core, covers a varied range. At one extreme is the doctrinal Islam of the *ulemas* (religious scholars), which, as we shall below, is not monolithic. At the other extreme is the 'nominal' Islam confined to expressions of abiding loyalty and sporadic participation in rituals. There is in the middle a broad spectrum of popular Islam with a variable relation to the *Shari'a*, and often 'contaminated' with alien influences. These not only flow from modern socio economic organisation but also other religions, such as Hinduism. The relation of Islam to the mosque and the tomb of a saint, two principal sites for public performances of religious rituals, vary across the range. In its austere version, the doctrinal Islam privileges the mosque as the sole public stage and eschews the veneration of living saints (*pirs* and *sufis*) and devotional visits to tombs of dead ones that occupy much of popular Islam (see van der Veer 1994). With only a minority being literate, a large majority of Pakistanis have only an indirect access to the *Shari'a*, via *ulemas*, mullahs (clerics) or various types of saints (*pirs*, *sufis*, etc.). Although officially Islam has no clergy and church, it has at its service an army of intermediaries of faith, both lay and professional, who are functionally akin to a clergy. Thus the characteristic of Islam is not the absence of a clergy but that entry to the ranks of clerics is unregulated. Drawn from various socio-economic groups, these intermediaries form the channel for the two-way traffic in influences between Islam and the society at large. The growing seepage of Islam in public life and the state in Pakistan since the late 1970s has gone in tandem with a massive growth in the numbers of mullahs and proselytisers. Investment in the religious infrastructure, mosques and *Madrassahs* (religious schools) has soared as investment in the public infrastructure of schools, hospitals and roads has dropped. The diversity of beliefs and practices that characterise the *umma* has two consequences: first, it gives rise to an incessant dialectics of revival and purification that is as old as Islam. Second, the Islamisation of the state beyond the expression of allegiance involves coercion and is highly divisive, even in a society such as the Pakistan with an abiding attachment to Islam. As an aside, the same is also true of the modernisation of popular Islam by decree in, for example, Tunisia or Turkey, such as banning the veil or the dawn-to-dusk fasting during the month of Ramadan in the Islamic calendar. The hold of Islam on the Pakistani state is not a simple reflection of the piety of the population, but depends crucially on the mundane politics of competition and conflict over rival agenda and power. Cynical political calculations more than salvation have been the motive force behind the promotion of Islam in public life. The oft-invoked absence of separation between the spiritual and the temporal in Islam does not cast much illumination on this relationship (see, for example, Gellner 1981). For the architecture of the state and the configuration of politics, which constitutes the temporal, are not constants but variables across time and space, a point that is eclipsed by the spectre of fundamentalism in the Islamic world. The relation of Islam to the state has been variable over history and across the Islamic world (see Madan 1997; Zubaida 1993).

There is enough of resemblance between Muhammad's and the present-day Islam to establish a genealogy between the two. But the doctrinal core of Islam, the *Shari'a*, although identifiable, has neither been unitary nor fixed once and for all (see Eickelmann and Piscatori 1996). It has undergone emendations and reinterpretations over time and across localities, and is traversed by sectarian schisms, such as that between Sunnis and Shia's. Each of these is further divided and there are also various heretic groups on the periphery of mainstream Islam. Sectarian cleavages have been and continue to be a major source of conflict and rivalry in the *umma*. To give an example, the first major civil strife in Pakistan was instigated in 1953–1954 by a demand by orthodox groups to the government to declare 'Ahmadis' (a heretic sect) a non-Muslim minority and to ban them from all key posts. The latter was a call for the dismissal of the then Foreign Minister of Pakistan. The *fatwa* (religious edict) of heresy against Ahmadis long predated the formation of Pakistan; what was new in the demand was that the *fatwa* be given a legal backing and non-Muslims be barred from holding any significant position in the government. The government refused to yield and appointed a committee of inquiry. The Munir report of the committee (named after the then Chief Justice) observed that government adjudication in theological disputes would fan religious conflicts rather than arresting them. However, two decades later in 1974, Zulfikar Ali Bhutto, not known for piety, engineered the declaration of Ahmadis as a heretic sect. Enshrined into the constitution, this excommunication would later confront the Pakistani government with the embarrassing problem of how to honour the first Pakistani Nobel laureate, Abdus Salam, who being a heretic Ahmadi merited the death penalty according to the Islamic law. The excommunication of Ahmadis set the precedent for pressing the power of the state in the service of Islam for political expediency, which in the 1980s would be used by the military government of General Zia to transform transgressions of Islamic commandments into criminal offences. As presaged by the Munir report, the introduction of the *Shari'a* into law instead of commanding a consensus provoked doctrinal dissension. In particular, it led to a sharpening of sectarian differences between the Sunnis, a large majority in Pakistan, and Shi'as, which in recent years have escalated into murderous warfare. Following the precedent set in respect to Ahmadis, militant Sunni groups are demanding the declaration of Shi'as as heretics also.

It might appear that the growing hold of Islam on the state and public life in Pakistan is a natural progression of communalist politics that led to the formation of Pakistan. There is a link but it is one which is indirect and mediated by internal politics in Pakistan. The Muslim communalist movement in the pre-partition India represented an anomalous combination of political mobilisation on religious lines but only in the service of temporal ends not of aligning the lives of the faithful with the *Shari'a*. The movement took the Muslim community as it existed and was led by worldly figures not by *ulemas*. Its cradle was not the *Madrassah* (religious school) but Aligarh a university founded at the turn of the nineteenth century to bring Western education to Muslims. Mawdudi, who would play a leading role in the movement for recasting Pakistan into an Islamic state, remarked:

> No trace of Islam can be found in the ideas and politics of Muslim League ... [Jinnah] reveals no knowledge of the views of the Qu'ran. ... All his knowledge comes from Western laws and sources.
>
> (Quoted in Nasr 1994: 20)

There were movements for Islamic revival, which predated communalist politics, but their relations with the Muslim League and Pakistan were ambivalent, ranging from open hostility to a grudging support. One revivalist strand, *Jamiyyat-ul-Ulma-i-Hind*, went as far as issuing a *fatwa* forbidding Muslims from joining the Muslim League. Another strand was represented by Mawdudi, who subscribed to the two-nations theory but favoured the creation of Pakistan only in so far as that would facilitate the establishment of an Islamic state (see Nasr 1994). The attitude of revivalist movements towards Pakistan may appear paradoxical, but it rested on the implacable logic that the partition of India would divide the Muslim community in the subcontinent, which is exactly what it did.

With the formation of Pakistan the relation between Islam and the state, which until then was a subject of utopian discourses, became a moot political issue. Created in opposition to secular India, Pakistan had to have an Islamic identity. On this there was a general consensus, but a wide disagreement on the extent of Islamisation. As indicated in the quotation by Mawdudi, Jinnah himself wanted the state to keep a discrete distance from religion. But he did not live beyond the initial turmoil of the partition. After Jinnah's death the relation between the state and Islam remained clouded in ambiguity. Pakistan took nine years to formulate its constitution and India only three (for an account of the peripatetic politics of constitution making, see McGrath 1996). This long gestation period was caused by two issues that have dogged Pakistani politics: first, the division of powers between the central government and provinces, each with a particular ethnic mix, and, second, the relation between Islam and the Pakistani state. Until the separation of Bangladesh in 1971, the relation between West and East Pakistan dominated the first, though there was a strong undercurrent of inter-provincial tension within West Pakistan. As for the second, the 1956 constitution did not go beyond the title 'Islamic Republic' and inconsequential commitment to upholding the *Shari'a*. Gauged in terms of the substantive imprint of Islam on laws and the functioning of the state, until the mid-1970s the hold of religion on the state was no greater in Pakistan than in India. This changed in 1974 when prime minister Zulfikar Ali Bhutto, in order to revive the flagging support for his regime, engineered the excommunication of Ahmadis and introduced various gestures of piety, such as shifting the weekly holiday from Sunday to Friday. It was only in the 1980s that there was a tangible movement towards the conversion of Pakistan into an Islamic state aided and abetted by two factors. The first was a military coup against Bhutto in 1977 led by General Zia who remained at the helm of the state until his death in 1988. The second was the establishment in 1978 of a communist regime in Afghanistan subsequently defended by Soviet troops. General Zia introduced various Islamic measures out of a mixture of personal piety and political cunning. It was the latter which determined the timing of various steps towards an Islamic state. General Zia skilfully promoted Islam to ward off the restoration of democracy. For example, the introduction of the *Shari'a* bill by General Zia in 1988 (just before his death in an air crash), was aimed at finding a new basis of legitimacy for his regime. The bill was never passed, but in the summer of 1998, the government of Nawaz Sharif resuscitated the bill coinciding with a worsening economic crisis in the train of nuclear tests. If passed, the bill would give a *carte blanche* to the executive to whatever it deemed necessary for implementing the *Shari'a*. It is important to emphasise that much of the Islamisation of Pakistan has taken place on the back of autocracy. Parties wedded to the establishment of an Islamic state have generally performed poorly in elections.

The combination of communists at the helm of the government in Kabul and a massive armed intervention by the Soviet Union managed to bring together various segments of Afghan society to wage a war with many faces and numerous combatants. It has been a war of liberation from a foreign occupation, a holy war against apostates and non-believers (*jihad*) and a marionette play by various countries to serve their own ends. The war acted as a lifeline for General Zia's regime. It brought substantial economic and military external assistance to not just the Afghan *mujahidin* (religious warriors) but also to Pakistan. It also posed enough of an external threat to Pakistan to enable General Zia to keep the demand for the restoration of democracy at bay. While Afghanistan was the theatre of war, Pakistan was the training and supply base for the fighters as well as the abode for millions of Afghan refugees. The Pakistani army and intelligence services were heavily involved in training and logistics (for a background, see Roy 1993). Waged as a *jihad*, the war complemented General Zia's aim of promoting Islam in Pakistan. The war not only rid Afghanistan of Soviet forces and their Afghan protégé but also spawned an Islam that would later cast a long shadow on Afghanistan in the shape of the Taliban regime and on Pakistan in the form of militant Islamic groups.

References

Ahmad, A. (1996) *The Indus Saga and the Making of Pakistan*, Karachi: Oxford University Press.

Ahmad, F. (1998) *Ethnicity and Politics in Pakistan*, Karachi: Oxford University Press.

Anderson, B. (1996) *Imagined Communities*, London: Verso Press.

Bose, S. and Jalal, A. (1997) *Modern South Asia: History, Culture, Political Economy*, London: Routledge.

Brass, P. R (1991) *The Politics of India Since Independence*, Cambridge: Cambridge University Press.

Brown, J. M. (1994) *Modern India: The Origins of an Asian Democracy*, Oxford: Oxford University Press.

Brubaker, R. (1992) *Citizenship and Nationhood in France and Germany*, Cambridge, MA: Harvard University Press.

Chaterjee, P. (1994) 'National history and its exclusions', in J. Hutchinson and A. Smith (eds) *Nationalism*, Oxford: Oxford University Press.

Choudhry, G. W. (1993) *The Last Days of United Pakistan*, Karachi: Oxford University Press.

Eickelmann, D. F. and Piscatori, J. (1996) *Muslim Politics*, Princeton: Princeton University Press.

Frynkenberg, R. E. (1993) 'Hindu fundamentalism and the structural stability of India', in M. E. Marty and R. S. Appleby (eds) *Fundamentalisms and the State: Remaking Politics, Economics and Militancy*, Chicago: Chicago University Press.

Gellner, E. (1981): *Muslim Society*, Cambridge: Cambridge University Press.

—— (1996) 'The coming of nationalism and its interpretation: the myth of nation and class', in G. Balakrishnan and B. Anderson (eds) *Mapping the Nation*, London: Verso Press.

Habermas, J. (1996) 'The European national state its achievement and its limits. On the past and future of sovereignty and citizenship', in G. Balakrishnan and B. Anderson (eds) *Mapping the Nation*, London: Verso Press.

Hardin, R. (1995) *One For All: The Logic of Group Conflict*, Princeton: Princeton University Press.

Hasan, M. (1997) *Legacy of a Divided Nation: India's Muslims Since Independence*, London: Hurst and Co.

Jalal, A. (1995) *Democracy and Authoritarianism in South Asia: A Comparative and Historical Perspective*, Cambridge: Cambridge University Press.

Kennedy, C. (1996) *Islamisation of Laws and Economy*, Islamabad: Institute of Policy Studies, The Islamic Foundation.

Madan, T. N. (1997) *Modern Myths and Locked Minds: Secularism and Fundamentalism in India*, Delhi: Oxford University Press.

McGrath, A. (1996) *The Destruction of Pakistan's Democracy*, Karachi: Oxford University Press.

Masica, C. P. (1993) *The Indo-Aryan Languages*, Cambridge: Cambridge University Press.

Miller, D. (1997) *On Nationality*, Oxford: Oxford University Press.

Narsr, S. V. R. (1994) *The Vanguard of Islamic Revolution: The Jama'at-Islami of Pakistan*, Berkeley: University of California Press.

Rahman, T. (1996) *Language and Politics in Pakistan*, Karachi: Oxford University Press.

Roy, O. (1993) 'Afghanistan: an Islamic war of resistance', in M. E. Marty and R. S. Appleby (eds) *Fundamentalisms and the State: Remaking Politics, Economics and Militancy*, Chicago: Chicago University Press.

Samad, Y. (1995) *A Nation in Turmoil: Nationalism and Ethnicity in Pakistan, 1937–1958*, Karachi: Oxford University Press.

Tambiah, S. J. (1996) *Levelling Crowds: Ethnonationalist Conflicts and Collective Violence in South Asia*, Berkeley: University of California Press.

Tamir, Y. (1993) *Liberal Nationalism*, Princeton: Princeton University Press.

Taylor, C. (1998) 'Modes of secularism', in R. Bhargava (ed.) *Secularism and its Critics*, New Delhi: Oxford University Press.

Van der Veer, P. (1994) *Religious Nationalism: Hindus and Muslims in India*, Berkeley: California University Press.

Weber, E. (1979) *Peasants Into Frenchman*, London: Chatto and Windus.

Weiner, M. (1995) *The Global Migration Crisis: Challenge to State and to Human Rights*: New York: HarperCollins.

Wirsing, R. G. (1998) *India and Pakistan and the Kashmir Dispute: On Regional Conflict and its Resolution*, London: Macmillan.

Ziring, L. (1997) *Pakistan in the 20th Century*, Karachi: Oxford University Press.

Zubaida, S. (1993) *Islam – the People and the State*, London: I.B. Tauris.

8 The changing temper of Indonesian nationalism

Michael Leifer

Nationalism and its uses

Indonesia is a country which glories in its nationalist past, exemplified by various days of commemoration; above all, that which marks the proclamation of independence on 17 August 1945. Independence from Dutch colonial rule was acknowledged internationally from 27 December 1949, but it is the earlier date of the onset of national revolution that is treated as the Republic's founding moment and the beginning of nation-statehood. When, in May 1998, an Indonesian student movement sought to sustain the momentum of their challenge to the personalised rule of President Suharto, they selected a day of nationalist significance for renewing their political protest. On 20 May 1908, a handful of reformist Javanese intellectuals had founded an organisation that they called *Budi Utomo* or 'Noble Endeavour'. As much cultural as political, *Budi Utomo* made a minimal impact on the Dutch colonial regime but it has come to be accepted as the first stirring of Indonesian nationalism. Accordingly, 20 May has been celebrated every year in Indonesia as National Awakening Day.

At issue in May 1998, however, was not an attempt to invoke nationalist symbolism against an alien power or indeed against internal forces within the Republic with separatist designs. The student movement invoked that symbolism in order to establish a basis in political legitimacy to their challenge to the country's authoritarian President who had been re-elected unopposed for a seventh consecutive five-year term of office in only the previous March in accordance with constitutional form. Nationalist symbolism was intended to serve a domestic political function of a defensive kind. It was invoked to protect President Suharto's student opponents from charges of anti-patriotic intent and not to inspire political mobilisation that had its separate source in the dereliction of a prolonged personalised rule. That episode, which preceded President Suharto's resignation from office the next day, to be succeeded by his vice-president, B. J. Habibie, is suggestive of the relatively subordinate role that nationalism had come to play in the public life of the Republic during his long tenure.

Nationalist sentiment did show itself in Indonesia in the following year, albeit not in any sustained robust form. It was displayed to a degree after the people of East Timor had voted overwhelmingly for independence from Indonesia in a plebiscite conducted by a United Nations (UN) mission on 30 August 1999. The Republic was then obliged to tolerate the intervention of a UN-sanctioned multinational force to restore order in the wake of orchestrated violence and destruction throughout the former Portuguese colony. The nationalist sentiment expressed over East Timor was not a nation-wide phenomenon; nor was it driven from the political centre as in Indonesia's past. Its locus was to be found in the sense of humiliation of the country's armed forces, which had never completely pacified East Timor since annexing the territory in 1975. It had its source also in a resentment of Australia's vocal criticism of Indonesia over East Timor and in its leading military role in the UN-sanctioned intervention.

Australia had been the principal Western state to have recognised Indonesia's incorporation of East Timor within the Republic. In consequence, its government had been able to conclude a treaty for the joint exploitation of the energy resources of the Timor Sea with its Indonesian counterpart. Canberra's change of political heart over East Timor was construed as an act of betrayal in Jakarta, despite President Habibie having taken the initiative in January 1999 to accord its people the right to choose between autonomy and independence. His rationale had been that Indonesia's international standing and prospects for recovery from economic adversity had been diminished by holding on to the former Portuguese colony which had become an unacceptable drain on national resources. Such a rationale indicated a willingness to exempt East Timor from Indonesia's national domain.

The circumstances surrounding East Timor's separation from Indonesia dented national pride but they did not give rise to a popular irredentist cause, which had been the case when the Dutch had withheld the western half of the island of New Guinea (now Irian Jaya) from the transfer of sovereignty. East Timor had never been a subject of a nationalist claim or a symbol of national fulfilment; its loss caused national resentment because Indonesia had been depicted as a pariah state over its maladministration of the territory. In the circumstances, irredentism was taken up primarily by indigenous East Timorese who had been recruited into Indonesia's armed forces and whose life-chances had been destroyed by the outcome of the plebiscite. Organised as so-called pro-integrationist militia, their purpose had been to wreak vengeance and to deny viability to an independent East Timor. Their scorched-earth policy satisfied the hurt pride of their patrons within Indonesia's armed forces who had been unable to come to terms with their military failure. In Jakarta and other major cities, despite a resentment of having an Australian-led multinational force imposed on Indonesia by the UN, public protest over East Timor was limited to small-scale and not nation-wide demonstrations.

East Timor falls outside of organic Indonesia defined with reference to Dutch colonial rule. Represented unsuccessfully by the armed forces as an issue of national integrity, it became a factor in the political struggle in the vacuum of power created with the downfall of President Suharto. In the event, those playing the nationalist card over East Timor failed to mobilise a nation-wide popular response either to the outcome of the UN-organised plebiscite or to the introduction of a UN-sanctioned multinational force into the ravaged territory.

The circumstances of the political downfall of Suharto and then the special case of East Timor would suggest that nationalism has long had its utility as a vehicle of political mobilisation at the centre of Indonesian politics. Under political pressure because of the country's acute economic adversity just prior to his contrived re-election in March 1998, President Suharto invoked the terms of Indonesia's constitution to justify resisting the prescriptions of the International Monetary Fund. His rationale that they were against so-called 'family principles' as embodied in article eight was treated with general derision, however. His interim successor, President Habibie upheld the integrity of Indonesia within its Dutch territorial inheritance against separatist movements in Aceh in northern Sumatra and in Irian Jaya, adjacent to Papua New Guinea. But he did not play the nationalist card in his unsuccessful attempt to hold on to high office, beyond passing criticism of Australia's alleged over-reaction to the crisis over East Timor. As indicated above, it was his initiative in January 1999 that paved the way for the United Nations supervised plebiscite in East Timor eight months later. It was also his decision to accept, albeit grudgingly, the authority of the United Nations Security Council in sanctioning the deployment of a law and order force to the territory. On 20 October 1999, the result of the plebiscite in East Timor was endorsed by consensus by the constitutionally-supreme People's Consultative Assembly (MPR), so excluding the territory from the national domain. His successor as President, Abdurrahman Wahid, chosen the same day by that Assembly, has endorsed that decision and has also called for reconciliation, and not irredentism, towards an independent East Timor.

This chapter seeks to explore the changing temper of Indonesian nationalism in the decades since independence. That exploration has been set against the background of political transformation within the Republic with the end of the Suharto regime in May 1998 and by the dramatic events in East Timor during 1999.

Nationalism, as indicated above, is an inherent part of Indonesia's political tradition. For some two decades after the end of the Pacific War, it was registered in a combative manner against real or imagined external adversaries. It was registered first against the Dutch, the former colonial power, not only in national revolution but also after independence over the irredentist cause of West New Guinea, and then against the British-inspired neighbouring Federation of Malaysia, which was denounced as a neo-colonial enterprise. During that period, nationalism was incorporated by the late President Sukarno within an emotive symbolism, described in acronym as *NASAKOM*, that was ostensibly intended to legitimise religious and communist as well as nationalist participation in the political process. In effect, that symbolism served a mobilising function within a competitive domestic politics with President Sukarno fending off the rival attentions of the armed forces and the Communist Party. Nationalism and allied symbolism were employed to underpin Sukarno's political centrality within the system of Guided Democracy that he imposed by decree in July 1959 to translate himself from a constitutional to an executive president.

From October 1965, fundamental political change began to take place in Indonesia in the wake of an abortive coup that was attributed to the country's Communist Party. By that date, the Republic was economically derelict and close to becoming a failed state. Nationalism invoked from the political centre had touched a genuine chord among a generation of Indonesians that had experienced revolutionary struggle against the Dutch. Its post-revolutionary significance and impact owed much, however, to the context of competitive politics within which it was employed. In that context, nationalism served as a cloak of legitimacy in a struggle among political rivals. Its use was symptomatic of the fragile condition of Indonesian politics and of the lack of a national consensus over the priorities of government and the spoils of office.

From March 1966, when President Sukarno was obliged to transfer effective power to army commander, Lieutenant-General Suharto, the temper and role of Indonesian nationalism began to change in a managed way. The characteristically frenetic populist quality of Indonesian politics was succeeded by a military-based order that placed the highest priority on stability justified in the interest of economic development. Politics took on a ritual, formalised quality that became far more guided even than during that period which the late President Sukarno had inaugurated in July 1959. For example, only three political parties were tolerated but Golkar, the government's electoral vehicle, was assured of overwhelming victory in every parliamentary election between 1971 and 1997 in which democracy was registered in form and not in any substance.

Although nationalist symbols were invoked as legitimising devices by the Suharto government, nationalism was not employed for the purpose of political mobilisation that had been the practice of its ill-fated predecessor. Indeed, under President Suharto's rule, a mobilising nationalism was conspicuous by its absence as an instrument of state policy, except as one ingredient of the state philosophy, *Panca Sila*, which will be addressed below. Indeed, on one occasion in an angry speech in Sumatra in 1980, President Suharto lumped together nationalists with others among his political detractors whose dissidence would not be tolerated.

At issue, in the light of the above introductory remarks, is why nationalism, which is an inherent part of Indonesian identity, has enjoyed such a low profile for the greater part of its existence as a state. At issue also is whether or not the nationalist fervour which was characteristic of the Republic's first two decades might well reappear. In the study of International Relations, it can be instructive to pose the question: why do wars end as well as why do they begin? Correspondingly, in the study of Nationalism, it may be instructive to ask why the temper as well as the role of nationalism may have been diluted in the case of a state created through a conspicuous act of nationalist will?

Before addressing these matters, it is as well to make clear that this chapter will be concerned primarily with the archipelagic-wide phenomenon of nationalism which was encountered, above all, by the Dutch from the end of the Pacific War when they sought to recover their colonial domain by force of arms. It will not be concerned specifically with any competing subordinate and frustrated nationalisms within the archipelagic state, except from the perspective of the central government. To that end, it merits pointing out that the Republic of Indonesia was born of a violent national revolutionary struggle which was ushered in by the circumstances of the surrender of the occupying Japanese forces at the end of the Pacific War. Nationalism was defined with reference to external foes and their domestic sympathisers, which included some indigenous ethnic groups within the archipelago, such as the Christian Ambonese who had been beneficiaries of colonial rule. The same internal definition applied also to the small but economically powerful ethnic Chinese community of migrant origin that had serviced the Dutch state in a comprador role to considerable advantage. Indeed, that role was replicated in servicing the interests of President Suharto's close family and business circle that attracted an economic nationalist resentment.

Although assimilation of a kind and the acquisition of citizenship have become increasingly common among Indonesia's Chinese, they have invariably been the object of the hostile and violent attentions of the *pribumi* or indigenous people. In the main, the *pribumi* have never regarded Indonesia's Chinese as an integral part of the national community and have resented their dominant economic role and close links to Suharto's regime and family circle. In extreme form that view was exemplified by the registration of acute social discontent and unrest during May 1998, itself a consequence of the economic adversity which had begun to afflict Indonesia from the latter part of 1997. Chinese property was a prime object of mob violence but the rape of Chinese women occurred also during the critical prelude to Suharto's resignation. With that tragic episode in mind, Indonesian nationalism may be seen to have been defined also with reference to a particular socio-economic legacy of Dutch rule which has persisted to the end of the twentieth century. The local Chinese have served, however, as a scapegoat for Indonesia's economic misfortunes rather than as the focus of a unifying neo-nationalism. The position adopted towards the tribulations of local Chinese by the successor government of President Habibie was ambivalent and less than responsible. However, he did not seek to capitalise on their resented economic role to mobilise nationalist feeling, while attacks on Chinese and their property ceased under his rule.

To return to our main theme, President Sukarno was eased from office in favour of Lieutenant-General Suharto who then held on to power for over three decades. Suharto inaugurated a so-called 'new order', without any intended allusion to fascist Europe of the 1930s. The change of regime was reflected in a radical revision of governmental priorities. A romantic autarchic nationalism was set aside and replaced by a concentration on economic development through an engagement with the international capitalist economy. The goal of a strong and respected Republic was articulated as a sober alternative. For example, in August 1969, President Suharto announced during an independence-day address that 'We shall only be able to play an effective role if we ourselves are possessed of a great national vitality'. That modern goal was approached, however, without any of the extravagant and rabble-rousing rhetoric that had distinguished the Sukarno era. No less a nationalist than Sukarno, and more directly involved as a soldier in national revolution, but totally different in style and manner, Suharto displayed a very different form of nationalist expression. For example, in registering Indonesia's leadership role beyond national bounds, he was content to express it through a founding membership of and an active participation in the Association of South-East Asian Nations (ASEAN). ASEAN was established in August 1967 as a multilateral instrument for regional reconciliation and not for national aggrandisement.

The fact of the matter is that the combative expression of nationalism with explicit external reference that was characteristic of Indonesia during the 1950s and the first half of the 1960s came to be set aside for a routine pursuit of national interests. That pursuit was based on the realisation that without economic development, Indonesia would not amount to much either regionally or globally. And that such development would require full co-operation with the sources of foreign capital, however dependent the initial relationship. It is with that routine expression of interest in mind, and in the light of the political downfall of Suharto and the drama of East Timor that a central question may be posed. To what extent does a vibrant nationalist tradition that is part and parcel of the political identity of the Republic find expression at the end of the twentieth century?

Nationalism and the Indonesian state

Indonesia in its archipelagic extent is best understood as a new state. It is not an example of a reversion to a sovereignty and to a political identity that had ante-dated colonial dominion. Historical empires may be readily located within the geographic ambit of the modern Republic but Indonesia is without historical antecedence within its contemporary bounds. Moreover, Indonesian nationalism developed not only in a characteristically negative reaction to colonial rule but also in a positive reaction to the territorial bounds of the colonial state which were assimilated wholesale into the nationalist claim. Some consideration was given in mid-1945, at the end of the Japanese occupation, to extending the claim to statehood beyond the Dutch domain into those of other colonial powers. Such a consideration was never pursued seriously at the time; nor has that aspiration been incorporated into an irredentist rationale, except opportunistically in justifying the integration of East Timor as the twenty-seventh province of the Republic in July 1976.

Indonesia, as identified as a new state, does not fit readily within Professor Anthony Smith's favoured model of nationalist provenance. Its identity is not rooted in a dominant ethnicity, even though the culturally distinctive Javanese comprise some 60 per cent of a national population of approximately 210 million. For one thing, the majority Javanese do not have an exclusive title to the island of Java but share it with the ethnically distinct Sudanese who are numerically prevalent in its western part. More importantly, the secular nationalist leadership that led the struggle for independence from the late 1920s conspicuously repudiated ethnicity as the source of national identity because of the considerable cultural diversity encompassed within Dutch colonial bounds. The nationalist leadership comprised modern men who had benefited from the limited educational opportunities provided by the colonial state. Their shared identity was based on a reaction to the racial barriers imposed by the colonial order and not on a sense of being part of a distinct ethnic community. They were concerned, above all, to avoid alienating any significant ethnic group within the archipelago. That would have been the case had the Javanese sought to base the state on their particular identity. The imperative of cultural diversity and religious tolerance was at the centre of five principles known as *Panca Sila* articulated by President Sukarno in June 1945 and subsequently adopted as the philosophy of the Indonesian state.

Civic and not ethnic nationalism was articulated as the basis of the claim to succeed the Dutch. At a historic nationalist Unity Congress in 1928, agreement was reached on establishing Malay, and not Javanese, as the *lingua franca* of the state in the making. Malay was the language most prevalent in Sumatra, and across the Strait of Malacca in British Malaya. It was also the language of archipelagic trade and had the advantage of being able to serve as a common tongue without registering the dominance of the majority Javanese. Repudiation of ethnic nationalism became a matter of practical politics given the cultural diversity encompassed by the Dutch colonial state. An attendant repudiation of a national identity defined in religious Islamic terms was at the core of *Panca Sila* which, above all, enjoined all Indonesians to worship a single deity but then permitted a free choice among such deities. Although *Panca Sila* was debased by its political abuse during the Suharto era, it registers the ideal notion of a civic nationalism.

It should also be noted that ethnic nationalism was conspicuously repudiated in successful pursuit of the irredentist claim to the western half of the island of New Guinea. That repudiation was given strength by the attempt by the Dutch during the struggle for independence to exploit ethnic differences in a move through a federal arrangement to cut the revolutionary Republic down to size. It found political expression early on after independence in August 1950 in the speedy dismantling of the initially-established federal Republic of the United States of Indonesia and its replacement by a unitary Republic.

Alternative dimensions of nationalism

Indonesian nationalism realised its statist aims through a combination of armed and diplomatic struggle. The period of national revolution between 1945 and 1949 was very much a defining experience in establishing the bases of political identity and legitimacy which has been relevant to foreign policy; for example, in judgements about the right of other states to exist from Malaysia to Kuwait. Although Indonesia's political elite have shared a common view about the international standing of the Republic, the post-independence drive for recognition and respect has taken two alternative forms which may be described respectively as the romantic and the modern developmental.

The romantic expression, which has been indicated above, was directed externally against the post-imperial Dutch over the irredentist issue of West New Guinea and against the British over Malaysia. Indeed, it was during the former episode that Indonesia declared its 'archipelagic principle' whereby all waters within straight base-lines connecting the outermost points of its outermost islands were deemed to fall within the exclusive sovereign jurisdiction of the Republic. At the time, in December 1957, it was a seemingly romantic revolutionary attempt to revise international maritime law that did not bear any relationship to Indonesia's competence to exercise such jurisdiction. It was intended to register the organic unity of the land and water of the distended archipelago known in the national language as *tanah ayer*.

Residual colonialism was the adversary in the case of West New Guinea, while neo-colonialism was identified as the adversary in the objection to the legitimacy of Malaysia, albeit made without a formal territorial claim in northern Borneo or indeed to East Timor. The challenges to the Dutch presence in West New Guinea and to the Malaysian project were represented within Indonesia as 'Confrontation', which took the form of acts of coercive diplomacy short of war. The repudiation of an alleged colonially-inspired redrawing of national boundaries within Indonesia's close environment led to a challenge to the status of the United Nations when exception was taken to Malaysia's election to a non-permanent seat on the Security Council. Apart from withdrawing from the United Nations in January 1965 in response to 'another absurd colonial manoeuvre', Indonesia set out, with Chinese support, to promote an alternative global institution based on a radical alignment of so-called 'New Emerging Forces'. China's Premier, Zhou Enlai, endorsed President Sukarno's proposal for a Conference of the New

Emerging Forces which, he suggested, could even become 'another United Nations, a revolutionary one which may be set up so that rival dramas may be staged with that body which calls itself the United Nations'. Needless to say, such a vainglorious enterprise was never realised. Indonesia returned contrite to the United Nations in September 1966 by which time President Sukarno was being eased from office.

The romantic form of nationalism identified with the person of the late President Sukarno and defined with reference to external adversaries was addressed, above all, to a domestic audience in a competitive political context. Nationalist claims were pursued in the case of West New Guinea but the prime functions of nationalist expression were domestic. They were employed not only to enable Sukarno to capture and sustain control of the Republic's political commanding heights but also to counter the disintegrative effect of centrifugal social forces based on ethnic sub-nationalism and military warlordism. In the event, Sukarno's nationalism proved to be self-indulgent and self-defeating as the economy deteriorated to a point of virtual stagnation and bankruptcy. That economic circumstance provided the context for regime change precipitated by internal political upheaval.

The distinctive romanticism registered by Sukarno was repudiated by his political successor, Suharto. He was no less a nationalist which he demonstrated in 1969 by his ruthless management of the determination of opinion in West New Guinea undertaken to satisfy the United Nations that Indonesia's territorial claim was supported by the local population. It had become evident, however, that Sukarno's romantic nationalism had not brought international respect but only derision in the West and foreboding within regional locale. In seeking an alternative expression of nationalist accomplishment, Suharto judged that without economic development Indonesia would count for very little. To that extent, his priorities corresponded with those of the country's first vice-president, Mohamad Hatta, who had argued unsuccessfully against sustaining the spirit of revolution and instead for post-revolutionary reconstruction and development. Hatta had resigned office in July 1956 in a feeble act of protest against the direction of national priorities, while the competitive nature of Indonesian politics facilitated the employment of a romantic nationalist symbolism. It was only with a regime change that it became possible to change national priorities in a fundamental way.

The revision of nationalist priorities

The romantic phase of Indonesian nationalism was brought to a halt through the political outcome of an abortive coup in October 1965. From March 1966, when Sukarno was disempowered by a military intervention in politics, national priorities were revised and radically expressed in political economy and foreign policy. National tradition was in no way repudiated but the goal of a strong and internationally well-respected Indonesia was pursued through engagement with the international capitalist economy on World Bank and International Monetary Fund terms. The new dependent pattern of foreign economic relations was justified and suffered in the interest of realising a national sense of entitlement through economic accomplishment.

In the more conventional area of foreign policy, Indonesia gave up its combative stance. By contrast, its government adopted an almost unique practice of political self-abnegation in its participation in regional co-operation. Within the ASEAN, Indonesia engaged in a pragmatic attempt to build confidence and trust with close neighbours and development partners in mind and also in an attempt to promote a political coalition against a perceived menacing China. Indeed, its measure of political self-abnegation proved frustrating to the country's foreign policy elite. On the fortieth anniversary of a seminal statement on Indonesia's ideal 'independent and active foreign policy' by former vice-president Mohamad Hatta in September 1948, a commemorative meeting was convened in Yogyakarta at which a call was made for the government to be more assertive in its conduct of foreign relations.

In Indonesia's case from the late 1960s, an assertive nationalism defined with reference to hostile external forces and internal political competition was given up, with one initial exception. The official explanation of the abortive coup of 1965 had identified Indonesia's Communist Party as culpable with support from the People's Republic of China. In October 1967, Indonesia suspended diplomatic relations with China which were not restored until August 1990. At issue was the interest of the military-based government in justifying its tenure and its policy of depoliticisation on the grounds that it had saved the country from a foreign-inspired plot. With substantial economic development and also the end of the Cold War, it no longer became necessary or practical to keep China at diplomatic arm's length. Moreover, it was then judged that such a diplomatic distance had to be reduced in order for Indonesia to play a more effective role in trying to resolve the Cambodian conflict and to realising its ambition of leading the Non-Aligned Movement. The pursuit of such priorities was not the same as lusting after nationalist goals in the Sukarno style.

The pursuit of nationalist interests

From its advent, the Suharto government sought to locate itself within a tradition of foreign policy that had been inaugurated during national revolution. To that end, it reaffirmed its commitment to an 'independent and active' foreign policy from which the Sukarno regime was alleged to have deviated. In practice, however, Indonesia conducted itself as part of the Western alignment of states, despite its founding membership of the Non-Aligned Movement that it eventually came to lead between 1992–1995.

Despite a determination to differentiate itself from the style and international alignments of its ill-fated predecessor, the Suharto government was consistent in its pursuit of Indonesia's interests and in the process demonstrated a notable continuity in foreign policy. For example, in 1967, its representatives were instrumental in shaping the declaratory terms of reference of ASEAN's founding document which registered national priorities for managing regional order on an exclusive resident-state regional basis which were consistent between the tenure of Sukarno and Suharto. A corresponding influence was exercised in 1971 in promoting and securing an alternative formula of a 'Zone of Peace, Freedom and Neutrality' to Malaysia's earlier proposal for neutralising South-East Asia through the vehicle of great power guarantees. At issue was the prerogative managerial role of regional states which Indonesia, as the largest among them, wished to assert to the exclusion of external powers. To that extent, Indonesia exercised a diplomatic centrality within ASEAN, albeit at a declaratory level which was not translated into practical operational expression.

In foreign policy, it is possible to identify a range of assertive Indonesian initiatives but without any accompanying nationalist rhetoric. For example, as indicated above, President Suharto did not have any qualms about the minimalist way in which his government fulfilled Indonesia's undertaking to the United Nations to permit an act of self-determination in Irian Jaya (West New Guinea) in order to secure international endorsement of the territorial transfer. Suharto persisted also in promoting recognition of the expansion of the Republic's maritime bounds that had been asserted initially during the Sukarno era. To that end, archipelagic status was sought and realised within the Third United Nations Conference of the Sea to find an acknowledged place within the Law of the Sea Convention that was concluded in 1982 and which came into force in 1994. Defence of archipelagic waters has remained a continuing national priority within the International Maritime Organisation (IMO) as Indonesia has sought to limit the number of archipelagic sea-lanes which it is obliged to establish under the UN Law of the Sea Convention.

Indonesia's brutal annexation of the eastern half of the island of Timor in December 1975 should be understood, without any implied justification, in terms of a strategic imperative determined by an archipelagic perspective. To that extent, it is possible to explain Indonesia's seizure of the former Portuguese possession as an act of strategic denial in a regional context marked by the success of revolutionary communism in Indochina earlier in 1975. The driving motivation was a determination to prevent an unacceptable ideological independence movement with menacing external affiliations from establishing an adjacent East Timor as a separate entity within the Republic's archipelagic ambit. Annexation was not the realisation of a declared irredentist nationalist objective but an attempt to secure the perimeter of the state from external subversion.

The issue of East Timor became a matter of acute international embarrassment for Indonesia whose human rights record within the territory has been widely condemned. Its annexation and then incorporation into the Republic was never recognised by the United Nations. From the viewpoint of Suharto's government, however, the matter of sovereignty in the face of local resistance and external condemnation became non-negotiable for a nationalist reason. Any tolerance of separatism in East Timor was deemed to be subversive of the integrity of the state that faced other separatist challenges in Irian Jaya and in Aceh, for example. Such objection to self-determination in the case of East Timor during the Suharto era was never made the subject of nationalist agitation, however. East Timor was non-negotiable also because it touched the personal pride of President Suharto who had authorised the annexation and who had conducted the ceremony of integration into the Republic.

One notable aspect of Indonesia's incorporation of East Timor in July 1976 was the rationale employed in its justification. President Suharto invented an ethnic nationalism in support of its incorporation into the Republic in direct contradiction to the civic version employed in claiming independence and additionally the western half of the island of New Guinea. Indeed, in order to assert its irredentist claim to that part of the Dutch colonial domain that was inhabited by Melanesian peoples, it had been imperative to reiterate that the Republic of Indonesia would comprise only the territorial extent of the former Netherlands East Indies and nothing more. At the ceremony in July 1976 inaugurating East Timor's incorporation, President Suharto pointed out, however: 'We do not regard you as newly arrived guests. We look upon you as our blood brothers who have returned to our midst in the midst of the big family of the Indonesian nation.' Here is an example of President Suharto paying deference to an ethno-symbolism of the kind identified by Professor Anthony Smith. Although subversive, in principle, it was not undertaken consciously at the expense of the national motto *Bhinneka Tunggal Ika* ('Unity in Diversity') which expresses the civic nationalism that served as the basis of the original claim to statehood.

Indonesia's proprietorial attitude towards East Timor under Suharto led also to a measure of deviation from a general policy of good neighbourliness pursued since the end of 'Confrontation' in the mid-1960s. For example, pressure was brought to bear on the Philippines and Malaysia when NGOs within those regional partners sought to organise meetings on East Timor with Indonesia placed in the role of political defendant. A nationalist strain was displayed at times also towards Western governments, especially in response to criticisms of the Republic's shortcomings over human rights. In March 1992, for example, an initiative was taken to disband the Inter-Governmental Group on Indonesia (IGGI) which had been set up in February 1967 in the Netherlands as an international aid consortium. That initiative was a nationalist reaction to a Dutch attempt to link aid flows to respect for human rights in East Timor where a massacre of young Timorese protesters had occurred in November 1991.

The aid consortium was then reconstituted in Paris in July 1992 as the Consultative Group on Indonesia (CGI) under the aegis of the World Bank and without Dutch participation. Indonesia's measure of latitude in the matter was an indication of the positive transformation in its economic circumstances over a quarter of a century. Such latitude was displayed also in the repudiation early in 1997 of an agreement reached with the United States to accept F16 aircraft on favourable terms intended originally for Pakistan because of US Congressional attention to human rights violations. Some nationalist sentiment was generated again in early 1998 when Michel Camdessus, the Managing Director of the International Monetary Fund (IMF), stood over President Suharto with arms folded in seemingly condescending mode as he signed a conditional agreement on financial assistance. By that juncture, however, President Suharto had become so discredited politically that any nationalist reaction was short-lived. He had become discredited because of national economic failure attributed to the corrupt nature of his administration. In the circumstances, the political will was lacking to confront the IMF in the same way that the IGGI had been six years previously.

By contrast with its predecessor, the interim-government of President Habibie showed itself willing to make an exception over East Timor. Initially, it offered a special autonomous status to the province, albeit short of independence, which led to a diplomatic accommodation with Portugal, the former colonial power which had long resisted Indonesia's annexation. In a surprising development in early 1999, he indicated a willingness to contemplate East Timor's reversion to Portuguese *cum* United Nations administration in a face-saving first step to independence. That concession reflected an unwillingness to continue to bear the material and diplomatic costs of holding the territory against the will of virtually all of its population. As indicated above, East Timor has never enjoyed a full nationalist resonance. For example, the status of the province was not an issue in parliamentary elections in June 1999 which were the most free and fair for over forty-four years. Indeed, those elections were notable for the absence of any serious nationalist issues among the forty-eight parties participating, despite some carping at the role of the IMF. Even more important, the session of the People's Consultative Assembly (MPR) that convened in the following October became totally absorbed in the first ever competitive election of an Indonesian president and vice-president as were supporters of alternative candidates camped outside the MPR building. East Timor's independence was accepted without a vote.

In the main, Indonesia's strident tradition of nationalism has been expressed externally in the post-Sukarno era primarily with reference to an apprehension of a rising China and internally with primary reference to the economic role of the local ethnic-Chinese community. That apprehension has a basis in historical memory of the pre-colonial era, the role of the ethnic-Chinese in dominating the country's economic life and in Beijing's alleged involvement in the abortive coup in October 1965. It has more recently been augmented through a sense of post-Cold War regional rivalry which has an economic and also a geopolitical dimension with China's maritime claims in the South China Sea intruding into the archipelagic waters of the Natuna Islands inherited by Indonesia from the Dutch. That apprehension found expression in a security agreement with Australia in December 1995 which, in principle, violated the non-aligned premise of Indonesia's foreign policy. That agreement became a casualty of Indonesian–Australian tensions over East Timor and was suspended by the government in Jakarta in September 1999. It is significant, however, that President Habibie did not seek to react politically to Beijing's limited diplomatic interventions after May 1998 on behalf of persecuted Indonesian Chinese. Any attempt to stir up anti-Chinese nationalist feeling would almost certainly have aggravated domestic disorder and impeded the Republic's economic recovery. The political downfall of President Suharto has not radically changed national economic priorities. None the less, a nationalist mood has revived in Indonesia in reaction to the interventionist role of the IMF as well as of attempts by foreign companies to hold Indonesia to over-priced commercial agreements negotiated with the minions of the Suharto regime. And despite the lack of popular interest in East Timor, a corresponding resentment has arisen of the way in which Indonesia has been traduced internationally over its handling of the territory. That mood has yet to be tapped or channelled to any effect by competing political forces.

Whither Indonesian nationalism?

Indonesia acquired statehood as an exemplar of civic nationalism and also as an exponent of revolutionary struggle as the most appropriate mode through which to define and express national identity against an obdurate colonial power. The late President Sukarno expropriated the rhetoric and symbols of a revolutionary nationalism in his own political interests. The effect was to extend the phase of nationalist struggle over two decades past the proclamation of independence. With the succession of President Suharto, Indonesian nationalism was deliberately made mute in its public expression and lost its exhibitionist quality in the interest of a radically revised political economy. Indeed, since then, nationalism, as a centrifugal activity within the archipelago, has been more of challenge to Indonesia than Indonesian nationalism has been to either regional or international order, despite the frustrated sense of regional entitlement held in Jakarta. The extent to which Indonesia under Suharto was willing to accommodate to economic dependence, instead of repudiating it Sukarno-like in his well-known statement 'to hell with your aid', was demonstrated in the way in which national pride was not allowed to get in the way of economic priorities. That pragmatic outlook was not revised by the interim administration of President Habibie.

Indeed, that administration found itself in a corresponding position of dependence to that experienced by former President Suharto in 1966, albeit in a very different strategic environment. It is one in which the West had lost its fear of a communist take-over and therefore could be uninhibited over applying economic pressure on Jakarta over self-determination in East Timor.

In recapitulation, Indonesian nationalism in challenging Dutch rule consciously repudiated an ethnic rationale defining itself exclusively with reference to the colonial territorial legacy. Post-independence, the nationalist ideal was sustained in a romantic irredentist phase whose rationale was to complete the revolution in its territorial extent as well as to keep alive its original spirit. An underlying motivation for employing revolutionary symbols and imagery was to serve a domestic function in a competitive political context in Sukarno's particular interest.

From the mid-1960s, however, Indonesian nationalism assumed a muted quality for reasons of political economy and regional co-operative security. None the less, the government of President Suharto was protective of national interests. That protectivism was displayed in the cases of Irian Jaya, Indonesia's archipelagic status and East Timor as well as in assuming the chair of the Non-Aligned Movement. It was displayed also in the view that Indonesia was entitled to a permanent seat on the United Nations Security Council.

The last truly robust expression of Indonesian nationalism occurred, however, during the early to mid-1960s driven by the competitive condition of domestic politics. Indonesia has now reached the end of a political era during which a quasi-monarchical ruler placed the highest premium on political demobilisation and stability and in which the only political competition was among courtiers. In the event, the provisional transfer of power in May 1998, that was accompanied and precipitated by violence, was relatively orderly compared to the bloody circumstances of 1965–1966 that had preceded President Sukarno's political downfall. President Habibie, as incumbent vice-president, succeeded to high office virtually by default, partly because it suited the armed forces leadership to make a constitutional virtue out of a political necessity in the interest of public order. Moreover, there was a notable absence of any exhibition of nationalist symbolism either among the beneficiaries of the transfer of power or among advocates of political reform.

That said, the exit of President Suharto raised popular expectations of political reform that is certain to mean greater political competition among Indonesia's cultural diversity, which includes an important Islamic dimension. Indeed, forty-eight political parties took part in the parliamentary elections in June 1999, although only five made a significant showing. Politics in Indonesia has become a much more open activity and political leadership will face demands for greater accountability from a legislature with genuine legitimacy. That development was demonstrated in the rejection of President Habibie's account of his stewardship by the MPR and his consequent decision to withdraw from the presidential contest, then won by Abdurrahman Wahid in October 1999. It is in such circumstances that a more strident nationalism could enter the political arena should opportunistic forces seek to exploit its mobilising potential. Indonesia's regional context is very different now, however, to that during the Sukarno era. There are no colonial presences to interpose in regional relationships, while those relationships have become encompassed within institutionalised structures of dialogue and co-operation, albeit weakened by economic adversity. And Indonesia after having been afflicted by an acute economic adversity has not recovered sufficiently to strike nationalist postures of the kind that enabled it to replace the IGGI with the CGI in 1992.

Indonesian nationalism persists as a political tradition and has revived to a degree with the political downfall of President Suharto. But it has become far more difficult to define and express with reference to an external other that provided its original source. Australia, with a population the tenth of Indonesia's, may seem a politically pretentious and irritating neighbour over East Timor but it has yet to inspire a unified nationalist passion, probably because it is difficult to regard as a serious threat. Moreover, the circumstances of the political downfall of President Suharto obliged his interim successor to concentrate on domestic economic priorities: a responsibility assumed also by President Abdurrahman Wahid. In such an exercise, which requires external, including IMF and World Bank support, any attempt at a romantic nationalist revival would be self-defeating for those in power in a more accountable political context. The circumstances of the political downfall of President Suharto and the dramatic events in East Timor would suggest that the nationalist card has not been played with any effect, and certainly not in the interest of managing a competitive domestic politics.

Fifty years after international acknowledgement of its independence, Indonesia's nationalism is most likely to be expressed through attempts to reassert a regional diplomatic role. Such a leading role was diminished by the impact of economic adversity and political turmoil. To reclaim such a role, Indonesia would need to demonstrate substantive evidence of economic recovery, which requires an inter-dependence with the global economy and its institutions. That conditional requirement places an obligation on Indonesia's new political leadership to conceive of the Republic's role in a similar way to that understood by former President Suharto. In August 1969, as indicated above, he had declared that: 'We shall only be able to play an effective role if we ourselves are possessed of a great national vitality'. Some three decades later, President Abdurrahman Wahid is confronted with the same challenge which also requires sublimating a romantic nationalist tradition.

Select bibliography

Anderson, Benedict R. (1972) *Java in a Time of Revolution*, Ithaca and London: Cornell University Press.

Cotton, James (ed.) (1999) *East Timor and Australia*, Canberra: Australian Defence Studies Centre.

Crouch, Harold (1978) *The Army and Politics in Indonesia*, Ithaca: Cornell University Press.

Dunn, James (1996) *Timor: A People Betrayed*, Frenchs Forest, New South Wales: ABC Books.

Feith, Herbert (1962) *The Decline of Constitutional Democracy in Indonesia*, Ithaca: Cornell University Press.

Feith, Herbert and Castles, Lance (eds) (1970) *Indonesian Political Thinking, 1945 1965*, Ithaca and London: Cornell University Press.

Frederick, William H. (1989) *Visions and Heat: The Making of the Indonesian Revolution*, Athens: Ohio University Press.

Jenkins, David (1984) *Suharto and His Generals*, Ithaca: Cornell Modern Indonesia Project.

Kahin, George McTurnan (1952) *Nationalism and Revolution in Indonesia*, Ithaca: Cornell University Press.

Legge, J. D. (1972) *Sukarno: A Political Biography*, London: Allen Lane.

Leifer, Michael (1978) *Malacca, Singapore and Indonesia*, volume 2. International Straits of the World, Alphen aan der Rijn: Sijthoff and Noordhoff.

—— (1983) *Indonesia's Foreign Policy*, London, Boston and Sydney: George Allen and Unwin.

McDonald Hamish (1980) *Suharto's Indonesia*, Blackburn, Victoria: Fontana/Collins.

Mackie, J. A. C. (1974) *Konfrontasi. The Indonesia-Malaysia Dispute, 1963–1966*, Kuala Lumpur: Oxford University Press.

—— (ed.) (1976) *The Chinese in Indonesia: Five Essays*, London: Nelson.

Palmier, Leslie (1962) *Indonesia and the Dutch*, London: Oxford University Press.

Polomka, Peter (1971) *Indonesia Since Sukarno*, Harmondsworth: Penguin Books.

Ramage, Douglas E. (1995) *Politics in Indonesia. Democracy, Islam and the Ideology of Tolerance*, London and New York: Routledge.

Reid, Anthony J. S. (1974) *Indonesian National Revolution, 1945–50*, Hawthorn, Australia: Longman.

Schwarz, Adam (1994) *A Nation in Waiting. Indonesia in the 1990s*, St. Leonards, Australia: Allen and Unwin.

Sukma, Rizal (1999) *Indonesia and China: The Politics of Troubled Relationship*, London and New York: Routledge.

Suryadinata, Leo (1996) *Indonesia's Foreign Policy Under Suharto*, Singapore: Times Academic Press.

Vatikiotis, Michael R. J. (1998) *Indonesian Politics under Suharto*, London and New York: Routledge.

Wehl, David (1948) *The Birth of Indonesia*, London: George Allen and Unwin.

Weinstein, Franklin B. (1976) *Indonesian Foreign Policy and the Dilemma of Dependence*, Ithaca and London: Cornell University Press.

9 Social capital and the imagined community

Democracy and nationalism in the Philippines

James Putzel

Introduction

In June 1998, the Philippines celebrated its 'centennial', but the anniversary was riddled with ambiguity as it marked the anniversary of both the declaration of the first independent republic in Asia and the colonisation of the islands by the United States. Since the stillborn birth of the first Philippine Republic in June 1898, the people of this repeatedly colonised archipelago have struggled to define what it means to be Filipino. With extreme ethnic and linguistic diversity, nationalism in the Philippines has been defined over time as an economic and political project, as is the case in many parts of the developing world where state units determined by colonial authority have little ethnic or linguistic coherence.

Philippine nationalism has been a hesitant nationalism and one that, by and large, has had little democratic content. The family and clan basis of economic ownership and politics has made the emergence of civicness particularly problematic. 'Social capital', which in Robert Putnam's thinking determines both democratic and economic prospects, has been confined largely to family networks.[1] A study of the Philippines suggests that there is nothing that intrinsically connects nationalism with democracy, and further, that there is much that is incompatible between these two great currents of modern politics.

Of course, if we were to accept Ernest Gellner's later propositions about nationalism as functional to industrial society it would put us on the terrain of many who see democracy as functional to capitalism.[2] The argument might then be that the Philippines needs simply to become more industrialised and more developed and in the process its national identity will be consolidated and democracy will be deepened simply to make capitalism work better. There is little in the Philippine story that inspires confidence in such functionalist explanations, however.

The 'imagined community' discussed by Benedict Anderson in his classic study of nationalism is imagined because people come together around a shared idea of a nation without necessarily possessing any personal connections.[3] Nationalism from this vantage point is more than an ethnic affinity and the connections that bind people are not personalist ones. Here there is a tension with a Putnamian notion of social capital that likewise transcends familial and ethnic boundaries but is premised on personal connections of an associational variety.

There is a version of nationalism that sees it as an historical political project wrapped up in ideas about liberty. Hobsbawm described early European nationalism in these terms.[4] However, much of the twentieth-century struggle for nationhood, for national independence, abandoned the idiom of liberty and the rights of man in favour of an economic project and political independence, often from colonial authorities themselves associated with democracy. While there was an echo of that enlightenment thinking in the movement leading up to the establishment of the first Republic in the Philippines, it never took hold, even in this early battle for national independence.

The problem with these theories of nationalism and democracy is that they curiously ignore the centrality of politics, political ideas and conscious political action, which in the end determine both the character of nationalism and the possibility of democracy. Gellner explicitly and purposefully ignores this in his attempt to show the functionalist character of nationalism to modernity. This is a convincing thesis, but one that cannot explain why nationalism sometimes incorporates a democratic vision while at other times it serves as the basis of authoritarianism and fascism.

The content of Philippine nationalism has never been particularly democratic. In fact, it is possible to argue that it has consistently eschewed democratic ideals. The nationalist project has been carried most forcefully by non democratic political currents of the right and the left. Nationalism has been defined in political terms merely as political independence. If anything, democracy, in the Philippines' particular historical experience, was associated with and tainted by US colonial rule. Nationalism has also been defined in economic terms in two economic nationalist projects: first, that of an elite deeply wrapped up in and marked by its origins in landed property; and second, that of a radical communist movement, which has been committed to peasant emancipation through an anti-democratic socialist project. In their uglier moments, economic nationalists have attempted to craft a Filipino identity in contradistinction to the Filipino-Chinese, attacking the community's entrepreneurs in an attempt to downplay the deep social divide between the wealthy and the poor among the mestizo population where no clear-cut dominant 'ethnie', in Anthony Smith's terms, has ever emerged.[5]

The 'Filipino identity' to the extent that one can employ such a label to any society as collective identity is constantly in the process of change and reinvention — has been deeply marked by its colonisers and the fact that independence finally came as a 'gift' from the Americans. The clearest unifying cultural characteristic of the population was the conversion of 85 per cent to Catholicism, but this too symbolised to some extent the legacy of colonialism. The Catholic character of the state has also prevented the full integration of Muslim communities in the south who have imagined a community in Islamic terms. Substantial numbers of Muslim people inhabiting territories that long resisted colonial authority are still determined to give this imagined community expression in an independent state in what is a hopeless cause given that they have become a minority in their own homelands with successive waves of government-sponsored Christian migration over the years.

With these ideas in mind, this chapter attempts to interpret the relationship between nationalism and democracy in the Philippines, focusing on six particular historic moments. In the last section, I offer a reflection on the possibility of marrying the democratic and nationalist impulses at the dawn of what some Filipinos have claimed will be a century of full national maturity and industrialisation.

Asia's first republic and first national liberation war

The independence movement that emerged in the late nineteenth century and the short-lived first republic were dominated by elite nationalism that ultimately had little democratic content. The fight to achieve independence brought together peasant aspirations under the authority of an elite economic nationalist project. This movement was ruthlessly suppressed by the United States in one of its first colonial adventures beyond the North American continent. More than 300 years of Spanish colonial rule over the archipelago bequeathed a system of patron-clientelism that formed the bedrock of the later social structure under US colonial authority.

The Philippines was among the earliest colonial outposts of Western Europe in South-East Asia. Colonisation began in the sixteenth century as a joint enterprise between the Spanish Crown and the Catholic friar orders (the Augustinians, Franciscans, Jesuits, Recollects and Dominicans). Spain treated the colony as an entrepôt in trade between the Far East and possessions in Central America, while Chinese merchants moved through the ports and into the interior to establish networks of production and trade. It was the British from their first occupation of Manila between 1762 and 1764, who became the main commercial force bringing the archipelago into the world economy as an exporter of agricultural commodities in the nineteenth century. Often, the most direct colonial masters in contact with ordinary people were the members of the friar orders whose proselytising mission was bolstered by the organisation of vast landed estates. The Spanish authorities incorporated traditional village leaders into their system of local rule. Forced labour and land-grabbing sparked successive, though usually localised, peasant rebellions. Over time an emergent Chinese-mestizo and

Spanish-mestizo elite, whose accumulation of wealth and land was frustrated by Spanish authorities and the friar orders, began to challenge colonial rule.

The earliest critics of Spanish rule emerged from amongst the educated mestizo – the *ilustrados* – at the beginning of the nineteenth century. Luis Rodriguez Varela, who was educated in France, published a series of books inspired by the Enlightenment and the French revolution. He called for the opening of free schools for the poor and local colleges of pharmacy, mathematics and navigation. Foreshadowing later economic nationalism, he demanded a limitation of Chinese economic activity and formed a society to promote indigenous economic interests.[6] By the late 1870s the first identifiably nationalist movement emerged advocating equality with, rather than independence from, the colonisers in the form of the Propaganda Movement.

The most famous of this tradition was José Rizal, whose political essays and satirical fiction written in the late 1880s and early 1890s inspired a generation.[7] Rizal attacked the autocracy of colonial rule and called for far-reaching reforms to avoid the outbreak of 'bloody revolution'. He argued for a free press and representation of the colony in the Spanish Cortes, linking civil liberties to a quest for economic improvement in the archipelago.[8] He founded the *Liga Filipina*, a semi-clandestine association made up of mainly professionals, small businessmen and landowners and commercially-oriented tenant farmers. Its aims as stated in its constitution included uniting the 'whole archipelago into one compact body' and the 'encouragement of education, agriculture and commerce'.[9] The Liga also was committed to establishing manufacturing and the modernisation of agriculture and actually attempted to raise credit for its members to pursue these goals.[10]

Rizal remained committed to a path of peaceful reform, even as his followers took up open rebellion against Spain in August 1896 and he awaited execution as its chief instigator. Andres Bonifacio, a Manila-based warehouse clerk or manager and a founding member of Rizal's Liga, formed the secret society of the Katipunan which sparked the aborted armed revolution.[11] The leadership of the Katipunan was consolidated more around the ideas of Freemasonry and a critique of the friar dominance of economic and political life, than a deep commitment to the *Rights of Man*. 'Liberty, equality and fraternity' was the slogan of the movement, but the guiding philosophy was a simple promotion of duties of 'a good life' akin to the Protestant ethic.[12] Before the revolution had been defeated, Bonifacio was executed by rivals within the movement and General Emilio Aguinaldo emerged from the Cavite provincial elite as the undisputed leader of a republican government that replaced the Katipunan. Defeated on the battlefield, Aguinaldo and other elite nationalist leaders were exiled to Hong Kong in December 1897.

It was the Spanish–American War that revived hopes for the revolution, when in May 1898 the Americans defeated the Spanish in Manila Bay and assisted the return of Aguinaldo and other exiled leaders to the archipelago. It was also this turn of events which brought more of the *ilustrado* elite behind the revolutionary cause. While the peasantry was mobilised as the fighting force of the revolution, their participation was as much motivated by duties to elite patrons who had joined the fray as it was by a sense that they were fighting for *kalayaan*, or 'freedom' – but not necessarily in nationalist terms.[13] Much of the elite courted by Aguinaldo remained convinced that the Philippines was not ready for self-government when the General and his followers declared an independent republic on 12 June 1898. The Malolos Constitution established the basis for a republican, but by no means democratic, government and one firmly under the authority of *ilustrado* men of privilege. Apolnario Mabini, who headed Aguinaldo's Cabinet as it faced war with the Americans, and who attempted to steer the government in a more democratic direction, to foster local democracy and taxation of wealth, was eventually marginalised.[14]

In February 1899, the US unleashed one of the bloodiest wars in the modern history of colonial empire building. It applied the techniques of battle perfected in its genocidal warfare against the indigenous people of North America to quash the new republic, which it refused to recognise.[15] Ignoring critics at home who formed an anti-imperialist movement, whose most prominent spokesman against American expansionism was the popular essayist and novelist Mark Twain, American troops were given wide authority to 'pacify' the rebellious Filipinos. The brutality of the conquest was illustrated by one of its most extreme protagonists, General Jacob Smith, who, when launching a campaign to bring the island of Samar under US authority in 1901, told his troops to turn it into a 'howling wilderness', saying 'Kill and burn, kill and burn, the more you kill and the more you burn the more you please me'.[16]

The motives of the US in colonisation were not unlike those that had originally led Spain to the islands – the Philippines was seen as an important base in the Asia Pacific for both geopolitical and commercial reasons. Once the revolution was defeated, the US courted the *ilustrado* elite in what became a colonial partnership.

Colonial rule, patronage and hesitant nationalism

The colonial state was built on an alliance between the US and an emergent land-owning oligarchy bred of the *ilustrado* elite. Ensuring the US a base in Asia and its corporate interests free access within the colonial territory, the Filipino oligarchy was given considerable political authority and opportunities for self-enrichment. The US colonial period saw the establishment of democratic institutions on a social foundation of patron–client relations and the dominance of a compromised nationalism among an elite whose interests were wedded closely to those of the coloniser.

The particular configuration of US colonial authority shaped the contours assumed by democracy and nationalism long after independence. Formal democratic organisations and institutions were established which mimicked those of the United States while power remained in the hands of an oligarchic elite, whose wealth originated in landownership, allied to powerful local *caciques* or 'political bosses'.[17] A Commonwealth Constitution adopted in 1935 laid out the framework of a unitary state where the executive power of the presidency was separated from the legislative power of a two-chamber Congress and an independent judiciary. Virtual universal adult suffrage was achieved by 1937 and regular elections were held for political offices at all levels of the government.

However, this formal democracy lacked the civic base that is central to the development of democracy. From 1916 until the Japanese invasion in 1942, political contests took place within the framework of a single organisation, the Nacionalistas. This was less a political party than a collection of clan alliances with competition maintained within one organisation due to its formal commitment to the cause of independence. Networks of patronage emanated from a relatively small number of powerful families that, together with often 'self-made' local strong men, dominated both the political and the economic spheres. The networks and shared norms spun from this system represented a kind of 'social capital', in James Coleman's terms, as they bestowed on power brokers advantages in the competition for wealth and political power.[18] While this type of social capital represented a real resource for powerful families and bosses, it served as a barrier to the deepening of democratic practice in society.

By the early 1930s, the economy that emerged under US tutelage was marked by sharp inequalities and increasing landlessness and rural impoverishment. Radical movements, including the Partido Komunista ng Pilipinas (PKP), emerged advocating social change often laced with the language of nationalism. The elite reacted with a weak social reformism – a poor imitation of Roosevelt's social-democratic measures in the US – and a nationalist veneer to undermine radical action.[19] Manuel Quezon, the most powerful indigenous politician in the islands, along with other prominent members of the Nacionalistas had long promoted a duplicitous nationalism. They openly called for independence from the US while secretly negotiating to delay independence for as long as possible.[20] Eventually, the Tydings-McDuffie Act of 1934 and the Commonwealth Constitution of 1935 were the formal institutional outcome of this, promising independence by 1945.

In the face of oligarchic power and the association of democracy with colonial rule, the nationalist project, like that challenging social inequity, came to be dominated by the Communist movement whose commitment to the democratic system was largely tactical. In the second half of the 1930s Communists and Socialists merged and extended critical support to Quezon's social reform programme in response to the Comintern's call for united front movements against fascism.[21]

A more conservative nationalism remained alive in the colony and was tapped by the Japanese after they invaded the islands between December 1941 and January 1942. A 'quisling nationalism' emerged in response to Japan's appeal to elite nationalists. While the leading members of the Commonwealth government, Manuel Quezon and Sergio Osmeña, fled the islands with General Douglas MacArthur, much of the leadership remained behind. With only a few exceptions the officials of the Commonwealth government collaborated with the Japanese occupation forces and presided over the declaration of an 'independent' Philippine Republic under Japanese tutelage. In the mid-1930s, Pio Duran had been an outspoken critic of Filipino subservience to colonial masters advocating the idea that the Philippines should put its faith in Asia and the Japanese.[22] This had been an undercurrent in Philippine nationalism since its defeat by the US, with figures like General Artemio Ricarte, who never accepted US rule and lived in exile in Yokohama until he returned with the Japanese invasion forces in December 1941.[23] Notable Filipino nationalists, like José Laurel who served as president during the war, demonstrated a deep ambivalence towards democracy.

Resistance to the Japanese persisted throughout the occupation – in a rather lacklustre fashion from fighters under the command of US intelligence and a much more vigorous movement linked to the PKP. The Party encouraged the formation of the People's Anti-Japanese Army, the Hukbalahap, which mounted a consistent resistance to the Japanese throughout the war.[24] This movement threatened to bring together those two historic impulses of peasant emancipation and national independence that characterised much of Asia in the first half of the twentieth century. The success of communism elsewhere in Asia was precisely in bringing together these two currents – nothing can better account for the victory of the Chinese revolution in 1949 or the long-fought victory of the Vietnamese. It was precisely because of experience elsewhere that the United States, upon its return to the islands at the end of the war, was intent on prising apart nationalist and peasant causes.

Maintaining the gulf between nationalism and the peasant movement

After MacArthur returned to the islands at the end of 1944 and the Japanese surrender, US forces began rounding up the Huks. Land reforms initiated by the resistance movement were revoked and the US set about supporting the reconstruction of a regime that would be amenable to its continued special relationship with the islands. With Quezon dead in exile, his vice-president, Sergio Osmeña became *de facto* president of a restored Commonwealth government. Apparently seeing Osmeña as too nationalistically inclined,

MacArthur backed Manuel Roxas as his choice for president in an election held on the eve of independence. The Nacionalistas split apart and the Liberal Party was established by Roxas who easily won the election. Independence was bestowed on the Philippines as a gift on 4 July 1946, a date designed to reinforce ties with the former colonial authority.

By the late 1940s, the new republic faced its first major internal political crisis. Dissatisfied by the post-war political settlement and the lack of social progress, the PKP found a receptive audience in the rural areas of Central Luzon, and relaunched guerrilla activities, this time against the Philippine state. With the state so closely tied to the US, once again a link between nationalist and peasant aspirations threatened to usher in a radical change. The government of President Elpidio Quirino was deeply indebted to the landowners and had unleashed a reign of terror in the countryside to put down peasant mobilisation, providing instead its greatest justification for expansion.[25]

The US responded to the threat with a two-pronged approach. First, concessions were made to economic nationalists. In what might seem today to be anachronistic, a mission sent by the International Monetary Fund (IMF) in 1950 concluded that the single biggest problem blocking the development of the economy was free trade.[26] The US allowed the imposition of import and foreign exchange controls, effectively endorsing an import-substitution policy. Of course, US companies established in the Philippines benefited from protection of the local market. These measures seemed enough to pacify malcontents among the business community.

The US also became actively involved in putting down the Huk uprising by fostering a reformist presidential candidate, Ramon Magsaysay, and sending in the notorious Colonel Edward Lansdale to take charge of physiological warfare against the armed guerrilla movement. An initial swing towards advocacy of a redistributive land reform was abandoned when the US and allies within the Philippine state were able to win victory over the communists without politically disruptive redistributive reforms.[27]

From this point on, elite economic nationalism assumed a deeply conservative character, particularly opposed to peasant demands for agrarian reform and always biased against agriculture in national development strategies. The 'Filipino First' policy promoted by President Carlos Garcia in the late 1950s was decidedly opposed to social reform. In seeking to bolster a 'class blind' nationalist idiom it resorted to an ethnic definition of the Filipino as 'not Chinese' and the latter were singled out as profiteers in both rhetoric and public policy.[28] While barriers to Chinese ownership in certain lines of business were only sporadically enforced and often used either as an instrument of extortion or to cajole investment in manufacturing, the net effect was to weaken a civil and civic definition of nationalism.

Authoritarian versions of nationalism: right and left

The wide gulf that separated the elite from the poor, of both the rural areas and the urban slums, and the Janus face of elite economic nationalism that under-pinned what was essentially a predatory state did much to weaken the legitimacy of the post-war democracy. Politics were characterised by competition between clan alliances with personalities easily switching from one party to the other simply to capture the spoils of the presidency in terms of access to patronage resources – the licenses and rents generated by import-substitution.

Ferdinand Marcos was elected to the presidency in 1965 on a platform of social reform. He succeeded in becoming the first president ever to be re-elected to a second term in 1969, but through a campaign that took the old adage of Philippine politics as a contest determined by 'guns, goons and gold' to new heights.[29] In the wake of this election the country saw a revival of peasant activism, the rise of a radical student movement (inspired in part by China and by the world-wide protest movement against US involvement in Vietnam). This proved to be a fruitful climate for a tiny new Communist Party of the Philippines (CPP), formed in 1968, to build up its cadre. Social activism also led to the re-emergence of nationalist sentiment among the elite that reached even into the Supreme Court, when, in 1972, it decided that all lands acquired by Americans since 1946 had been illegally acquired and would be subject to confiscation by 1974.[30]

It was these events that provided the backdrop for Marcos' declaration of martial law in September 1972. Marcos' motive clearly was to stay in power as he was prohibited by the constitution from running for another term in 1973. Nevertheless, his authoritarian move enjoyed considerable support from the business community and, as it turned out, from the United States.[31] During the consolidation of his 'New Society', Marcos spouted a spurious nationalist rhetoric. It was a kind of hybrid economic nationalism pursued in official rhetoric while being America's ally in a hostile Asia, especially as the Vietnam War went bad for the US.

The continued presence of the US bases and later the association of the US with the World Bank as a major source of external support for what became an increasingly corrupt regime, gave the anti-dictatorship struggle a particularly nationalist character. Dictatorship presented an opportunity for the weak CPP to expand its forces. However, while successfully seizing the nationalist mantle and the cause of the peasantry, its ideology prevented the party from developing a democratic philosophy despite its claim to promote 'national democracy'. 'United fronts' with elite opponents to Marcos paid lip-service to democracy, but the practice of communist linked cadres continually convinced potential elite allies that the radical movement had no commitment to democracy. Consistent democratic nationalists were figures like Senator José Diokno and Senator

Lorenzo Tanada, who desperately tried to forge unity between the increasing numbers of elite opponents to Marcos and the radical movement. However, they became exasperated with the Communists' failure to submit to basic democratic principles within the opposition.[32]

Marcos' declaration of martial law politicised the Philippine military, which until that time had largely remained on the periphery of politics. When the ageing dictator's regime began to crumble after 1983, the young colonels who opposed him attempted to craft an ideology in the idiom of nationalism. They turned to the work of Nilo Tayag, a former Secretary General of the CPP who defected to the government and elaborated an ideology of nationalism. This conservative nationalism inspired the ambitious military officers who after failing to defeat Marcos on their own, rallied behind the claims of Cory Aquino to have won a snap presidential election in February 1986.

During the last two years of the Marcos dictatorship a rising opposition to Marcos from within the elite began to articulate a programme for the restoration of democracy and liberalising economic reform. Because of the continued support of the Reagan-led White House for Marcos this movement increasingly assumed a nationalist rhetoric. Even Cory Aquino, whose slain husband had been a long-time friend of the US, came out openly against the maintenance of US bases on Philippine territory. For a short time, the pro-democracy movement took on a decidedly nationalist character.

People Power Revolution and the quest for national maturity

In February 1986, the now famous 'People Power Revolution' catapulted Corazon Aquino into power on the heels of a military revolt. The success of Aquino's subsequent restoration of democracy was couched in decidedly patriotic and nationalist terms. The courageous fashion in which the crowds stared down Marcos loyalists in the Armed Forces of the Philippines in a showdown on Epifanio de los Santos Avenue (EDSA) gave rise to a genuine national pride. To some extent this moment fulfilled the spirit of 1898 and a sense of national maturity emerged perhaps for the first time in Philippine history. But it was the nationalist character of the Aquino regime's early rhetoric combined with the new government's initially soft line on the Communist Party and its New People's Army that most disturbed conservatives in the White House and the US Congress.

In response, Aquino wasted little time and, as every president had done before her, she set about establishing her pro-American credentials. She bowed to the wishes of the US and made repeated concessions to rebellious officers in the AFP and assumed a more intransigent stance towards the communists. Most notable was Aquino's decision to reverse her position on the maintenance of the US bases in the country – perhaps the single most significant symbol of compromised nationhood.

Rather than ushering in a democratic revolution, Aquino presided over a restoration of the old pre-martial law order. Politics remained marked by a system of clan politics that was content to maintain a shallow democracy. A new constitution approved in 1987, while incorporating some limitations on executive power and some important social reforms, was largely based on the 1935 Commonwealth Constitution. However, the new constitution did reinforce restrictions on foreign ownership and foreign investment in certain strategic sectors.[33] Congressional elections held later that year saw the election of a House of Representatives largely peopled by veteran clan politicians or their relatives.[34] An historic opportunity squandered by Marcos was again squandered by Aquino when she turned her back on proposals for a far-reaching redistributive agrarian reform in deference to what in reality were weakened and emaciated landed interests.[35] Nevertheless, Aquino's democratic regime opened up a new space for the expansion of civil society.

Two developments during the Aquino presidency had important implications for nationalism and democracy in the country. First, in September 1991, against Aquino's expressed wishes, the Senate took an historic decision asking the US to remove its military bases from Philippine territory. Of course, upholding and executing this decision was made a great deal easier by the growing lobby in the US for drastic cuts in overseas bases, the changing strategic equation in Asia with the collapse of the Soviet Union, and the fact that one of the bases was utterly destroyed by the eruption of the Mount Pinatubo volcano. Nature (or God as most Filipinos would put it) intervened to complete the Filipino nationalist agenda. Nevertheless, the removal of the bases after the EDSA Revolution, did give the country a sense of full nationhood that it had never achieved before.

The second development was the rise of non-governmental organisations (NGOs) as a major actor on the local and national scene.[36] This represented the rapid expansion of an associational realm – a civil society – that had long been dominated by business associations and charitable organisations sponsored by the elite. Several factors contributed to this surge in NGO activity. First, accelerated non-armed political activity and expanded development work in response to economic hardship during the last four years of the decaying Marcos regime resulted in the emergence of a wide variety of NGOs throughout the archipelago. Second, mass defections from the CPP of an educated and socially committed cadre that had become disenchanted with communism provided NGOs with a seasoned leadership who had expansive social networks. Third, the availability of considerable sums of money from developed country governments, northern NGOs and international development agencies provided both a massive expansion in the funds available to local NGOs and an incentive to establish such organisations to tap into the bonanza.

Of course, it is easy to exaggerate the importance of NGOs, whose influence over national decision-making remains limited and whose own practice is riddled with problems of inefficiency and a lack of accountability.[37] Nevertheless, for the first time a major group of social reformers, appeared committed to constructing the types of networks and associations that can build up a civic-based social capital. The rapid rise of NGOs provided an opportunity for the development of a form of civic engagement less marked by the patron–client relations of the past and not confined to specific communities of business families like the Filipino-Chinese. The nationalism which NGO leaders inherited from the radical movement was imbibed with a democratic content – bringing to the fore the vision of reformers like the late Senators Diokno and Tanada whose aim had been the creation of a social movement that was both nationalist and democratic. The point to stress here is that it is through the promotion of political ideas and through specific political actors that nationalism can be rendered in democratic terms. While the appearance of NGOs did not mean that this would occur, it did open up possibilities where few existed before.

A general and a movie star attempt to redefine the nation

General Ramos' ascension to the presidency in 1992, marked both the stability of the new democratic order in the country, and the rehabilitation of many who had served the Marcos regime – a process that was fully completed with the election of Joseph Estrada in 1998. President Ramos attempted to craft a new economic project for the country, finally breaking from the influence of elite economic nationalism that had amounted to the protection of old family empires and stalled development.

Liberalisation of trade and privatisation of government assets were accelerated. Revenues thus obtained brought the budget into balance for the first time in years, but in deference to his elite supporters in Congress, Ramos backed away from taxation reform that could have established the basis for long-term fiscal strength. The former general's administration succeeded in modest economic growth and important reforms in the banking sector that left the country in a slightly better position than most of its neighbours to face the financial crisis which engulfed the region from July 1997.

Given his long association with the United States, being a West Point graduate and in close contact with the Pentagon during his many years of service in the AFP, Ramos was cautious about appearing too deferential to the Americans. He promoted a foreign policy that sought to strengthen the Philippines' ties with Asia – both Japan and neighbours in the Association of South East Asian Nations (ASEAN). This effort began during the Marcos presidency where it became increasingly clear that over the long term, the Philippines' developmental fate would be determined much more by its place within a rising Asian economy than by old links with its former coloniser. This shift is represented in material terms by the rising importance of Japanese investment, lending and foreign assistance in the country's economy.

At home the Ramos administration had a mixed impact on the shape and character of national identity. He consciously sought to paint his presidency as one committed to national unity and reconciliation. Blessed with the self-destruction of the communist movement, Ramos was able to devote his attention to first bringing back into the fold rebellious military officers who had staged several *coup d'état* attempts against his predecessor and then to reaching a peace agreement with armed Islamic separatist groups based on the southern island of Mindanao.

In September 1996 he reached a peace agreement with the Moro National Liberation Front (MNLF) whereby the organisation that had waged a 20-year battle with government troops would lay down its arms, its fighters would be integrated into the security forces and a Southern Philippines Council for Peace and Development would be created under the authority of MNLF Chairperson Nur Misuari. Misuari went on to become the governor of the Autonomous Region of Muslim Mindanao. Fulminations of the Christian settler population were not enough to scupper the agreement and the war-weary forces of Misuari were ready to lay down their arms. But it was not a full peace as the rival Moro Islamic Liberation Front (MILF) remained on the sidelines, waiting to recruit those who would be disaffected with Misuari if peace brought little economic improvement to the island. Nevertheless, Ramos succeeded in dampening the fire of Islamic nationalism though he was not able to extinguish it altogether.

A more disturbing trend emerged as the government sought to cushion effects of its reforms with a new nationalist rhetoric directed against Chinese-Filipinos. This was most evident in the speeches of Ramos' national security adviser, General José Almonte. Almonte equated 'crony capitalism' with Chinese-Filipino business, renewing fears in the community that once again they would become the target of government coercion.[38] In 1995, when the country suffered from a rice shortage largely caused by government miscalculations of the harvest and underestimation of import needs, officials pointed their fingers at 'hoarding' among Chinese-Filipino rice traders. Most worrying for the Filipino-Chinese community was the weak-kneed response by the government with the escalation of kidnappings for ransom targeted mainly at Chinese-Filipino business families. In fact, subsequent investigations saw consistent involvement in the kidnappings by former members of the security forces. The revival of anti-Chinese messages emanating from circles close to the government was the uglier side of politics during the Ramos administration. Despite the significant assimilation of Chinese-Filipinos within the Philippines, deep-rooted prejudices remain just below the surface among the mestizo majority.

Ramos did little to put national politics on a more democratic path. Just as he won the presidency by relying on traditional clan-based politics, he endorsed an old-style politician, Speaker of the House, José de Venecia, for the presidency in 1998. In doing so, Ramos underestimated the appeal of his popular vice-president, former movie star Joseph Estrada, and overestimated de Venecia's ability to mobilise traditional clan networks to secure a victory. Given that eleven candidates were competing for the presidency, Ramos must have believed that the business community's fear of an Estrada presidency combined with endorsements for de Venecia from the military and Islamic politicians in the south would be just enough to defeat Estrada.

However, Estrada's populist appeals to the common person created an unstoppable bandwagon and he won a landslide victory. In the manner of populists everywhere, Estrada drew from a wide cross-section of the political spectrum. NGOs and the left found his economic nationalist and pro-poor rhetoric attractive. Estrada had been active in the Senate's campaign against the US bases. At the same time he was a traditional politician *par excellence*. He had the solid backing of Eduardo Cojuangco, the biggest civilian ally of the late President Marcos. The former movie star was close to the Marcos family and its extended political network having been part of it during his long stint as mayor of San Juan in Metro Manila during the Marcos presidency. In the final stages of his campaign he enlisted the support of bankers and mainstream economists and promised responsible government.

Once in office, Estrada, ever the political chameleon, dropped any hint of economic nationalism and engaged in negotiations over new visitation rights for the US military. Soon he reopened the debate over constitutional reform, but attempted to win support from the business community by arguing that the main objective of reform should be to remove constitutional provisions limiting foreign investment. He promised not to extend his term of office beyond the six-year limit as Ramos had hoped to do when his supporters launched a stillborn effort at amending the constitution.

Estrada maintained his commitment to a 'pro-poor' agenda, but failed to elaborate a detailed programme to implement it. The top positions in his Cabinet all went to individuals committed to the liberalisation programmes of the Ramos administration, while political portfolios were distributed between his own loyalists and those close to the Marcos and Cojuangco networks. Estrada's attempt to be all things to all people allowed him to maintain popular support well into his six-year term of office.

Captivated by their access to the halls of power, the NGOs hoped to influence the shape of the Estrada presidency. He promised renewed action on agrarian reform and appointed long-time activist Horacio Morales, formerly with the National Democratic Front during the years of dictatorship and later head of the Philippine Rural Reconstruction Movement. It is difficult to imagine the populist movie star – who served for years under Marcos, who ran for the Senate in 1987 on a platform with one of Cory Aquino's most hated adversaries, the former

Defence Secretary Juan Ponce Enrile (known to have instigated military officers to overthrow her government) and who teamed up with Marcos stalwart Eduardo Cojuangco – presiding over a period of democratic renewal. In fact, early on in his presidency he took a very hostile stance towards those newspapers and journalists who expressed criticisms of his administration, leading to the closure of the country's oldest paper – the *Manila Times* – and the near bankruptcy of its most independent-minded paper, the *Philippine Daily Inquirer*.

In this context of a somewhat embattled democracy, the NGOs' enthusiasm for decentralisation and a constitutional reform that would see the presidential system replaced by a parliamentary one may be misguided. Decentralisation and parliamentary government are not equal to democratisation in a climate where local power constellations are still dominated by clan and kin networks and local bosses. While the elections in 1998 saw an unquestionable victory for Estrada's populism, elections to the House of Representatives and provincial and local governments were still determined by the power of clans and political bosses. Imelda Marcos sat in the House as a representative of her home province, her daughter was elected congresswoman from Ferdinand Marcos' home province while Ferdinand Jnr became governor.

Conclusion

Democratic deepening in the Philippines requires the formation of stable political parties based on programmatic politics replacing the shifting alliances around personalities bred by clan politics and populism. There is some objective basis for the pursuit of such politics, both in the business community and the widening associations of civil society.

There is a tension between nationalism and democracy in every country. In fact, more often than not, nationalism is more conducive to anti-democratic practices with its appeals beyond class and individual rights. The withdrawal of US bases from the Philippines removed one of the few remaining targets of nationalist campaigns. Slowly, Tagalog is replacing English as the language of communication between elites from different regional and linguistic communities. It is still possible that an ugly, ethnically-defined nationalism could re-emerge in a time of economic crisis as was illustrated in the mid-1990s during Ramos' tenure in office. Just below the surface there is still an openness among the mestizo majority to racism towards Chinese or indigenous tribal minorities that mirrors the racism prevalent in so many northern democracies. Military rebels who attempted to overthrow the Aquino government couched their mission in nationalist terms and dissent from that quarter remains a possibility in the future.

Nationalism and democracy are compatible only when the idea of the nation is defined in democratic terms. Activists in the expansive associational sector are best situated to pursue that redefinition. It is there as well that social capital can be accumulated through the multiplicity of networks and shared values and norms that derive from continued interaction, but this will only serve democratic ends if the networks and organisations created operate with democratic rules and carry democratic values.

Notes

1 Robert Putnam, *Making Democracy Work: Civic Traditions in Modern Italy* (Princeton: Princeton University Press, 1993).
2 Ernest Gellner, *Nations and Nationalism* (Oxford: Basil Blackwell, 1983).
3 Benedict Anderson, *Imagined Communities: Reflection on the Origin and Spread of Nationalism* (London, Verso, 1983).
4 Eric Hobsbawm, *The Age of Capital, 1845–1875* (London: Abacus, 1985), chapter 5.
5 Anthony Smith, *The Ethnic Origins of Nations* (Oxford: Blackwell, 1986).
6 Nick Joaquin, *A Question of Heroes* (Manila: National Book Store, 1981), pp. 31–2.
7 Rizal's most famous works were his novels, *Noli me tangere* (*The Lost Eden*), 1887 and *El Filibustrismo* (*Subversion*), 1891.
8 José Rizal, 'The Philippines within a century', *La Solidaridad* (September 1889–February 1890), reprinted in G. F. Zaide, *José Rizal: Asia's First Apostle of Nationalism* (Manila: Red Star Book Store, 1970), and his 'The indolence of the Filipinos', 1890, also reprinted in Zaide.
9 Cited in Zaide, ibid., p. 237.
10 G. Fischer, *José Rizal, Philippin 1861–1896: un aspect du nationalisme moderne* (Paris: Maspero, 1970), pp. 82–5.
11 Nationalist historians have tried to paint Bonifacio as a leader of the lower classes but evidence seems to confirm that he was relatively well-off and well-connected. See Jonathan Fast and Jim Richardson, *Roots of Dependency: Political and Economic Revolution in Nineteenth-Century Philippines* (Quezon City: Foundation for Nationalist Studies, 1979), pp. 68–70.
12 Ibid., chapter 10.
13 On the complex character of peasant aspirations, see Reynaldo Ileto, *Pasyon and Revolution: Popular Movements in the Philippines, 1840–1910* (Quezon City: Ateneo de Manila University Press, 1979).
14 Cesar Adib Majul, *Apolonario Mabini, Revolutionary* (Manila: National Heroes Commission, 1964).
15 Luzviminda Bartolome Francisco, 'The first Vietnam: The U.S.–Philippine War of 1899', *Bulletin of Concerned Asian Scholars*, vol. 5, no. 4 (December 1973).
16 Francisco; James Putzel, *A Captive Land: The Politics of Agrarian Reform in the Philippines* (London, Manila and New York: Catholic Institute for International Relations, Ateneo de Manila University Press and Monthly Review Press, 1992), pp. 51–2.
17 Benedict Anderson, 'Cacique democracy in the Philippines: origins and dreams', *New Left Review*, no. 169 (May–June 1988), pp. 3–31. See my review of the peculiarities of the democratic system in 'Survival of an imperfect democracy', *Democratisation*, vol. 6, no. 1 (Spring 1999), pp. 198–223.
18 James Coleman, *The Foundations of Social Theory* (Cambridge, MA: Harvard University Press, 1994), chapter 12.
19 Rene Ofreneo, *Capitalism in Philippine Agriculture* (Quezon City: Foundation for Nationalist Studies, 1980), p. 25; and Renato Constantino, *A History of the Philippines* (New York: Monthly Review Press, 1975), pp. 350–4.

20　Theodore Friend, *Between Two Empires: The Ordeal of the Philippines, 1929–1946* (New Haven, CT: Yale University Press, 1965); and Bonifacio Salamanca, *The Filipino Reaction to American Rule, 1901–1913* (Quezon City: New Day Publishers, 1984), p. 147.

21　Alfredo B. Saulo, *Communism in the Philippines: An Introduction* (Quezon City: Ateneo de Manila University Press, 1990), chapter 4.

22　David Joel Steinberg, *The Philippines: A Singular and Plural Place* (Boulder, CO: Westview Press, 1990), pp. 97–105.

23　Salamanca, *The Filipino Reaction*, p. 158.

24　Benedict Kerkvliet, *The Huk Rebellion: A Study of Peasant Revolt in the Philippines* (Berkeley: University of California Press, 1977).

25　Renato Constantino and Letizia Constantino, *The Philippines: The Continuing Past* (Quezon City: Foundation for Nationalist Studies, 1978), pp. 213–21.

26　Cited in Alejandro Lichauco, 'The international economic order and the Philippine experience', in José R. Vivencio (ed.), *Managing the Future: The World Bank and the IMF in the Philippines* (Quezon City: Foundation for Nationalist Studies, 1982), pp. 12–48.

27　Putzel, *A Captive Land*, pp. 85–105.

28　Yoshihara Kunio, *Philippine Industrialization: Foreign and Domestic Capital* (Quezon City: Ateneo de Manila University Press, 1985), chapter 5; and Teresita Ang See, 'The socio-cultural and political dimensions of the economic success of the Chinese in the Philippines', in Ellen Huang Palanca, *China, Taiwan, and the Ethnic Chinese in the Philippine Economy* (Quezon City: Philippine Association for Chinese Studies, 1995), pp. 93–106.

29　Amando Doronila, 'The transformation of patron–client relations and its political consequences in postwar Philippines', *Journal of Southeast Asian Studies*, vol. 16, no. 1 (March 1985), pp. 99–116.

30　Walden Bello, David Kinley and Elaine Elinson, *Development Debacle: The World Bank in the Philippines* (San Francisco: Institute for Food and Development Policy, 1982), pp. 138–9.

31　The best general account of US support for Marcos is Raymond Bonner, *Waltzing with a Dictator: The Marcoses and the Making of American Policy* (New York: Vintage Books, 1987).

32　See Putzel, *A Captive Land*, chapter 5; and James Putzel, 'Managing the "main force": the Communist Party and the peasantry in the Philippines', *Journal of Peasant Studies*, vol. 22, no. 4 (July 1995), pp. 645–71.

33　*Constitution of the Republic of the Philippines*, adopted by the Constitutional Commission of 1986, Article 12, sections 10 and 11.

34　Institute for Popular Democracy, *Political Clans and Electoral Politics: A Preliminary Research* (Quezon City: Institute for Popular Democracy, 1987), section 5.

35　Putzel, *A Captive Land*, chapters 6–11.

36　The best account of the role of NGOs in the Philippines is Gerard Clarke, *The Politics of NGOs in South-East Asia: Participation and Protest in the Philippines* (London: Routledge, 1998).

37　See James Putzel, 'Non-governmental organisations and rural poverty', in G. Sidney Silliman and Lela Garner Noble (eds), *Organizing for Democracy: NGOs, Civil Society and the Philippine State* (University of Hawaii Press, 1998), pp. 77–112.

38　See, for instance, the interview with Margaret Thomas in *Business Times*, 9–10 July 1994.

10 Nationalism and the international order

The Asian experience

James Mayall

As Anthony Smith rightly points out in chapter 1 of this volume, the modern world is made up of nation-states. As he also notes, this was not always so. It is the transition from a more diverse social and political world to one in which the units, at least formally, conform to a single pattern, that has led historians, political scientists, sociologists and anthropologists to investigate the causes of the rise of nationalism, the characteristics of the nation itself (as distinct from the claims of nationalist doctrine), and whether nations can survive without states, and if so, under what circumstances.

From the perspective provided by the study of international relations, it is more often the consequences of nationalism for the international order, and the modifications that entry into international society induces in successful nationalist movements, that is of primary interest. Since for most of the twentieth century, international relations have been dominated by the Western powers – and hence by their ideas about the relationship of national rights to state power and to international order – it is worth asking to what extent the Asian experience of nationalism, as reviewed in this book, has conformed to these conceptions or challenged them.

Because students of international relations have generally been concerned with consequences, they tend to be indifferent, or at least agnostic, about the claims of primordialists and modernists concerning the origins of nations. However, there is one sense in which the study of international relations may support at least some versions of the modernist account. It has been said that the state makes war and war makes the state. Since it is ultimately the anarchical nature of international relations that makes war possible, and since to succeed in war, states must be able to command loyalty and sacrifice, this formula might be more accurately stated as follows: the international system allows the state to make war, and states make nations.

Japan, which at first sight can be claimed with equal plausibility by the primordialist and modernist camps, is a case in point. As Ian Nish argues in chapter 5, before the Meiji restoration, the Japanese 'generally lived in their clan communities and probably had less conception of a nation or nationality than of the class to which they belonged in their feudal society'. The same kind of observation would have been made of many European societies a century before. But, as Nish also notes, 'there is nothing so effective for developing the nationalist spirit as war'. By the time Japan had emerged victoriously from wars against China and Russia and in the First World War, Japanese national identity was firmly established. So, we should also ask whether, as is sometimes argued, the formative role of war in nation-building is a peculiarly Eurocentric idea, or whether, as the Japanese example suggests, it is also borne out by the evidence from Asia.

Before turning to these questions, it may be useful to sketch the standard picture of international society, particularly as it has evolved under the impact of nationalist ideas. The origins of the modern states-system are generally traced to the end of the European wars of religion in the middle of the seventeenth century. It was the elevation of the principle of state sovereignty over other non-territorial principles of authority, the formal proscription of religious (ideological) war, and the elaboration of a diplomatic system of resident embassies with extra-territorial but reciprocated privileges, that made possible modern international society. It was a society of princes not of peoples. At first it did not include non-Western rulers, whose external relations were organised separately in ways that sometimes touched the Western world (and visa versa) but did not penetrate to the point where each side had to revise its view of the other as barbarian. As Western power and expansion increased and intensified, much of Asia was either conquered – and hence deprived of any status within international society (for example, the Indian subcontinent, the Dutch East Indies, the Philippine archipelago, Malaya, and so forth) – or was forced into an essentially subordinate role and on Western terms (for example, China, Japan).

Nothing essentially changed until 1919, when an attempt was made to redraw the map of Europe along national lines and in accordance with the principle of national self-determination. The idea that the people should be sovereign, rather than the dynasts, had been around since the American and French revolutions; but in 1919, not even Woodrow Wilson intended it to apply to the non-Western world. However, since the idea of popular sovereignty had been conceived in universalist, not in culturally specific, terms, it was seized upon by nascent nationalist movements throughout the colonised and subdued countries of Asia. The latter, starting with Japan, were the *first* to successfully challenge the Western conception of international society as a closed club; the others had to wait until after the Second World War to claim, in Pandit Nehru's words, their 'rendezvous with destiny'. But although there were exceptions here and there, they shared with earlier European nationalists, a desire to join the society of states on equal terms, not to change it. The original principle – to each prince his own religion – had been tacitly changed to each nation its own territory, but the international borders of these territories had been drawn by the emperors not the nationalists.

Those who had succeeded to the national real estate at the time of decolonisation were generally resistant to any who came after – Uigars, Punjabis, Kashmiris, etc. – claiming that they too were nations, whose fundamental rights had been ignored.

Against this background, this chapter will examine what can be said in relation to Asia, and in contrast with other parts of the world, by considering three points: first, the meaning of national self-determination; that is, was it conceived as a political principle for dislodging alien rule or as a popular principle for mobilising the population and legitimising the government? Second, attitudes to secession and irredentism; i.e., on what grounds are secessionist movements resisted and irredentist claims advanced, and are there significant and idiosyncratic regional variations? And third, the relationships of nationalism to democracy and minority protection; i.e., are some Asian nationalisms, civic and democratic and does the international system constrain or permit alternative kinds of nationalism in Asia?

National self-determination

The problem posed for international order by the attempt to make the principle of self-determination the criterion of international legitimacy was exposed in Europe, not Asia. It arose because it proved impossible to redraw the political map without leaving minorities trapped within the new, so-called, nation-states that succeeded to the Hapsburg, Hohenzollern, and Ottoman empires after 1918. The new dispensation was problematic because, in the East, the absence of democratic traditions led the nation to be imagined as a community of blood ties, in other words in exclusive and narrowly ethnic terms.

This pattern finds some echoes in Asia but not many. Japan is a relatively homogeneous society and although China is ethnically diverse, the Han are so dominant – making up around 85 per cent of the population – that their rulers have never felt the need to press the ethnic basis of their national identity. The partition of the Indian subcontinent comes closest to the European experience. The case was argued on the grounds that there were two nations – albeit defined in religious and communal rather than ethnic terms – and that one of them, represented by the Muslim League, could never be free without a state of its own. As in post-1918 Europe, the partition of the Indian subcontinent led to massive population transfers and left the minorities that remained behind more vulnerable than they had been under the empire.

Such analogies should not be pressed too far. The real contrast between Asia and Europe lies, on the one hand, in the nature of the imperial order against which nationalists pitted themselves, and on the other, in the differences between the kinds of state to which they laid claim. The doctrine of national self-determination originated in the previously centralised states of the north Atlantic sea-board. In these countries, as Ernest Gellner has pointed out, the rise of nationalism – that is the demand that political and cultural boundaries should be congruent – required little more than a kind of *ex post facto* ratification that the state in fact belonged to the people.[1] Except in Ireland, it did not require substantial territorial revision. In Eastern and Southern Europe, however, there were no centralised states – and hence no well established national political cultures – with the result that the largely rural populations had to be mobilised against dynastic rule along ethno-cultural lines. In these circumstances, where the nation did not exist, it was simply invented.

In Asia, as in Europe, nationalism arose in opposition to imperial rule. But whereas in Europe, when the dynasts were finally overthrown, they disappeared from the scene, in many cases leaving the nationalists to create nation-states *de novo*, in Asia the end of empire had two entirely different consequences. First, the European imperial powers did not cease to exist; they simply withdrew to their own homelands, from where they continued to exercise considerable economic, military and political influence. This meant that they were almost inevitably used as models for nation- and state-building; it also meant that they were available as targets, that the quest for national self-determination could be continued after independence and by other means. It found expression, for example, in Sukarno's brief attempt to mobilise the 'new emerging forces' against Western economic and political domination, and in Nehru's partial closure of the Indian economy at home, and his identification of imperialism with war and hence of anti-colonial nationalism with non-alignment and peace.

The second consequence of European imperial withdrawal in Asia was that, in contrast to Europe, it mostly left the nationalists in possession of existing states. Like governments everywhere, they faced the problem of legitimising their rule – and so were attracted by the economistic ideas of nation-building that were then in vogue – but they usually took over existing colonial structures of government and administration, in the name of the nation. The political class was able to monopolise the symbols of nationalism without taking seriously ethnic or cultural arguments for self-determination. Indeed, decolonisation and self-determination were regarded as unproblematic synonyms: self-determination was thus a political principle for dislodging alien rule rather than an instrument of popular mobilisation aimed at legitimising the government. Of course, in the early years, it was often difficult to distinguish between the two, and the former normally emerged triumphant. It is in those cases where these observations do not hold – most notably in Pakistan which had to invent a state and a nation simultaneously – that the aftermath of the transfer of power most resembles the European pattern.

Secession and irredentism

The insistence that the nation should belong to, and indeed be defined by, the state is not peculiarly Asian. Indeed, throughout the Cold War, it was one of the few propositions on which east and west, north and south was united. The collapse of communism and the end of the Cold War briefly encouraged the belief that the prospects for successful secession and/or irredentism had dramatically improved. But, although the communist world – like the liberal empires before it – shattered into its constituent parts, there is little evidence to support this view. The most that might be said – as the case of East Timor illustrates – is that the end of the Cold War has removed some, but certainly not all, of the obstacles faced by secessionists in obtaining the international recognition and support on which success depends.

The East Timor case provides the most telling evidence, not only of the opportunities but also of the constraints faced by secessionists. Before turning to it, however, it may be worth asking whether there are significant regional variations – within Asia and in contrast to other parts of the world – in attitudes towards irredentism and secession? If there were, it would challenge the view of a single international system based on a common understanding of sovereignty and territorial integrity. Three propositions can be advanced in support of this challenge: that faith rather than territory defines the *umma* (the community of the faithful) and hence the nation within Islamic societies; that pre-modern concepts of political authority such as suzerainty exercise an influence in Asia that they have lost elsewhere; and that there is a greater tolerance of territorial adjustments for geo-political or strategic reasons than in the West. Let us consider each in turn.

Islam

The Islamic revivalists and anti-imperial writers of the early twentieth century, such as the Indians, Muhammed Iqbal and Syed Amir Ali, emphasised the pan-Islamic, rather than territorial basis of Muslim identity. Tahir Amin describes Iqbal's view that for Muslims, 'ethnic, racial and territorial differences have limited utility and are recognised for purposes of identification only'.[2] It is also true that, whereas the conventions of modern statecraft and international jurisprudence developed from the subordination of the religious to the secular power in Christian Europe, no parallel self-denying ordinance was ever adopted by Muslim rulers. In this sense, the *jihad* is a living tradition, while the Crusade is a dead one. On the other hand, it is not at all clear what difference all this makes at the level of practical politics. As Amin also points out, the leading Muslim nationalist leaders of the post-colonial age were either supporters of liberal capitalism, such as Ayub Khan of Pakistan or Suharto in Indonesia, or national socialists, such as Zulfikar Ali Bhutto in Pakistan or Sukarno of Indonesia. Neither their fundamental ideas nor their attachment to territorial sovereignty can be easily differentiated from their Western counterparts.

The one successfully forced secession of the Cold War era resulted from the dismemberment of Pakistan and the creation of Bangladesh. But the defeat of the Pakistan army in East Bengal was accomplished by Indian forces and the rebellion seems to have owed little to specifically Islamic ideas about state and nation, except in the negative sense that Islam proved an inadequate basis on which to forge a national identity between people who were separated by 1,000 miles of Indian territory. The peaceful separation of Singapore from the predominantly Muslim Malaysia was certainly influenced by communal considerations (most notably the Malay fear of being swamped by ethnic Chinese) but these fears were economic and political rather than religious.

Suzerainty

The Chinese communists, like the Bolsheviks in Russia, had originally flirted with the principal of national self-determination as a way of attracting ethnic minorities away from the Nationalist government. A resolution of the first All-China Congress in 1931 held out the prospect of independence for minority peoples:

> in districts like Mongolia, Tibet, Sinkiang, Yunan, Kweichow and others where the majority of the population belongs to non-Chinese nationalities, the toiling masses of these nations shall have the right to determine for themselves whether they wish to leave the Chinese Soviet Republic and create their own independent state, or whether they wish to join the Union of Soviet Republics, or form an autonomous area inside the Chinese Soviet Republic.[3]

This tolerance of minorities did not survive the revolution. On acquiring power in 1949, Mao Zedong's first public speech was entitled, 'The Chinese People have stood up'. Succession, rather than self-determination was to define the new China, a move which Mao accomplished by endorsing Sun Yat-Sen's doctrine of China's five races – the Han, Tibetans, Uighars, Mongols and Manchus. Succession was to the area from which, whenever they were able, the imperial centre had traditionally claimed the right to extract tribute. To drive the point home, China annexed Sinkiang and Tibet, which during the period of imperial decline had lapsed into *de facto* independence. The forceful incorporation of Tibet in 1950 – the one minority homeland where the indigenous population outnumbered the Han – caused an international outcry, but it was not challenged by the United Nations because Britain and India, the two states most immediately concerned, had always accepted Beijing's theoretical suzerainty over the territory.

Chinese opposition to post-Cold War 'peace support' operations, most stridently expressed in Kosovo, is clearly influenced by the government's desire to contain demonstration effects amongst their own minorities. As other chapters in this volume make clear, Sinification and assimilation policies have had limited success. At the same time, there is little evidence to suggest that Western bumper stickers urging the cause of Tibetan freedom have made serious inroads into China's will to maintain its control, if not its authority, over the country

The geo-political imperative

The claim that there was an inalienable right to self-determination introduced a disturbingly subversive element into the established international order. To try and contain the damage in the 1960s, the new African states revived the principle of *uti possidetis*, first formulated in the nineteenth century by Latin American countries, as a means of short-circuiting a vicious round of irredentist and secessionist conflicts after the withdrawal of Spanish power. By this time most of Europe's Asian colonies were already independent, and it is arguable that, when power was being transferred, they were less respectful of established colonial boundaries, than countries in other regions. Not only did China ignore both world opinion and the *de facto* independence of Tibet, India also had no compunction in absorbing Goa and Hyderabad. In these cases, invasion was euphemistically renamed as a police action. The Indian government also made it clear that it regarded territorial consolidation – and in Sikkim and along the north-east frontier – strategic depth in relation to China, as more important than popular aspirations. To the extent that important elements in the Congress Party had never been fully reconciled to partition, geo-political considerations also played a part in India's decisive role in the creation of Bangladesh. *Uti possidetis* in South Asia is a convenient defence against further fragmentation, but did not stand in the way of opportunistic national expansion in the past.

Strategic considerations were also important in the construction of the post-colonial Indonesian state. At the time of decolonisation – identified by Michael Leifer in this volume as the romantic phase of Indonesian nationalism – Sukarno and his followers insisted on the authenticity of their own movement by reference to an act of deliberate self-creation. (The contrast was with Malaysia, which they regarded as a neo-colonial creation of the British.) They laid claim to the Dutch East Indies, not on ethnic grounds, but because they had constituted themselves as the nationalist successors to the Dutch by an act of will. The confrontation with Malaysia was not about the boundaries that should define the successor states but about whether it was possible to create a genuine nation-state in collaboration with the former imperial power. It was only in 1975 when the opportunity arose to consolidate the archipelagic state by annexing East Timor that the Indonesians opportunistically introduced an ethnic justification for breaching the *uti possidetis* principle.

In the final analysis, however, the case of East Timor suggests that Asian attitudes to irredentism and secession are not significantly different from those in other parts of the world. With the exception of Bangladesh, the state has successfully fought off separatist challenges to its authority in India, Pakistan, the Philippines, Myanmar and Sri Lanka. There are understandable fears that the 'secession' of East Timor may provoke separatist pressures elsewhere in the sprawling Indonesian archipelago. But, while it is impossible to be sure what the international reaction would be in the event of a further Indonesian inspired 'ethnocide', international support for East Timor would not by itself establish the precedent.

The reason is that under the conventional interpretation of national self-determination as decolonisation, East Timor should have become an independent state within its colonial borders. International acquiescence in Indonesia's annexation of the Portuguese colony has to be viewed in the context of increased Cold War tensions following the establishment of communist regimes in Cambodia, Laos and Vietnam, and the Portuguese coup of April 1974. This brought down the fascist government in Portugal itself but led rapidly to the emergence of Afro-Marxist regimes in Angola and Mozambique that were linked by treaty to the Soviet Union. But acquiescence did not involve formal recognition any more than it did of Israel's occupation of the Golan Heights or Morocco's of the northern part of the former Spanish Sahara. Ironically, only Australia, which later reversed its position and led the UN mandated peace-making force into the territory in September 1999, formally recognised the annexation. This is not the place to debate whether the UN was wise to accept President Habibe's offer of a referendum in East Timor, with the timetable and conditions that accompanied it. But it is clear that in pressing the claims of the East Timorese, they were upholding the principle that all colonies had a right to independence, not supporting secessionist self-determination in general.

Nationalism and democracy

In terms of the final question raised at the beginning of this chapter, Asian nationalisms also seem to be more similar than dissimilar to those in other parts of the world. In some countries – India, Japan and the Philippines are the most long lasting examples – there has been no fundamental difficulty in expressing national identity through a democratic constitution. In others, the appearance if not always the reality of democracy has been maintained, while in others such as Cambodia under Pol Pot or Myanmar, pathological variants of ultra-nationalism have periodically usurped the state.

From this perspective, the significant contrast is arguably not between European, Asian and African variants of nationalism, nor between primordialist and civic variants, but between anti-colonial (or in the case of China and Japan anti-Western) nationalisms and the rest. Several Asian nationalist movements have claimed to represent a historical and cultural identity stretching back far beyond the colonial period, but they have seldom claimed the right to independence on the basis of ancestral descent. The assertion of Japanese nationhood was the result of a deliberate choice to emulate the liberal capitalist route to modernity, the post-revolutionary Chinese assertion the socialist route to the same goal. The anti-colonial movements in the Indian subcontinent, the Dutch East Indies, Malaya, Ceylon[4] and elsewhere, borrowed eclectically from the liberal and socialist models, but these were political not ethnic nationalisms, whose leaders were convinced that the removal of alien power was necessary for the modernisation of their societies.

Given these origins, it might be expected that Asian nationalism would be more easily reconciled with democratic government than in those parts of the world where the nation is defined in a narrow and ethnically exclusive way. The weakness of this argument is that it operates only at the level of official nationalist rhetoric and largely ignores social and political realities. It is not merely, as James Putzel concludes of the Philippines in chapter 9, that 'nationalism and democracy are compatible only when the nation is imagined and defined in democratic terms', it is that such definition requires more than an act of will by nationalist leaders.

Most of the states discussed in this book are ethnically, linguistically and religiously diverse, even if prolonged co-existence has, in most cases, also produced an overarching political culture, or at any rate a *modus vivendi*. For a democratic culture to take root in societies where social divisions make it hard for people to define themselves primarily as citizens, either traditional institutions must be adaptable to democratic purposes, as in India where social life depends crucially on mechanisms for alliance building, or there must be credible constitutional guarantees to protect the rights of minorities.

As we have seen, Asian nationalists have been, if anything, less responsive than those elsewhere to providing such guarantees, although they may come to an informal political accommodation with a minority population as the Malays did with the Chinese in Malaysia. As long as the political class refuses to engage in constitutional reform to accommodate minority and communal interests, democracy is likely to prove unstable and prone to military coups or oligarchic take-over. A Gellnerian analysis would suggest that this is the result of an unresolved conflict between competing groups to capture the state and so elevate their own folk or low culture to a position from which it can become the national culture for the state as a whole.[5] But this suggests that the territorial map is in fact more malleable than is, in fact, the case. As the October 1999 coup in

Pakistan suggests, without a pre-existing territorial title, to which reference back can be made, the constitution is more vulnerable than the state itself. This is true in Asia, but certainly not only there.

Notes

1   Ernest Gellner, *Conditions of Liberty, Civil Society and its Rivals* (London: Hamish Hamilton, 1994), pp. 113–18.
2   Tahir Amin, *Nationalism and Internationalism in Liberalism, Marxism and Islam* (Islamabad: International Institute of Islamic Thought, 1991), p. 67.
3   Quoted in Walker Connor, 'Ethnology and the peace of South Asia', *World Politics*, 22 (1) (October 1969), pp. 51–86.
4   See, for example, Elie Kedourie, *Nationalism in Asia and Africa* (New York: World Publishing Company, 1970).
5   Ernest Gellner, *Nations and Nationalism* (Oxford: Blackwell, 1983); *Nationalism* (London: Weidenfeld and Nicolson, 1997).

Index